IN
GOD
WE
TRUST?

RenewedMinds

RenewedMinds, an imprint of Baker
Academic in partnership with the Council for Christian Colleges & Universities,
publishes quality textbooks and academic resources to guide readers in
reflecting critically on contemporary
issues of faith and learning. While
focused on the needs of a Christian
higher-education curriculum, Renewed-
Minds resources will engage and benefit
all thoughtful readers.

The Council for Christian Colleges & Universities is an association of more
than ninety-five member colleges and universities, each of which has a
curriculum rooted in the arts and sciences and is committed to the integration of biblical faith, scholarship, and service. More than thirty Christian denominations, committed to a variety of theological traditions and
perspectives, are represented by these member institutions. The views
expressed in these volumes are primarily those of the author(s) and are
not intended to serve as a position statement of the Council membership.
For more information, please use one of the following addresses:

www.cccu.org

council@cccu.org

The Council for Christian Colleges & Universities
321 Eighth Street N.E.
Washington, D.C. 20002-6518

IN
GOD
WE
TRUST?

Religion and American Political Life

Edited by
Corwin E. Smidt

A RenewedMinds Book

Baker Academic
A Division of Baker Book House Co
Grand Rapids, Michigan 49516

Published by Baker Academic
a division of Baker Book House Company
P.O. Box 6287, Grand Rapids, MI 49516-6287

Printed in the United States of America

Library of Congress Cataloging-in-Publication Data

In God we trust? : religion and American political life / edited by Corwin E. Smidt.
        p.   cm.
    "A RenewedMinds book."
    Includes bibliographical references and index.
    ISBN 0-8010-2261-4 (paper)
    1. Religion and politics—United States. I. Smidt, Corwin E., 1946–

BL2525 .I55 2001
261.7′0973—dc21   2001016162

For information about academic books, resources for Christian leaders, and all new releases available from Baker Book House, visit our web site:

http://www.bakerbooks.com

Contents

101913

Contributors

Michelle Donaldson Deardorff did her undergraduate work in political science and history at Taylor University and her M.A. and Ph.D. at Miami University in Oxford, Ohio. She has taught at Millikin University (Decatur, Illinois) since 1991 and is currently Associate Professor of Political Science. Dr. Deardorff's research and publications have focused on lower federal court rulings in pregnancy discrimination and abortion controversies. She has also written on northern school desegregation and the federal courts.

Frank Guliuzza received his Ph.D. from the University of Notre Dame and is Professor of Political Science and due-process officer at Weber State University in Ogden, Utah. In addition, he is pre-law adviser and coaches Weber State's intercollegiate mock-trial team. He has published articles and reviews in a number of journals, including the *Marquette Law Review*, the *Drake Law Review*, the *Williamette Law Review*, the *Journal of Politics,* the *Review of Politics*, *PS: Political Science & Politics*, *American Political Science Review*, and *Academe*, and has recently written the book *Over the Wall: Protecting Religious Expression in the Public Square* (SUNY Press, 2000).

James L. Guth obtained his Ph.D. from Harvard University and is Professor of Political Science at Furman University. He is author of numerous scholarly articles and chapters on religion and politics, and is co-editor of *The Bible and the Bible Box* (Westview, 1991) and *Religion and the Culture Wars* (Rowman & Littlefield, 1996), and coauthor of *The Bully Pulpit*: *The Politics of Protestant Clergy* (University Press of Kansas, 1998).

Stacey Hunter Hecht obtained her Ph.D. from the University of Minnesota and is currently Assistant Professor of Political Science at Bethel

College in St. Paul, Minnesota. Her dissertation focused on welfare policy in the United States. Her research on public policy, Christianity and politics, and undergraduate teaching has been presented at several national conferences.

Daniel J. B. Hofrenning is Associate Professor and Chair of the Political Science Department at St. Olaf College. He has written a book on religious lobbying, *In Washington but Not of It: The Prophetic Politics of Religious Lobbyists* (Temple University Press, 1995). He has also written journal articles and numerous op-ed pieces and magazine articles on a range of political topics. He teaches classes in public policy and American politics, particularly courses in religion and politics, political parties and campaigns, and environmental policy. After studying at Luther Seminary, he did his graduate work in political science and public policy at Duke University and at the University of Minnesota.

Lyman A. Kellstedt received his Ph.D. from the University of Illinois and is Professor of Political Science at Wheaton College. He is also an author of a large number of scholarly articles and chapters on religion and politics, and is coeditor of *Rediscovering the Religious Factor in American Politics* (M. E. Sharpe, 1993) and *Religion and the Culture Wars* (Rowman & Littlefield, 1996), and coauthor of *The Bully Pulpit: The Politics of Protestant Clergy* (University Press of Kansas, 1998).

Doug Koopman teaches political science, specializing in American politics, and also serves as the Program Director for the Paul B. Henry Institute for the Study of Christianity and Politics at Calvin College. His research specialty is Congress, specifically the U.S. House of Representatives. He has published a number of works in this area, including *Hostile Takeover* (Rowman & Littlefield, 1996), a book about the House Republican Party from 1980 through its rise to majority status in 1995, which won a *Choice* magazine award as one of the best new books on U.S. politics. Before beginning his teaching career at Calvin, Koopman worked for fifteen years on Capitol Hill in a variety of staff positions for individual members of Congress, congressional committees, and leadership offices. A graduate of Hope College, he holds a Master of Theological Studies degree from Wesley Seminary, and the M.A. and Ph.D. degrees in American politics from the Catholic University of America in Washington, D.C.

Stephen V. Monsma is Professor of Political Science at Pepperdine University in Malibu, California. His books include *Positive Neutrality: Letting Religious Freedom Ring* (Greenwood Press, 1993) and *When*

Sacred and Secular Mix: Religious Nonprofit Organizations and Public Money (Rowman & Littlefield, 1996). His most recent publications are *The Challenge of Pluralism: Church and State in Five Democracies* (Rowman & Littlefield, 1997) and *Equal Treatment of Religion in a Pluralistic Society* (Eerdmans, 1998), both with J. Christopher Soper.

Corwin E. Smidt received his Ph.D. in political science from the University of Iowa and holds the Paul Henry Chair in Christianity and Politics and serves as Executive Director of the Paul B. Henry Institute at Calvin College. Author and coauthor of a variety of articles on religion and politics, he is coeditor of *Sojourners in the Wilderness: The Christian Right in Comparative Perspective* (Rowman & Littlefield, 1997) and coauthor of *The Bully Pulpit: The Politics of Protestant Clergy* (University Press of Kansas, 1998).

J. Christopher Soper obtained his Ph.D. in political science from Yale University in 1992 and is currently an associate professor of political science at Pepperdine University in Malibu, California. He is the author of numerous articles on religion and politics. His most recent publications are *The Challenge of Pluralism: Church and State in Five Democracies* (Rowman & Littlefield, 1997) and *Equal Treatment of Religion in a Pluralistic Society* (Eerdmans, 1998), both with Stephen Monsma.

Jeff Walz is an Assistant Professor of Political Science at Concordia University Wisconsin (CUW). Following the completion of graduate work at the University of Nebraska-Lincoln, and a one-year replacement teaching position at Wheaton College in Illinois, Walz joined the CUW faculty in 1997. He teaches courses in American government, introductory politics, the presidency, religion and politics, and related areas. His research has appeared in the *American Review of Politics*, *Political Research Quarterly*, *Publius: The Journal of Federalism*, and the *Southeastern Political Review*. He is currently examining the connection between religion and politics among Lutheran pastors.

John G. West Jr. is an Associate Professor of Political Science at Seattle Pacific University and a Senior Fellow at the Seattle-based Discovery Institute, where he runs the program on religion, liberty, and civic life. He holds a B.A. in communications (editorial journalism) from the University of Washington and a Ph.D. in government from the Claremont Graduate School. His publications include *The Politics of Revelation and Reason: Religion and Civic Life in the New Nation* (University Press of Kansas, 1996) and *The Encyclopedia of Religion in American Politics* (Oryx Press of Kansas, 1996), which he coedited and for which he wrote the introductory overview essay. He also coedited *The C. S. Lewis Readers' Encyclopedia* (Zondervan, 1998), which won a Gold Medallion award for best biography of 1998 from the Evangelical Christian Publishers Association. He has contributed articles to a variety of publications and books, including *Religion and Liberty*, *Policy Review*, *Wake Forest Law Review*, *The American Enterprise*, *The Encyclopedia of the American Constitution*, *The Encyclopedia of the American Presidency*, and *Permanent Things*.

Peter Wielhouwer is Associate Professor in the Robertson School of Government at Regent University. He received his Ph.D. from the University of Georgia. His research has focused on parties and elections and has been published in the *American Journal of Political Science*, the *American Politics Quarterly*, and the *Journal of Politics*.

Thomas Young is a graduate student at Regent University Law School and the Robertson School of Government, where he is pursuing a joint J.D. and M.A. in public policy.

Preface

This text is designed primarily as a supplemental volume for introductory courses in American politics. Most texts for such courses give little, if any, attention to the role of religion in American political life. This volume seeks to address this void, and, as a result, it is structured to parallel most textbooks used in introductory courses on American politics.

The authors of the various chapters are Christian scholars. They are scholars in that they have published books or refereed journal articles related to the chapter's topic: a short biography of each author appears before this preface. Each author is not simply a scholar, but a Christian scholar, as each is a member of Christians in Political Science, an association of Christians who work in the field of political science. Finally, almost all teach in relatively small, denominationally affiliated, liberal-arts institutions. Thus, not only are the authors of this volume likely to know the kinds of topics that will engage undergraduate students, but they are also well equipped to know the level of discussion and analysis that will challenge, but not overwhelm, students enrolled in such courses.

Each chapter in this volume was originally written for presentation at the Conference of Christians in Political Science held at Calvin College, June 17–20, 1999, hosted by the Paul B. Henry Institute for the Study of Christianity and Politics. Each author was invited to prepare a paper related to his or her area of expertise, and each paper was revised following the conference in light of discussion and suggestions. This cooperative process by Christian scholars who understand the needs of undergraduate education has resulted in a volume that, I believe, should prove a valuable, engaging, and stimulating supplemental text for courses in American politics. I trust that this volume will stimulate students not only to study the relationship between religion and American politics in greater depth but also to do so with greater analytical sensitivity. Finally, I hope that this volume will motivate some students to consider, as well as to choose, the study of the relationship between religion and politics as an academic field of study and personal vocation.

Corwin E. Smidt
Calvin College

1

Differing Perspectives on Politics among Religious Traditions

J. Christopher Soper

What is the proper political role for the Christian church? Should Christians turn to the government to resolve such issues as abortion or poverty, or is it better for religious believers to focus on the life of the church? While the answer to such questions may to some seem self-evident, they divide Christians into differing camps. In fact, since the Protestant Reformation of the sixteenth century, Christians have understood politics and their role as citizens in different ways. The churches that emerged from the Reformation emphasized alternative biblical themes, and, as a consequence, they taught their adherents to view their political calling as Christians differently. These teachings ranged from Anabaptism, which viewed the state as an alien force that Christians were called to confront by means of radical discipleship, to a Reformed theology that understood government and politics to be an arena for the unfolding of God's purposes in the world.

This religious diversity played itself out most notably in the United States, a nation of immigrants. Immigrants brought with them their religion, which included teaching about the Christian's social and political responsibility to the state. This chapter highlights the political teaching of five theological traditions: Reformed, Anabaptist, Lutheran, Roman Catholic, and Black Protestant. These five perspectives embody powerful intellectual traditions rooted in hundreds of years of Christian history. In many ways these perspectives define how Christians in these traditions are taught to think about politics and their responsibility to the state. Each of the five has been important in the development of Christianity in the United States.[1]

This chapter also contends that a church's social and political theology is powerfully affected by culture. Historically, for example, churches that have been a part of the majority have turned to the government to shape the culture of the community according to their religious values. Majority churches do not perceive a deep tension between religion and the state because the church and the wider society involve the same culture and basic values. Minority churches or religious perspectives, by contrast, have been more likely to question the legitimacy of a close union between religion and politics because the state has subjected them to various types of social and political discrimination (Lipset 1981). Important to remember is that the status of churches has changed in America's two-hundred-year history. What once were minority faiths (Baptist, Methodist, Roman Catholic) have become part of the cultural and political mainstream. For the most part, a church's political vision changes to reflect its new status in society.

The connection between religion and culture—theology and society—is complex, but what will become clear in this chapter is that both have been important in determining how churches in the United States understand their political responsibilities. This chapter first explores what each of the five traditions teaches about politics and how such teaching may have affected how believers have come to understand their political role in America. The chapter next focuses on how America's social and cultural environment has left its imprint on each of the traditions.

Christian Perspectives on Politics

The Christian perspective that has had the most impact on American churches is Reformed Protestantism. The preeminent religious principle in Reformed thought is the absolute sovereignty of God. John Calvin (1509–64), the primary architect in the sixteenth century of a Reformed vision, did not view God's sovereignty passively, in the sense that God was the supreme legislator and creator of the laws of nature who then

14

stood aside as they worked their way out in human history. Calvin's notion implied, instead, God's continual involvement in and relevance to every aspect of the world (Meeter 1960). Taking its cue from the first chapters in the Book of Genesis, a Reformed perspective emphasized that God created the world *and everything in it*, and called it good. There can be no justification, then, for a Christian to reject the world; Christ's followers are instead called to shape and influence the world around them.

To achieve this goal, Calvin sought to transform Geneva, Switzerland (a community he helped lead), into a model of the kingdom of God. This did not simply mean proclaiming the good news of God's coming kingdom; it also implied that its arrival would be demonstrated in every part of society, including politics, the arts, music, and education, all of which would rest squarely under the sovereignty of God. Abraham Kuyper, the nineteenth-century Dutch statesman and philosopher, expressed this Reformed vision well: "There is not a square inch on the whole plane of human existence over which Christ, who is Lord over all, does not proclaim: 'This is mine!'"

While Reformed Protestantism does not discount the reality of human sin, the implication of this perspective is that the redeemed have both the obligation and the capacity to remake the world in light of God's purposes for it. The philosopher Nicholas Wolterstorff uses the term *world formative Christianity* to describe what was at the time a new and radical idea in Christianity, that the structures and institutions of the material world were religiously significant and that Christians could become agents for positive social renewal (1983).

The political ramification of this Reformed perspective is clear: Christians have a duty to use the political order to reflect God's glory (Stone 1983). Because God is sovereign over all the earth, there can be no strict demarcation between religion and politics. The Christian must make every effort to transform aspects of culture that are not consistent with God's intentions for the world. Seen in this light, political activism becomes a natural and faithful response for the redeemed when pushed into the world of politics.

The Anabaptist/Mennonite tradition offers a profoundly different vision. Anabaptism emerged in the early sixteenth century as an alternative to the Lutheran and Reformed wings of the Protestant Reformation. The primary theological themes of Anabaptists were the creation of the true church based on the model of the New Testament as they understood it, and radical Christian discipleship patterned along Jesus' teaching in the Sermon on the Mount (Littell 1964). For Anabaptists, the church was the visible community of the redeemed. It was a voluntary association of those who had been called by God to restore the apostolic church and who were committed to a life lived in obedience to Christ's teaching. The world outside of the church was fallen; the church was the vehicle through which God worked in the world. The Anabaptist ethic was one of nonconformity to the world, which included a commitment to pacifism, service, and the way of the cross (Gustafson 1978).

The Anabaptist ecclesiology and ethic resulted in a dualism between the church and the world, which led its believers to have an ambiguous relationship to the state and politics. Using H. Richard Niebuhr's famous categories of Christian ethics, Anabaptists saw a strict demarcation between Christ and culture (Niebuhr 1951). In politics, they opposed any state-enforced religious conformity. As Franklin Littell notes, "They felt most strongly of all about the union of church and state. They believed that no individual might rightly be compelled by the magistrate in the matter of faith" (1964, 65). It was not simply that Anabaptists did not trust the state to make the *right* religious choices for its citizens. Instead, they argued that it was beyond the state's legitimate function to make *any* religious claim on its citizens.

Anabaptism certainly knows little, if anything, of the Reformed teaching that Christians have a responsibility to ensure that earthly rule reflects God's kingdom. There is almost nothing in Anabaptism to suggest that Christians should take an active part in the state's functioning (Wogaman 1988). To the extent that the church has a political role in Anabaptism, it is indirect: the church stands in judgment of the state, which inevitably depends on power and the sword to pursue its mission. By contrast, the church should be a living example to the world of how a life lived in commitment to Christ's ethic of nonresistant love should look. Sociologically, Anabaptists were a classic "sect," a voluntary association of religious believers that lived in a relatively high state of tension with their environment.[2] Anabaptists were also like many sects before and after them in that they faced severe persecution from the state—whether Roman Catholic or Protestant—which reinforced their skepticism about worldly politics.

A Lutheran perspective on politics differs in important respects from the Reformed and Anabaptist teaching. The founder of this perspective was Martin Luther (1483–1546), whose most important and creative contribution to the world of politics was his concept of *two kingdoms*. Luther drew a rigid distinction between the sacred and secular worlds. To Luther, such a distinction was perfectly compatible with human nature and existence. As he wrote in his famous treatise *Freedom of a Christian*, "Man has a twofold nature, a spiritual and a bodily one" (1961, 53). These realms are represented by two kingdoms, governed by characteristics unique to each system. The kingdom of God is the world of faith. In it "a Christian is a perfectly free lord of all, subject to none" (53). This freedom must be absolute because "no external thing has any influence in producing Christian righteousness" (54). In the spiritual world a Christian needs "neither laws nor good works, but, on the contrary is injured by them if he believes that he is justified by them" (67). Because religious freedom was so important in working out one's salvation, Luther made the revolutionary claim that the power of the state must be strictly limited in the spiritual world.

Yet we live in the physical world, and in this life the Christian "must control his own body and have dealings with men" (67). The freedom that is unlimited in the spiritual world must, because of the totality of human sin, be restricted in the earthly world by laws and institutions. In this world, "a Christian is a dutiful servant of all, subject to all" (53). While the state has no role in the spiritual world, therefore, Luther concluded that a Christian's outward behavior in the physical world must be governed by strict rules, under legitimate authorities.

Luther did not, however, expect much from politics. In Luther's view, political institutions existed to limit the social consequences of human sin. Without laws and rulers the world might fall into chaos. While he no doubt believed that all creation belonged to God, Luther's emphasis on human corruption made it difficult for him to see the state as having any function beyond the maintenance of social control. As the theologian James Gustafson notes about Luther's conception of the state: "It really cannot be the basis for developing a more positive common good" (1978, 14). The absolute separation of the earthly and spiritual kingdoms in Luther's theology leads logically to the conclusion that the two realms have little impact on one another. In contrast to Calvin, Luther held out little hope that the spiritual world could or should inform the world of politics. There is little sense in Luther's writing that Christians ought positively to bring gospel principles to bear on their politics.

In many respects, the picture drawn by Luther about politics is similar to that of the Anabaptists. Like them, he was skeptical about what the state could or should try to accomplish in spiritual matters. This similar premise, however, led Luther to a different conclusion about the Christian's attitude toward the world of politics. The Anabaptists' emphasis on Christian discipleship led them to argue that the church must resist the state because the state is based on force, coercion, and violence. Luther, by contrast, claimed that as long as the state made it possible for Christians freely to pursue their more important spiritual calling, they should be dutiful citizens and accept the political status quo. The Lutheran perspective on politics, in short, stands firmly on the side of a conservative political ethic in that Luther did not believe that Christians should seek radically to reform the political status quo.

Given the Catholic church's nearly two-thousand-year history, it is difficult to generalize about a single Roman Catholic perspective on politics. One important strand of that tradition comes from Augustine of Hippo's fifth-century work, *City of God*. In that work, Augustine (354–430) argues that there is a fundamental contrast between the world (the City of Man) and Christianity (the City of God). Augustine uses the city metaphor to show how the nature of one's love, or allegiance, dictates one's social behavior. The City of Man is made up of people who try to find their satisfaction within the world. In the City of God, by contrast, people direct their attention beyond the temporal world, to God. Augustine believed, however, that the City of God was an invisible reality that would not be fully realized until the end of the world. As such, it was not possible to determine who ultimately belongs to which of the two cities, and he consistently stated that the church was not the City of God on earth.

The implication for politics in an Augustinian viewpoint is acquiescence to the state as a fundamentally established institution with limited purposes. The state was necessary to check the consequences of human sin in the City of Man. But Augustine argued, as did Luther after him, that political quietism should be the norm for believers, as their primary goal is spiritual union with God. Augustine's famous aphorism, "Thou hast made us O Lord for thyself, and our heart shall find no rest till it rest in thee," captures this idea that the physical world is less significant than the spiritual world.

Despite his intentions, Augustine's work was eventually used by the Catholic church to support the idea of a unified Christian commonwealth (Maddox 1996). Christendom, which emerged in the Middle Ages, saw the church as the de facto City of God on earth. Abandoning Augustine's notion of limited government purposes, the church advocated a vision of a hierarchically structured state with extensive areas of influence that operated in close alliance with the church. The political implication in this Catholic perspective was that the church as an institution had a political mission to provide unity in the world by organizing and ruling all people according to biblical injunctions.

The Protestant Reformation challenged the presumption that the Catholic church would, or could, have this kind of unified political power. While the church gradually modified its view in light of this Protestant threat, it did not abandon it. The church retained key principles of this Christendom idea until well into the twentieth century, including that the government should have a public profession of religion, that the church should be protected by the state, and that the spiritual was superior to the temporal order. The church expressed skepticism about democracy and frequently allied itself with authoritarian governments (Molnar 1980).

The Second Vatican Council (1962–65) introduced a fundamental change in the political attitudes of the Roman Catholic church. Pope John XXIII called the council to renew the life of the church and to bring up to date its teaching, discipline, and organization. The legislation that came out of the meetings had an enormous influence in changing the attitudes of the church to other religious bodies, both Christian and non-Christian, and in how the church viewed the world of politics. Instead of affirming the inherited Catholic position that the state ought to be subservient to the interests of the church, Vatican II supported the ideals of a liberal political democracy: separation of church and state, respect for religious diversity, and adherence to individual freedoms. Far from abandoning its political role, however, the church reaffirmed the significance of the church's political witness to its social justice tradition. In the aftermath of Vatican II, the church views its political mission as providing a prophetic voice on behalf of such issues as poverty, abortion, war, and peace.

The fifth and final perspective is that of Black Protestantism. In contrast with the other four perspectives, Black Protestantism is not as closely associated with a particular thinker or a specific church tradition. Instead, Black Protestantism emerges principally out of the social and political experience of African Americans in the United States. The most formative of those experiences for blacks was their enslavement until the end of the Civil War in 1865 and the state-sponsored discrimination that followed for the next century. During this time, religion served as a refuge for the African American community, the church being one of the few institutions in which blacks were relatively safe and free.

In the context of this oppression, the black church forged a theology based on the biblical themes of Jesus' liberation of the poor and oppressed and of God's miraculous delivery of his chosen people. This is not surprising given the historical treatment of blacks in the United States. Religion provided a means of escape and a cause for hope among black slaves. A popular black spiritual written during the time of slavery asked rhetorically, "Didn't my Lord deliver Daniel, then why not every man?" For the black church the answer was clear: God would and could deliver blacks from their oppression. Liberation and freedom have remained the key themes for blacks who continue to face discrimination and inequality. As James Cone, a leading black theologian, notes, "It does not matter what oppressors say or do or what they try to make us out to be. We know that we have a freedom not made with human hands" (1975, 140).

Despite its commitment to the liberation of African Americans, the black church has not consistently been politically active. In the decades following the Civil War, the vast majority of blacks lived in the South, where their political freedom was severely limited. Political quietism was the norm for the black church because blacks feared for their lives if they became politically active. This changed dramatically during the civil rights movement of the 1950s and 1960s. Led in large part by black clergy, the movement gradually mobilized the black church to political activism as a natural and appropriate response to the biblical themes of liberation and freedom. Since that time, Black Protestantism, more than any other church tradition, has emphasized that political activity is a legitimate and necessary way to improve the lives of African Americans.

Given this diversity of perspectives on politics within Christianity, one might ask why such diversity exists and which of these five traditions has the "correct" understanding of the Christian's social and political role. For various reasons, however, there is no escaping this multiplicity of points of view and no simple answer to the question of which of these traditions is "correct." First, it needs to be recognized that Jesus' life in the New Testament does not provide a clear political blueprint for Christians who seek to be faithful to his witness politically. Jesus himself was never directly involved in politics. He did not form a political party, hold or seek a political office, organize a political protest, or seek directly to influence the policies of the leading political figures of his day (Pilate, Herod, Caesar). Far from offering a systematic answer to the question of the proper relationship between politics and the Christian faith, the few statements Jesus made about politics provide ambiguous guidelines at best. For example, in the famous story in which the Pharisees ask Jesus if it was lawful to pay taxes to the emperor (a most political question), Jesus gives them a cryptic answer that can and has been interpreted by Christians in a number of ways ("Give to Caesar what is Caesar's, and to God what is God's"; see Matt. 22:15–22).

Various passages and stories in the Old and New Testaments point believers in different directions as they seek to understand the relationship between faith and politics. One example is the voice of the Old Testament prophets, who urge God's people to challenge the political status quo and to work tirelessly for justice, mercy, and peace for the oppressed. A second, and very different, model comes from Paul's counsel to believers in Romans 13 to obey the governing authorities that have been instituted by God. As they have sought to understand their political obligations, these five Christian traditions have drawn upon particular texts in the Bible and emphasized different themes. Each tradition has tried to be faithful to what the Bible teaches on politics, but the particular historical and cultural context out of which they have emerged has influenced the biblical themes they have highlighted or neglected. It is no surprise, for example, that the preeminence of the Roman Catholic church during the Middle Ages led it to highlight passages that called on Christians to be good citizens of the state. By contrast, the political repression that Anabaptists experienced at the hands of Protestant and Catholic magistrates led them to emphasize Scriptures that challenged the political status quo. In a sense, then, each of the five traditions may be viewed as having "a" correct (or at least defensible) approach to politics, but not "the" correct approach.

This is not to suggest, however, that all interpretations of the Bible on questions related to politics are equally valid. One of the principal tasks of theologians and social ethicists is to give a compelling and thorough account of what the Bible teaches on politics by weaving the themes and passages in the Scriptures that speak to the church's political role (Yoder 1972; Sherratt and Mahurin 1995). But this task exceeds the confines of this chapter.

Religious Perspectives in American Politics

The Colonial Period

What influence did these religious perspectives have on politics in the United States? Two of the three leading denominations in the early years of the republic (Congregational and Presbyterian) were theologically Reformed. These Puritan settlers saw the state as an extension of their religious calling, and they tried to make the political order consistent with their religious principles. The Puritans turned to the state to control the religious affairs of the new nation, passing laws and regulations designed to support their idea of what constituted a Christian civilization (Hatch 1989).

Reformed churches, however, faced increasing religious competition in the United States from immigrants from other traditions. A variety of Anabaptist churches, for example, immigrated to America during the colonial period. Mennonites, Hutterites, Amish, Baptists, and others came to America to practice their faith without governmental restriction, but colonial governments instituted their own forms of religious orthodoxy that were in many respects as restrictive as those in Europe (Murrin 1990). The Calvinist clergy tried to use politics to defuse their

21

religious competition. In many communities, Reformed churches received subsidies from the government to hold their services in public buildings without charge, while other churches did not receive such subsidies. In addition, while the Constitution's establishment clause ensured that the national government would not have an officially established church, state governments could have an official church, and many did until the early part of the nineteenth century.

The political reality "on the ground" fits perfectly with the Anabaptist theology that the state and its politics could not be trusted with religious affairs. From the Anabaptists' perspective, the attempts by Reformed clergy to control their religious practices were nothing more than the use of political means to extend the domain of Reformed religious and cultural practices. Anabaptists supported the American Revolution in large part because they hoped it would topple the religious establishments of the day. They also enthusiastically joined Madison and Jefferson after the war had ended in the fight for the separation of church and state. There was, again, a perfect symmetry between Anabaptist theology and their political interests as members of a minority sect.

Reformed churches also faced a challenge from the religious awakenings of the seventeenth and eighteenth centuries. The churches that benefited most from the religious revivals were not the Reformed churches, but the upstart Methodist, Disciples, and Baptist denominations. As the sociologists Roger Finke and Rodney Stark (1992) have noted, these "evangelical" churches understood the religious needs of a frontier population better than their Reformed counterparts, and, as a consequence, there was a surge in the growth of their churches. The Calvinist clergy conspired with public officials to define the camp meetings the revivalists used so effectively to recruit church members as disturbances of the peace or as violations of other statutes, but their attempt to restrain the new churches failed miserably. By the middle decades of the nineteenth century, the Presbyterian and Congregational churches no longer had a political monopoly over their religious competition.

It would be unfair to dismiss these actions as nothing more than an attempt by Reformed churches to preserve their religious monopoly in the face of increasing competition. While that is part of the story, Reformed clergy sincerely believed that evangelical churches were religiously and culturally harmful. Given their Reformed notion of God's sovereignty, it not only made sense for them to use politics to restrain these "dangerous" evangelicals, but it was also a religious mandate.

It is ironic that the Baptists, with their radical social and political ethic, would have been so effective at spreading their religious message in America. As historian Nathan Hatch notes (1989), however, the Baptist theology was in many ways perfectly suited to emerging American cultural values. Baptists' stress on believers' baptism, congregational autonomy, a called rather than a professional clergy, and the individual's ability to interpret Scripture resonated deeply with America's democratic and populist political culture. In addition, the Baptists proved willing and able to adapt their message effectively to local needs, which in this case meant embracing an evangelical religious piety that was in many ways theologically Reformed. The Baptist church in America, then, became a mixture of Anabaptism and Calvinism.

What impact did this have on politics? Reformed churches did not abandon the world of politics. Their theological views on God's sovereignty dictated that they work to transform the world, and for the most part they continued to try to do that. While they lost the numbers battle to the more evangelical denominations, members of Reformed churches retained a high social status that gave them privileged access to the political process in the twentieth century.

Evangelical churches also turned to the state for religious ends. This was not surprising for the Methodists, who emphasized personal holiness and believed that the world could, and should, be freed from the taint of sin. Political action for the Baptists, however, seemed wholly inconsistent with their religious heritage. As a persecuted sect during the colonial period, Baptists supported a theology of opposition or indifference to the state. This became harder to sustain as Baptist churches became large, successful, and integrated into American culture. The various Baptist churches did not fully abandon their commitment to church-state separation, but they dropped the idea that the state was a fundamentally alien force that Christians ought to oppose. In light of their social mobility, Calvinists offered a competing political vision for the church, and Baptists became more open to using politics to remake the world according to their religious vision.

The Postwar Protestant Establishment

The immigration of large numbers of Roman Catholics, Lutherans, Jews, and other ethnic religious groups in the middle and latter decades of the nineteenth century also affected how the churches viewed politics. The Lutheran communion in the United States, for example, quintupled in size between 1870 and 1910. While there was a tremendous diversity among the various Lutheran churches (at one point there were sixty-six independent church organizations), there was an underlying unity of faith and practice among these newly arriving Lutherans. For the most part, Lutherans, along with Roman Catholics and other immigrant religious groups, wanted to preserve their identity, language, religious traditions, confessions, and doctrines (Hertz 1976). Religious minorities created a parallel society with their own schools and other institutions to protect themselves from Protestant influences.

This "insurgency of foreigners" posed, in the minds of many Reformed and evangelical clergy, a threat to the values of the American Christian civilization. As the historian Sydney Ahlstrom notes (1972), a common-core Protestantism emerged as these churches sought to protect and defend their shared cultural values in the face of this immigrant challenge. The politically dominant churches viewed Lutherans and Roman Catholics as religiously and culturally suspect, and they used the government to try to impose their religious values on these immigrants.

The political expression of this religious impulse took many forms. At one extreme were efforts to restrict legal immigration so that fewer Catholics, in particular, could settle in America. The American Protective Association, formed in 1887, helped to revive grassroots anti-Catholicism as it wrote pamphlets emphasizing the subservience of Catholics to the pope in Rome. The Prohibition movement can also be understood as a conflict over religious values. To Reformed and evangelical Christians, Prohibition was an effort to purge the world of the sin of alcohol. Lutherans, Roman Catholics, and Jews, however, had very different values on alcohol consumption; to them, Prohibition was nothing more than the imposition of a Protestant religious ethic on their culture.

The battle between Protestants and Catholics was particularly intense in the public schools, which were designed in part to assimilate immigrants into American culture. As a rule, public schools could have religious exercises until well into the twentieth century, and local school boards frequently encouraged "Protestant" exercises that Catholics and other religionists bitterly opposed. In response, Lutherans, Catholics, and other minorities established their own schools to preserve their language and religious traditions in a hostile American setting. Not to be outdone, the state of Oregon tried, with an amendment in 1922 that required children from eight to sixteen to attend public schools, to compel Catholics and Lutherans to integrate into the state-run school system. The Supreme Court, however, overturned the law in *Pierce v. Society of Sisters* (1925).

The political efforts by the dominant churches reinforced the theological skepticism that Lutherans had about trusting the state with religious affairs. Lutheran immigrants brought a conservative and confessional theology to the American church (Kuenning 1988). In politics, this meant a rigid reformulation of Luther's theology that discouraged the application of religious principles to politics and sought to separate the Christian from the secular state. Instead, the church placed a renewed emphasis on the principle that God's kingdom was otherworldly and that no amount of social reform could usher in the millennium. As noted above, Luther did not advocate a Christian separation from the world or active opposition to the state by the church. Luther believed that government had an important role to play, even though he preferred the state to keep out of religious affairs. Lutherans in America were, consequently, dutiful citizens and involved in politics, but they did not try to get the state actively to transmit their values. They simply wanted the government to stay out of religious affairs.

The situation for Roman Catholics was more complicated. As a minority church facing religious persecution, Catholics had an interest in keeping church and state as separate as possible, a viewpoint that the American Catholic church gradually began to articulate in the late nineteenth century. This was not, however, perfectly consistent with the inherited Catholic perspective on politics. The papal encyclicals of Pope Leo XIII (1878–1903) reaffirmed the idea that the government should make a public profession of the faith and that the church should use the state to protect its own institutional interests. The Vatican also warned the American church of the dangers of the separation of church and state, or what it called "Americanism" (Segers 1990). The American Catholic church walked a fine line between articulating the official positions of the church, while paying attention to its unique situation in the United States. What is particularly ironic is that while the church was viewed by many Protestants as potentially subversive and dangerous because of its allegiance to Rome, Roman Catholics made every effort to prove their loyalty and patriotism to America.

The split between religionists during this post–Civil War period also played itself out in party politics. Through a detailed analysis of election returns, political scientist Paul Kleppner (1970) has demonstrated that the most significant cleavage in late-nineteenth-century America was between members of pietistic and liturgical churches. Pietists, who were a combination of Reformed and evangelical Christians, were part of the de facto religious and cultural establishment. They sought to use politics to help usher in God's kingdom; they voted for the Republican Party, which was more likely to support their efforts. Members of liturgical churches (Roman Catholics and Lutherans) felt the sting of state-sponsored discrimination and fought vigilantly against state encroachment on their churches. They wanted the government to stay out of the affairs of the church and supported the Democratic Party, because it favored personal freedom and state neutrality regarding religion.

The Modern Era

The modernist controversy in the early twentieth century had a profound impact on the structure and politics of American churches. The theological debate pitted liberals, who sought to reconcile the Christian faith with modern science and changing social conditions, against conservatives, who reasserted the traditional teaching of the church. Each of the five religious perspectives struggled with the modernist challenge at some point in the century. But, overall, during the twentieth century there was a gradual realignment of denominations into liberal and conservative camps based on the position that they took on the modernist controversy. In addition, though churches continue to be as involved in politics as they have ever been, when they make political statements, they do so less within the framework of their particular theological tradition.

With the exception of a few ethnic churches (the Reformed Church in America and the Christian Reformed Church), theologically Reformed denominations (Presbyterian and Congregational) sided with the liberals in this theological dispute. Because it placed greater emphasis on the social and political transformation of society than on the salvation of individual sinners, a liberal theology proved to be conducive to political action. Churches that adopted a liberal theology (Presbyterian, Congregational, Northern Baptist, Disciples of Christ, Episcopal) joined forces to support the Social Gospel movement in the early part of the twentieth century.

The theologically liberal churches also had the highest status in American society and therefore had greater access to political elites in government. Because of their strategic location, these so-called mainline churches had more political power than their numbers might have indicated. This was particularly true in the decades immediately following the Second World War, when mainline churches had an organized presence in Washington, D.C., that dwarfed that of their conservative counterparts (Fowler, Hertzke, and Olson 1999). Mainline churches effectively used their access and influence to lobby Congress on civil rights and other political issues in the 1960s.

The largest of the historically Anabaptist churches, the Southern Baptist Convention (SBC), allied itself with the conservative or evangelical side of the modernist debate. In contrast with liberal churches, evangelicals initially shied away from politics. Their conservative theology emphasized the primacy of religious conversion rather than social transformation and was not as conducive to political action as liberal theology. In addition, evangelical churches were socially marginal in national politics. While they periodically engaged in politics on issues of personal morality, evangelicals generally refrained from the kinds of political efforts that engaged liberal churches in the early decades of the twentieth century. Their focus, instead, was on theological debates within the church.

The growth of evangelical churches in the latter half of the twentieth century changed the political calculus. By 1970, Southern Baptists were the largest Protestant denomination in America, and other evangelical and fundamentalist churches grew rapidly as well. This coincided with the decline of membership in the historically mainline, liberal Protestant churches. At the same time, evangelicals were improving their economic and social standing. Jimmy Carter, a Southern Baptist and self-described born-again Christian, was elected president in 1976, indicating the rising social status for theologically conservative Christians in general and Southern Baptists in particular. Instead of being socially insignificant because of their theological views, conservative Christians were increasingly a part of the political and cultural mainstream.

Evangelicals were motivated to become politically active by their antipathy to the liberal social norms and practices of the 1960s and 1970s. Evangelical Christians formed a number of political organizations to defend deeply held values on such issues as abortion, pornography, and gay rights. Southern Baptists and other evangelical churches became active first in the Moral Majority and later the Christian Coalition out of a conviction that politics was necessary to reinforce their religious views, especially on an American culture that had left their values behind. Evangelical churches now compete with mainline churches for influence in the policy-making process (Hertzke 1988).

Because of their cultural isolation, Lutherans initially ignored the modernist controversy that was dividing the Protestant religious world into evangelical and mainline camps in the early part of the twentieth century. This sectarian isolation did not, however, last for long. Lutherans became increasingly integrated into American society as the century progressed, and, as a consequence, it became more difficult for them to maintain their linguistic, cultural, and religious distinctiveness. Lutherans, in short, gradually became assimilated into American society and have been increasingly affected by religious and cultural trends outside of the denomination. By the end of the Second World War, a clear demarcation had emerged within the Lutheran communion that mirrored the larger Protestant world. A union of three Lutheran churches in 1982 formed the Evangelical Lutheran Church in America (ELCA), which represents the church's more liberal wing, while two separate organizations, the Lutheran Church–Missouri Synod (LCMS) and the Wisconsin Evangelical Lutheran Synod (WELS), champion the church's conservative tradition.

The Roman Catholic church reconciled itself with the modernist debate in its Second Vatican Council. As noted earlier, the council brought a fundamental change in the church's liturgy, organizational structure, and in how it viewed its political role. Vatican II affirmed the values of America's political democracy and encouraged the process of Catholic social integration. The church did not abandon its political vision, but the Catholic hierarchy now articulates positions on various social justice issues rather than simply defending the institutional interests of the church (Byrnes 1991). As with many Protestant churches, there is a division within American Catholicism between traditionalists, who reflect a more conservative religious and political position, and modernists, who advocate a more liberal view. The split manifests itself over political issues (abortion, capital punishment, economic justice) and religious concerns (women's ordination, attitudes toward gays in the church).

Black Protestantism is unique among the five religious perspectives because it combines a strongly evangelical theology with generally liberal political views. African American Christians are more religious than the rest of the population and, by large margins, they have conservative theological views. They are not, however, politically conservative. Blacks do have traditional views on abortion and the role of women, but they are liberal on gay rights, civil rights, and economic issues. The latter set of issues tends to take precedence within black churches and among African American interest groups.

One of the consequences of the modernist controversy is that it has led toward a gradual restructuring of American churches (Wuthnow 1988). The old religious fault line that divided religious believers by denomination gradually gave way to a new cleavage based on a commitment of churches to a liberal or conservative theology and worldview. Liberals stress the themes of religious and political choice, diversity, and progress. Conservatives, on the other hand, emphasize the importance of traditional religious and cultural values. One of the results of this realignment is that the shared religious heritage and distinctive beliefs of denominations do not matter as they once did. This restructuring has encouraged churches to work across denominational lines for religious and political purposes. Liberal Presbyterians find that they have more in common with liberal Catholics, Jews, African Americans, and secular elites than they do with conservative members of their own church.

While active in politics, churches are less likely to offer a unique or distinctive theological perspective on politics. Historically Reformed churches, for example, are involved in contemporary politics; they pass numerous resolutions at annual meetings, and work with other churches on various peace and justice issues. The link between this activism and the churches' theological heritage, however, is far less clear than it once was. One is hard pressed to find explicit reference in denominational pronouncements for why a Reformed perspective on politics dictates a particular position, or even a certain attitude toward the political world. It is less a "Reformed" perspective that the lobbying offices of the Presbyterian Church in the United States of America (PCUSA), the United Church of Christ (UCC), and other historically Reformed churches offer than a liberal, even secular, viewpoint on politics.

The five-million-member Evangelical Lutheran Church in America is increasingly indistinguishable from other Mainline Protestant churches. An illustration of the Lutheran integration into the mainline world is a recent decision by the church to declare full communion with the Reformed Church in America, the PCUSA, and the UCC. In its politics, the ELCA acts like other mainline churches. It has a Division for the Church in Society that helps to establish social policy, lobbies the government to enact favorable legislation, and works with other church organizations that share its political vision. Over the years the church has articulated a generally liberal stand on such issues as the environment, the death penalty, and race relations, to name a few. The division describes its mission in this way:

> The church takes a public stance because of the faith it confesses. *If God is active in all arenas of life* [my emphasis], God's people must bear witness in society, for example, when God's purposes of mercy and justice for all are being violated. This typically occurs through the development of social statements—the most authoritative form of social policy—that address significant broad areas of social concern and emerge out of a process of extensive and inclusive deliberation in this church. (Evangelical Lutheran Church in America 1999)

This is essentially a Reformed statement on the relation between the church and the world. There are, of course, many ways to interpret Luther on the subject, but it is hard to imagine that he believed that the church should bear witness to "broad areas of social concern" if that meant active political involvement by the church. What is even clearer is that the division's statement contradicts the history of the Lutheran church in America in that, historically, it did not seek to transmit its social values through political action.

At the other end of the political spectrum is the Ethics and Religious Liberty Commission of the Southern Baptist Convention. As late as 1989, the commission was a small lobbying organization for the church that rented office space in Washington, D.C., and worked primarily on issues of religious liberty. Under the leadership of Richard Land, it has become a multimillion-dollar organization that owns its own building, has a visible political presence in the city, and takes political stands on a panoply of political issues. Remarkably, given the SBC's largely Anabaptist heritage, in a recent issue of their publication, *Light*, Land outlined a defense for American involvement in Kosovo using the classic Catholic just-war doctrine (Land 1999).

Ethnic churches are a possible exception to this trend. The Mennonite Church, for example, has a very effective organization in Washington that lobbies on issues directly related to the church's Anabaptist heritage, particularly pacifism (Miller 1996).

The 2.6-million-member Lutheran Church–Missouri Synod has kept a strong commitment to the historical confessions of the Lutheran Church. It emphasizes Luther's two-kingdom theology in its statements on politics:

> The primary mission of the church, according to our Lutheran belief, is the preaching of the Gospel and the administration of the sacraments. The government, on the other hand, has the divinely given mandate to provide for the temporal peace and tranquility of its citizens. So we Lutherans advocate a certain institutional separation but functional interaction between church and state. (Lutheran Church–Missouri Synod 1999)

The cost of keeping fidelity to a particular heritage, however, is that both the Mennonite Church and LCMS have remained on the fringes of American culture. The LCMS, for example, takes conservative positions on social and moral issues, but the church refuses to engage in any ecumenical endeavor with churches that do not share their commitment to the historic confessions of the Lutheran Church, which is basically the entire evangelical world. The Mennonite Church, by contrast, is politically liberal, but its commitment to pacifism and nonviolent resistance is not the norm for most mainline churches.

Despite these exceptions, however, the general trend is toward a new religious landscape in which the churches defend differing political positions with little thought given to the unique perspective on politics offered by their denominational heritage. Religion and theology are still important for the political choices made by churches and individual Christians (Guth et al. 1997), but those decisions are less likely to reflect the particular traditions of the denominations involved. But an even more sober assessment asserts that political activism itself may well contribute to secularizing the political message of Christians, as Christian groups, in an effort to reach as large an audience as possible, downplay their distinctive theological heritage and rely on secular arguments to defend their positions (Hofrenning 1995).

References

Ahlstrom, Sydney E. 1972. *A Religious History of the American People*. New Haven: Yale University Press.

Byrnes, Timothy. 1991. *Catholic Bishops in American Politics*. Princeton, N.J.: Princeton University Press.

Cone, James H. 1975. *God of the Oppressed*. New York: Seabury.

Evangelical Lutheran Church in America, Division for Church in Society. 1999. "Why and How Does the ELCA Address Social Concerns?" http://www.elca.org/dcs/addressingsocial.html

Finke, Roger, and Rodney Stark. 1992. *The Churching of America, 1776–1990*. New Brunswick, N.J.: Rutgers University Press.

Fowler, Robert Booth, Allen D. Hertzke, and Laura R. Olson. 1999. *Religion and Politics in America*. 2d ed. Boulder, Colo.: Westview.

Gustafson, James M. 1978. *Protestant and Roman Catholic Ethics*. Chicago: University of Chicago Press.

Guth, James, et al. 1997. *The Bully Pulpit: The Politics of Protestant Clergy*. Lawrence: University of Kansas Press.

Hatch, Nathan O. 1989. *The Democratization of American Christianity*. New Haven: Yale University Press.

Hertz, Karl H. 1976. *Two Kingdoms and One World: A Sourcebook in Christian Social Ethics*. Minneapolis: Augsburg.

Hertzke, Allen D. 1988. *Representing God in Washington: The Role of Religious Lobbies in the American Polity*. Knoxville: University of Tennessee Press.

Hofrenning, Daniel J. B. 1995. *In Washington but Not of It: The Prophetic Politics of Religious Lobbyists*. Philadelphia: Temple University Press.

Kleppner, Paul. 1970. *The Cross of Culture: A Social Analysis of Midwestern Politics, 1850–1900*. New York: Free Press.

Kuenning, Paul P. 1988. *The Rise and Fall of American Pietism: The Rejection of an Activist Heritage*. Macon, Ga.: Mercer University Press.

Land, Richard. 1999. "Kosovo: Do We Pay Now or Later?" *Light: The Ethics and Religious Liberty Commission of the Southern Baptist Convention* (May–June): 2.

Lipset, Seymour Martin. 1981. *Political Man: The Social Bases of Politics*. Expanded ed. Baltimore: John Hopkins University Press.

Littell, Franklin H. 1964. *The Origins of Sectarian Protestantism*. New York: Macmillan.

Luther, Martin. 1961. "The Freedom of a Christian." In *Martin Luther: Selections from His Writings*, edited by John Dillenberger. Garden City, N.Y.: Anchor.

Lutheran Church–Missouri Synod. 1999. "An Introduction to the Lutheran Church—Missouri Synod." http://www.lcms.org/introlcms.html

Maddox, Graham. 1996. *Religion and the Rise of Democracy*. New Haven: Yale University Press.

Meeter, H. Henry. 1960. *The Basic Ideas of Calvinism*. Grand Rapids: Grand Rapids International Publications.

Miller, Keith Graber. 1996. *American Mennonites Engage Washington: Wise as Serpents, Innocent as Doves?* Knoxville: University of Tennessee Press.

Molnar, Thomas. 1980. *Politics and the State: The Catholic View*. Chicago: Franciscan Herald.

Murrin, John. 1990. "Religion and Politics in America from the First Settlements to the Civil War." In *Religion and American Politics: From the Colonial Period to the 1980s*, edited by Mark A. Noll. Oxford: Oxford University Press.

Niebuhr, H. Richard. 1951. *Christ and Culture*. New York: Harper.

Segers, Mary C., ed. 1990. *Church Polity and American Politics: Issues in Contemporary Catholicism*. New York: Garland.

Sherratt, Timothy R., and Ronald P. Mahurin. 1995. *Saints as Citizens: A Guide to Public Responsibilities for Christians*. Grand Rapids: Baker.

Stone, Ronald H. 1983. *Reformed Faith and Politics*. Washington, D.C.: University Press of America.

Wallis, Roy. 1982. *Sectarianism*. New York: Wiley.

Wilson, Bryan. 1961. *Sects and Society*. Berkeley: University of California Press.

Wogaman, J. Philip. 1988. *Christian Perspectives on Politics*. Philadelphia: Fortress.

Wolterstorff, Nicholas. 1983. *Until Justice and Peace Embrace*. Grand Rapids: Eerdmans.

Wuthnow, Robert. 1988. *The Restructuring of American Religion: Society and Faith Since World War Two*. Princeton, N.J.: Princeton University Press.

Yoder, John Howard. 1972. *The Politics of Jesus*. Grand Rapids: Eerdmans.

Teaching Tools

Discussion Questions

1. What are the similarities and the differences in how the five religious traditions view politics?
2. In what ways has American culture affected the social and political teaching of churches over time?
3. Describe the political impact of the immigration of large numbers of Lutherans, Roman Catholics, and other religious minorities at the end of the nineteenth century.
4. What was the political impact of the modernist controversy on America's churches?
5. Analyze the difference between how a liberal and a conservative theology viewed politics in the early part of the twentieth century.
6. How would you explain that Christians and Christian churches view politics so differently?

Topics for Student Research

1. Using the appropriate website below, research the social and political teaching of your denomination. What are the key biblical texts

and/or concepts that contribute to your church's understanding of a Christian's social and political obligation? Does your denomination take official positions on social and political issues? If so, describe some of those positions. If your church does not take an official stance on issues, how does it explain the relationship between religion and politics?

2. Compare the social and political teaching of at least two denominations on at least two contemporary political issues. Do the churches take the same or different stances on the issues? What kinds of arguments do they provide for the positions that they take? What are the theological and scriptural bases for their views?

3. What do you believe that your faith requires of you in social and political involvement? Is faith primarily a personal matter of individual salvation or does it also require you to do something to change the political world around you? Should your faith inform your politics? If so, in what ways? What theological and/or scriptural resources do you use to defend your position?

Denominational Websites

Denomination	Web Address
African Methodist Episcopal (AME) Church	www.amecnet.org
American Baptist Churches in the USA (ABC-USA)	www.abc-usa.org
Assemblies of God	www.ag.org
Christian Reformed Church in North America	www.crcna.org
Churches of Christ	www.church-of-christ.org
Church of God in Christ	www.cogic.org
Episcopal Church	www.dfms.org
Evangelical Lutheran Church in America	www.elca.org
Lutheran Church–Missouri Synod (LCMS)	www.lcms.org
Mennonite Church USA	mcusa.mennonite.net
Presbyterian Church (U.S.A.)	www.pcusa.org
Presbyterian Church in America (PCA)	www.pcanet.org

Reformed Church in America	www.rca.org
Roman Catholic Church	www.nccbuscc.org
Seventh-Day Adventist Church	www.adventist.org
Southern Baptist Convention	www.sbc.net
United Church of Christ	www.ucc.org
United Methodist Church	www.umc.org

For the web addresses of additional churches, go to:
www.forministry.com/Denomination

2

Religion and the Constitution

JOHN G. WEST JR.

Religion shaped the development of the U.S. Constitution of 1787 in important ways. This chapter examines the distinctive contribution of religion to the development of the U.S. Constitution, as well as the limitations of its contribution. The first part of the chapter briefly discusses whether the Constitution was intended to set up a completely secular political system or a Christian commonwealth, followed by a second section that examines the diversity of religious beliefs held by those who drafted the Constitution. The third section analyzes the text of the unamended Constitution for clues on the role of religion in America's political system, while the fourth section explores the religious roots of the political theory of the Constitution—including the Puritan idea of covenant, the belief in human sinfulness, and the recognition of religious liberty. The chapter concludes with a brief discussion of political controversies that have caused some religious believers to challenge the Constitution's authority. Included in this discussion are the efforts to abolish slavery and to amend the Constitution to recognize the authority of Jesus Christ.

The American Constitution: Godly or Godless?

The Constitutional Convention had been meeting for only a few weeks when a crisis erupted. Delegates from the four smaller states demanded equal representation in the Senate, fearful their rights would be trampled without it. Delegates from the larger states balked, and the small-state delegates threatened to walk out. Tempers flared, members of the Convention insulted each other, and deliberations deadlocked.

Just as the Convention seemed about to disintegrate, the oldest delegate rose to speak. At 82, Benjamin Franklin was accorded more than a little deference by the rest of the Convention. "[T]he very heavens obey him, and the clouds yield up the lightning to be imprisoned in his rod," wrote fellow delegate William Pierce (Farrand 1966, 3:91).

Franklin proposed a three-day adjournment to cool tempers, supplemented by the hiring of a chaplain, who would "introduce the business of each day by an address to the *Creator of the universe . . .* beseeching Him to preside in our council, enlighten our minds with a portion of heavenly wisdom, . . . and crown our labors with complete and abundant success!" (Farrand 1966, 3:471).

The youngest delegate at the Convention, twenty-seven-year-old Jonathan Dayton from New Jersey, continues the story:

> The words of the venerable Franklin fell upon our ears with a weight and authority, even greater than we may suppose an oracle to have had in a Roman senate! A silent admiration superseded, for a moment, the expression of that assent and approbation which was strongly marked on almost every countenance; I say *almost*, for *one* man was found in the Convention, Mr. H—, from—, who rose and said, with regard to the first motion of the honorable gentleman, for an *adjournment*, he would yield his assent; but he protested against the second motion, for the appointment of a chaplain. He then commenced a high-strained eulogium on the assemblage of *wisdom*, *talent* and *experience*, which the Convention embraced . . . and concluded by saying, that therefore he did not see the necessity of calling in *foreign aid!* (Farrand 1966, 3:471–72)

Ignoring "this impertinent and impious speech," according to Dayton, Washington and the rest of the Convention immediately ratified both the call for a chaplain and an adjournment. The subsequent recess was spent in "free and frank" consultations, the result of which appeared in the morning session three days later. As soon as the chaplain had closed his prayer, a compromise was secured on the organization of the Senate according to the existing plan.

36

Thus occurred the miracle at Philadelphia. At the very point the Convention was about to break apart, passion and self-interest gave way to reason and self-sacrifice as delegates humbled themselves before the supreme lawgiver of the universe. Or so it was supposed by those who read the above account, which first appeared in the respected *National Intelligencer* in 1826 (Farrand 1966, 3:467 n. 1). Evangelicals quickly appropriated the story in order to vindicate the pious character of the founding. Here was positive proof that the framers had remembered God while drafting the Constitution.

That prayers were initially proposed by a Unitarian rather than a Christian proved but a minor irritant. Evangelical Thomas Grimké equated Franklin with the biblical Cornelius, the Roman centurion in Acts 10 who believed in one God. Grimké added that subsequent events at the Convention bore witness that God had heard the delegates' prayers. "The result must convince us, that the supplications of our Cornelius and of his fellow-worshipers, were 'had in remembrance before God,'" declared Grimké in a Fourth of July oration in 1833. "Order arose out of chaos; Light, out of darkness; Discord was exchanged for Unanimity; the jealous, proud and selfish States, became bound to each other, as by the indissoluble bond of perpetual wedlock . . ." (Grimké 1833, 15).

There was only one problem with this account, as James Madison pointed out to Grimké in a letter in 1834: It wasn't true (Farrand 1966, 3:531). Franklin had made the speech, but his proposal for prayers had been tabled (Farrand 1966, 3:531; Madison 1987, 209–10).[1] In some respects, however, the truth or falsity of the narrative was the least interesting part of the affair. The extraordinary thing was that Americans should even be interested in prayer at the Constitutional Convention. The Constitution expressly forbade religious tests for national office, and by the 1820s tax support for churches had ended in every state but one. Yet American Christians remained insatiably curious about the religious beliefs of the Founding Fathers and the relationship between religion and the Constitution.

The politics of the time helps explain why. By the 1830s, Evangelical Protestants in America were coming under sharp criticism for their involvement in public life (West 1996, 134–36). When evangelical reformers objected to the opening of post offices on Sundays because they believed it violated religious liberty, they were accused of being traitors to the Constitution by Congressman (later Vice President) Richard Johnson (Johnson 1834, 1:229–31). When missionaries sought to defend the treaty rights of the Cherokee, they were similarly labeled "canting fanatics" by Congressman Wilson Lumpkin (Lumpkin 1907, 68). Freethinker Frances Wright, meanwhile, told audiences around the country that Christianity was nothing more than superstition and urged them to withdraw their support from churches and religious charities (D'Arusmont 1972, 45–46, 65–66). It is little wonder that evangelicals during this period sought reassurance that Christianity was a legitimate part of America's constitutional order. The result was a lively debate about religion and the Constitution that continues to the present day.

On one side of this debate have been advocates of what might be termed the "Christian Constitution" thesis. In their view, America's Constitution was intended to establish a Christian republic in which the government operated under God's laws, in which Christianity (or at least religion in general) was encouraged by the government, and in which faith played a key role in the nation's public life. According to advocates of this position, all of America's Founding Fathers may not have been Christians, but they were overwhelmingly influenced by a Christian worldview and regarded Christianity as fundamental to a healthy political order. The Reverend Jaspar Adams provided a classic articulation of this position during the 1830s in his widely read sermon, "The Relation of Christianity to Civil Government in the United States" (Dreisbach 1996c).[2] The Christian Constitution thesis continues to resonate among many evangelical Christians today, popularized by David Barton in videos such as *America's Godly Heritage* and Christian pop singer Carman in his song "America Again" (Barton 1995; Carman 1998). More nuanced versions of this argument have been offered over the past couple of decades by theologian Francis Schaeffer, constitutional lawyer John Whitehead, and educators Gary Amos and Richard Gardiner in their book *Never Before in History: America's Inspired Birth* (Schaeffer 1981; Whitehead 1982, 190; Amos and Gardiner 1998).[3] According to Amos and Gardiner, "Christianity was a central and pervasive force in the early development of America, and the political principles enshrined in our Founding documents can be directly traced to the Christian context of the Founders" (1998, v).

Taking up the other side of the debate have been proponents of what some have provocatively termed the "godless Constitution" (Kramnick and Moore 1996). In their understanding, the Constitution's framers intended to establish a purely secular republic in which religion would be largely confined to the private sphere. According to Isaac Kramnick and R. Laurence Moore, "The principal framers of the American political system wanted no religious parties in national politics. They crafted a constitutional order that intended to make a person's religious convictions, or his lack of religious convictions, irrelevant in judging the value of his political opinion or in assessing his qualifications to hold political office" (1996, 23). Advocates of this view usually argue that America's founders were predominantly Enlightenment figures who were either nominally religious or avowed skeptics. In the words of historian Gordon Wood, "At best the Founding Fathers only passively believed in organized Christianity and at worst they scorned and ridiculed it" (1980, 359). Walter Berns goes further, claiming that the founders believed that religion had to be "reformed and rendered harmless" in the new republic they created and arguing that one of their goals was "the subordination of religion" (1986, 214, 223).

As we will see, variations of these two views have played a role in most of the discussions involving religion and the Constitution throughout American history, whether those discussions have focused on the religious beliefs of the Constitution's framers, the treatment of religion in the Constitution's text, or the role of religion in the political theory of the Constitution.

Religious Beliefs of the Framers of the Constitution

Interest in the religious beliefs of America's Founding Fathers dates back at least to the Adams-Jefferson presidential contest of 1800, when one of the major campaign controversies focused on the religious beliefs of candidate Thomas Jefferson. Opponents of Jefferson painted the election as a stark choice between "God and a Religious President" and "Jefferson and no God" (Miller 1960, 265 n. 34). Ironically, both John Adams and Thomas Jefferson were Unitarians, but Adams hid his heterodox beliefs more effectively than Jefferson (West 1996, 49–53, 56–67). By the 1830s, controversy had erupted over whether George Washington was a Christian. In the pages of the *New York Free Inquirer*, freethinker Robert Dale Owen claimed that Washington was a Deist, and in lecture halls his associate Frances Wright boldly asserted that "Washington was not a Christian. . . . [H]e believed not in the priest's God, nor in the divine authority of the priest's book" (Boller 1963, 15–16).[4] Defenders of Washington's piety responded in 1836 with *The Religious Opinions and Character of Washington*, a 414-page tome by E. C. M'Guire that depicted the general as devoted to constant prayer, the frequent taking of communion, and the diligent observance of the Christian Sabbath (M'Guire 1836). Interest in the religious beliefs of the Founding Fathers has continued up to the present, generating books with such titles as *"In God We Trust": The Religious Beliefs and Ideas of the American Founding Fathers*; *Faith of Our Fathers: Religion and the New Nation*; and *The Faith of Our Founding Fathers* (Cousins 1958; Gaustad 1987; LaHaye 1987; also see Johnson 1919; Eidsmoe 1987; Boller 1963).

Contrary to depictions of the founding generation as dominated by Deists and apologists of the Enlightenment, nearly all of the founders who participated in the Constitutional Convention had ties to traditional Christian churches. The Episcopal Church claimed the majority of delegates (twenty-nine), while Presbyterians and Congregationalists were the next-best-represented groups, claiming nine and seven delegates, respectively. Most remaining delegates were affiliated with the Methodist, Lutheran, or Dutch Reformed churches. Two members of the Convention—Daniel Carroll of Maryland and Thomas FitzSimmons of Pennsylvania—were Roman Catholics (Bradford 1982). There was only one confirmed Unitarian among the group—Benjamin Franklin—and he refrained from speaking openly about his beliefs (West 1996, 15–25).

Some of the framers were probably only nominally Christian, but others took their spiritual commitments very seriously. Two delegates had been clergymen, and several others were active lay leaders in their respective churches. Congregationalist Abraham Baldwin had been a licensed preacher and served as a military chaplain during the Revolutionary War. In 1781, he was even offered a professorship of divinity at Yale, but he declined the post and became a lawyer instead (Bradford 1982, 214). Episcopalian William Johnson (future president of the institution now known as Columbia University) helped organize the Protestant Episcopal Church in America during the later years of his life (Bradford 1982, 34). Episcopalian Charles Cotesworth Pinckney eventually served as president of the Charleston Bible Society and as vice president of the American Bible Society (Zahniser 1967, 272). Methodist Richard Bassett of Maryland was perhaps one of the delegates most active in lay ministry. A close friend of Bishop Francis Asbury, Bassett freed his slaves under the influence of Methodist teaching. "Mr. Bassett is a religious enthusiast," wrote fellow delegate William Pierce. ". . . He is a Man of plain sense, and has modesty enough to hold his Tongue. He is . . . in high estimation among the Methodists" (Farrand 1966, 3:93).

The religious beliefs of some of the better-known leaders at the Convention are more difficult to uncover. Convention president George Washington was an active member and vestryman of the Episcopal Church, and he clearly believed in a personal God who intervenes in human affairs. However, he refrained from partaking of Holy Communion during parts of his adult life, and his beliefs about the divinity of Christ are unclear (West 1996, 36–41). The religious beliefs of James Madison are even murkier. He had studied under the Reverend John Witherspoon at the Presbyterian College of New Jersey, and he spent his college days wondering about whether his name was "enrolled in the Annals of Heaven" (Madison 1962–, 1:75). But surviving writings from Madison's later years give little indication of either his religious beliefs or practices as an adult (West 1996, 67–73).

How the religious beliefs of the framers influenced their political beliefs is unclear in many cases, but, for a few individuals, connections can be drawn. James Wilson, probably the most gifted legal theorist among the founders, developed a comprehensive view of law and society that drew upon the Christian natural law tradition (largely via the works of Anglican Richard Hooker) and emphasized the importance of setting up a society in which reason, conscience, and the Bible teach the same duties and by their combined efforts move society in the right direction (Wilson 1967, 1:144).[5]

Religion and the Text of the Constitution

Whatever the personal religious beliefs of the framers, a more important issue is how religion was dealt with in the actual constitutional text. When examining the text of the original Constitution, perhaps the most remarkable feature relating to religion is its lack of religious language. Unlike many other public documents of its period (the Declaration of Independence and various state constitutions, for example), the federal Constitution nowhere pays homage to the Supreme Being or even to the importance of civic virtue (Dreisbach 1996b, 928). Claiming that the lack of God in the Constitution "was no oversight," Isaac Kramnick and R. Laurence Moore argue that it demonstrates a specific intent on the part of the framers to create a "godless document" that would establish a purely secular republic (1996, 27). The records of the Constitutional Convention provide scant support for such a thesis. According to extant accounts of the Convention, there was no debate about God in the Constitution's preamble, and it is risky to try to draw conclusions about intent based on silence. When asked why members of the Convention did not include the customary invocation to God in the preamble, Alexander Hamilton reportedly replied, "We forgot it" (Adair and Harvey 1974, 147 n. 8).

Given the political context of the period, probably the best explanation put forward about the lack of a reference to God in the Constitution relates to federalism, the belief that United States was actually a federation of smaller and largely autonomous republics. While the Constitution of 1787 sought a stronger national union for limited national purposes, the fact remains that most people still regarded the state, not the nation, as the primary unit of political community under the new Constitution. Even George Washington, an ardent supporter of a stronger national government, wrote to his friend Marquis de Chastellux in 1788 about his hopes, not for the new republic, but for "our rising Republics" (Fitzpatrick 1931–44, 29:485). Accordingly, the framers likely regarded state constitutions as the most appropriate place to invoke God and morality, and most came from states with constitutions that did. The framers also may have been concerned about infringing on state prerogatives in this area. Given the lack of evidence during the debates at the Constitutional Convention, we will never know for sure.

The most explicit mention of religion in the unamended Constitution is the prohibition of religious tests for federal office. According to Article VI, "no religious Test shall ever be required as a Qualification to any Office or public Trust under the United States." Religious tests were a standard feature in many of the existing state constitutions, and they typically denied atheists or non-Christians the right to hold public office. On the surface, this is perhaps the strongest evidence that the framers sought to separate religion from politics under the new Constitution. But, in reality, the motivation behind the ban on tests is as unclear as the reason why God was left out of the preamble. The records of the Constitutional Convention again shed little light on the matter. While certain delegates apparently disagreed with the ban on religious tests, the vote on the amendment proposing the ban was unanimous (Farrand 1966, 2:461, 468).[6] It would be wrong to conclude from the ban that the framers were necessarily opposed to a role for religion in politics—or even that they were indifferent to the religious beliefs of public officials. As Daniel Dreisbach points out, "Some delegates at the Philadelphia Convention who endorsed the federal ban had previously participated in framing religious tests for their respective state constitutions" (1996a, 294). In addition, Christians of the time were divided over the usefulness of religious tests. Many believed that such laws violated the rights of conscience that ultimately protected Christians from persecution, and even some who wished to elect only Christians to public office thought that religious tests were next to useless and merely promoted hypocrisy. An unscrupulous politician, after all, could feign belief in certain doctrines whether he actually believed them or not.[7] The principle of federalism also likely came into play (Dreisbach 1996a, 294–95). Many churches feared granting the national government power over religious beliefs lest the new government use that power to favor one group of churches over another. Again, however, we cannot be certain about the reason for the adoption of the ban given the limited data from the Convention itself.

In addition to the ban on religious tests, Article VI of the Constitution allowed public officials to declare their allegiance to the new Constitution "by Oath or Affirmation." This was likely an effort to accommodate the views of Christians, such as Quakers, who believed—based on Jesus' instructions in Matthew 5:33–37—that swearing oaths was contrary to the Bible. The only other mentions of religion in the original Constitution were incidental. The clause dealing with the veto power of the president (article I, section 7) provides that the president shall have ten days to consider a bill for veto, "Sundays excepted." This paid deference to the traditional observance of Sunday as the Sabbath by most Christian denominations. Finally, the Constitution dated itself both from the year of national independence and "in the Year of our Lord."[8]

Trying to construct an overall argument from these limited references about the role of religion in the Constitution's text is problematic. Perhaps the most one can say is that the framers demonstrated a concern for religious liberty by enacting the ban on religious tests for public office and by allowing public officials to declare their support for the Constitution by affirmation instead of oath; and the framers paid deference to the religious customs of the day through the Sundays-exception clause.

Religion and the Theory of the Constitution

While religion may play a minor role in the actual text of the Constitution, that is not the case when it comes to its political theory. Though the intellectual influences that shaped American constitutionalism were many and diverse, it is beyond serious question that the Protestant tradition played a key role in shaping both the institutions and the ideas embodied by the Constitution of 1787.

Perhaps the most fundamental idea taken from the Protestant tradition was the idea of constitutionalism itself. God may not be mentioned in the preamble, but the words "We the People . . . do ordain and establish this Constitution" resonate with Puritan compact theory. The Puritans began as reformers within the Anglican Church in England during the reign of Queen Elizabeth, and a key group within Puritanism believed that local congregations ought to rule themselves by means of a voluntary compact among their members (see McLaughlin 1932, chaps. 1 and 2; Kelly and Harbison 1976, 14–19). This Puritan idea of compact as the source of communal authority in the church easily transferred to political institutions. Robert "Trouble-Church" Browne, an early leader of a Puritan faction known as the Separatists, argued that "an agreement of the people" was the correct foundation for civil government as well as church government (McLaughlin 1932, 21). Hence, when Puritan Separatists on the *Mayflower* anchored off America in the early 1600s, they decided that they needed a compact in order to provide the proper basis for their new government. So forty-one of the passengers signed what became known as the Mayflower Compact, declaring "solemnly and mutually in the Presence of God and one of another [that we] combine ourselves together into a civil Body Politick, for our better Ordering and Preservations, and Furtherance of the Ends aforesaid" (Schultz, West, and Maclean 1999, 275).

Later compacts supplied the basis for governments at settlements in New Hampshire, Providence, Hartford, and along the Connecticut River. Perhaps the most significant of these documents were the Fundamental Orders of Connecticut, which "for all practical purposes [were] the first of modern written constitutions" (Kelly and Harbison 1976, 17). As is true of modern constitutions, "they were a written compact of the people by which a fundamental frame of government was erected" (Kelly and Harbison 1976, 17).

Citizens of the Massachusetts Bay Colony did not explicitly form a compact for civil government, a compact of sorts already having been formed at the colony's founding. Nevertheless, the same ideas about government by compact permeated Massachusetts. Boston minister John Cotton declared that "all civill Relations are founded in Covenant. . . . For . . . there is no other way whereby a people . . . free from naturall and compulsory engagements, can be united or combined together into one visible body to stand by mutuall Relations, fellow-members of the same body but only by mutual Covenant; as appeareth between husband and wife in the family, Magistrates and subjects in the Commonwealth, fellow-citizens in the same cities" (McLaughlin 1932, 69). The pervasiveness of compact theory in Puritan New England supplied an important building block in the development of American constitutionalism, and its fullest expression was in the Constitution of 1787.

A second religious contribution to the Constitution concerned the view of human nature implicit in the document. Unlike later revolutionaries in France and Russia (and later American intellectuals such as Ralph Waldo Emerson), leaders of the American Revolution carried with them few illusions about human perfectibility. "If men were angels, no government would be necessary," wrote James Madison in Federalist No. 51 (Rossiter 1961, 322). Madison's implication, of course, was that men were far from angelic. That is why the Constitution created a government so limited by checks and balances. The founders' distrust of human nature had deep roots in the Christian emphasis on human sinfulness, which pervaded much of American colonial history, especially in Puritan New England. One cannot read the sermons of Puritan clergy without being confronted by the darker side of human nature and its implications for limiting government power. In the words of Reverend Cotton, it is a necessity "that all power . . . on earth be limited, Church-power or other. . . . It is counted a matter of danger to the State to limit Prerogatives; but it is a further danger, not to have them limited . . ." (Miller and Johnson 1963, 1:213). The Puritans' realism about human nature cast a long shadow, and historian of religion Sydney Ahlstrom did not exaggerate when he suggested that "the *Federalist Papers*[,] . . . as well as John Adams's defenses of the American constitutions, can be read as Puritan contributions to Enlightenment political theory" (1972, 363).

While the Christian tradition helped provide key aspects of the political theory embodied by the Constitution, it would be wrong to claim that the founders somehow thought they were establishing a government explicitly derived from the teachings of the Bible, or even that they believed that "biblically revealed higher law offers the only reliable guide to personal and national health" (Whitehead 1982, 190). While Christians throughout American history have advanced such claims about the founders, there is little evidence to support such claims, which reveal ignorance of the theory of knowledge prevalent at the time the Constitution was written.[9] Both Christians and non-Christians among the founders believed that reason and revelation taught the same truths when it came to earthly matters, and so there was little reason to draw a sharp distinction between the two. In the words of the Reverend John Witherspoon, James Madison's old teacher at the College of New Jersey, "If the Scripture is true, the discoveries of reason cannot be contrary to it; and therefore, it has nothing to fear from that quarter" (Witherspoon 1982, 64). Because of their view of the unity of truth, Christians among the founding generation saw little need to try explicitly to derive a political system from the Bible. There was nothing anti-religious in this view; indeed, it was grounded in the Christian natural law tradition articulated by a long line of Christian thinkers, including Augustine, Aquinas, Hooker, Calvin, and Luther.[10] In the view of Christians during the American founding, all truth came from God, and therefore all true ideas were available for use, whether they came from Christianity or derived either from antiquity or the Enlightenment—intellectual traditions from which the founders borrowed liberally for such ideas as the separation of powers, bicameralism, and the extended republic (Lutz 1984; Adair 1974; Pangle 1988; Barlow, Levy, and Masugi 1998).

If treating the Constitution as explicitly derived from the Bible is wrong, it is equally erroneous to regard the Constitution's political theory as somehow anti-religious, as some scholars have alleged. Walter Berns, for example, argues that the Constitution is radically anti-Christian because it did not mandate government support for religion and because the founders advocated religious freedom, a concept that Berns claims "derives from a non-religious source" that is "incompatible with Christian doctrine" (1986, 215). Berns's view is misguided for a variety of reasons. First, as pointed out earlier, the Constitution set up a federal system in which most matters were left to the states and localities. Some delegates to the Constitutional Convention probably did favor government aid to churches, but they would have thought such aid should be determined by local communities, not the national government. A more fundamental problem is Berns's claim that the founders sought to undermine traditional religion because they believed in religious liberty. Berns is correct that the leading American statesmen of the time all embraced religious liberty, but he is wrong to think that the concept of religious liberty was somehow anti-Christian. While there were influential Enlightenment theorists hostile to traditional Christianity who advocated religious freedom, the origins of the concept were largely within the Christian tradition itself. During the earliest days of Christianity, in fact, religious liberty was the standard doctrine among Christians. During the second century, church father Tertullian argued that "it is a fundamental human right, a privilege of nature, that every man should worship according to his own convictions: one man's religion neither harms nor helps another man. It is assuredly no part of religion to compel religion" (*To Scapula*).

During the seventeenth century, the Christian case for religious liberty was made by American colonist Roger Williams. Starting out as a Puritan, Williams became a Baptist and ended up a "Seeker." He was indefatigable in his support for the rights of conscience, and he explicitly founded Providence, Rhode Island, as "a shelter for persons distressed for conscience." Williams's literary legacy includes *The Bloudy Tenent of Persecution* (1644), in which he pressed a vigorous case for religious toleration more than four decades before John Locke's more celebrated *Letter on Toleration* (Stokes and Pfeffer 1964, 13–16; Miller and Johnson 1963, 1:219–24). Williams condemned religious persecution squarely on Christian grounds, arguing that persecution contradicted the meek example of Jesus and promoted fraudulent conversions. In Williams's view, the separation of church and state was good for the church because it helped safeguard its purity.

In America, the case for religious liberty was largely made by people arguing from the same vantage point as Williams. They advocated the rights of conscience in order to safeguard religion rather than to restrict it. Often they sought to protect the rights of fellow believers. That was the idea that animated the Roman Catholic founders of Maryland, for instance. They wanted Maryland to serve as a haven for Catholics; in the process, they created a colony that protected the liberties of Protestants as well. Quaker William Penn similarly envisioned his colony of Pennsylvania as a place where fellow believers could find refuge from the persecution they had suffered in England. The colony subsequently guaranteed complete freedom of worship for all who believed in "one

Almighty God" (Stokes and Pfeffer 1964, 11–13, 18–19). By the time the Constitution was written, the most numerous supporters of ending tax support for churches in America continued to be devout Baptists, Methodists, and Presbyterians rather than devotees of the French Enlightenment such as Thomas Paine and Thomas Jefferson.[11]

Even if the Constitution is not explicitly anti-religious, some scholars claim that it is so implicitly because it downplays the political needfulness of religion. In ancient and medieval political philosophy, religion was regarded as a cornerstone of political life because it promoted cultural cohesion and civic morality. Framers such as James Madison, however, appeared to reject this traditional view of religion's civic role. Far from relying on religion to promote cohesion and civic morality, Madison emphasized in Federalist No. 10 that "neither moral nor religious motives can be relied on as an adequate control" of the factional strife of politics (Rossiter 1961, 81). Indeed, religion could help promote social disorder rather than contain it by inflaming the passions of citizens and breaking them into factions. According to Madison, the true solution to the "violence of faction" in politics was not religion or religiously motivated morality, but structural checks and balances in the Constitution that could harness human selfishness in order to supply "the defect of better motives" (Rossiter 1961, 322).

By separating the powers of government among different branches, the framers set up a system in which "ambition would be made to counter ambition," and government officials in one branch would find it in their interest to resist encroachments by officials of another branch (Rossiter 1961, 322). In short, the government under the new Constitution appeared to be a machine that could run itself without the extraneous moral support traditionally supplied by religion. In the words of George Will, it was "almost as though the Founders thought they had devised a system so clever that it would work well even if no one had good motives—even if there was no public-spiritedness" (1983, 133).

Did the framers believe that they had fashioned a secular republic that could replace the need for religion and religiously inspired moral convictions with checks and balances? Not really. It is true that defenders of the Constitution sometimes talked this way, but the Constitution was not written in a vacuum, and one needs to understand the broader political context. One of the chief complaints leveled against the new Constitution by its detractors was that it relied too much on the virtue of the new rulers for its proper operation. The dissenting members of Pennsylvania's ratifying convention, for example, charged that in the new charter "it appears that the liberties, happiness, interests, and great concerns of the whole United States may be dependent upon the integrity, virtue, wisdom and knowledge of 25 or 26 men" (Allen and

Lloyd 1985, 62). During the Virginia ratifying convention, Patrick Henry similarly declared that "all the good qualities" of the proposed national government were founded on the "supposition that our American governors shall be honest." But if the new rulers turned out to be "bad men," he added, the new Constitution's "defective and imperfect construction puts it in their power to perpetrate the worst of mischiefs" (Allen and Lloyd 1985, 134). Finally, a writer using the nom de plume Cato warned readers of the *New York Journal* against placing such an "unbounded" confidence in their rulers "as the advocates and framers of this new system advise" (Allen and Lloyd 1985, 168).

Given these repeated warnings about the Constitution by its opponents, it became imperative for defenders of the new charter to emphasize its various safeguards rather than to expound on the role of religion and virtue in the new government. To emphasize the latter themes would have been to play into the hands of the Constitution's detractors.

There was another reason, mentioned above, why the architects of the Constitution likely deemphasized the role of religion and morality: federalism. The institutions designed to promote virtue and character formation—churches, schools, and similar organizations—were based at the local level, and the states clearly wanted matters to remain that way. It made little sense to focus debate over the Constitution on institutions that everyone agreed the new government should have no authority to control.

Having said this, there is plenty of evidence that the founding generation was acutely aware of the need for virtue among the citizenry to make its venture in self-government possible—and of the crucial role played by organized religion in cultivating this virtue. George Washington expressed the common sentiments of many Americans when he wrote in his farewell address that "of all the dispositions and habits which lead to political prosperity, religion and morality are indispensable supports" (Fitzpatrick 1931–44, 35:229). Far from believing that the Constitution was a machine that would run itself, the founders knew that the citizens had to be self-controlled and honorable for free government to work. In the words of Benjamin Franklin, "Only a virtuous people are capable of freedom. As nations become corrupt and vicious, they have more need of masters" (Franklin 1905–7, 9:569). Countless clergymen of the period sounded the same theme. Congregationalist minister Nathanael Emmons, for example, argued that "vice, by destroying these moral and social ties, effectually saps the foundation of freedom, and completely prepares a people for the shackles of slavery. For nothing but the rod or arbitrary power is sufficient to restrain and govern a people, who have lost their virtue, and sunk into vice and corruption. Such a people are neither fit to enjoy, nor able to assert and maintain their liberties. They must be slaves" (1842–50, 2:47).[12] Most founders further agreed that the way this civic virtue was cultivated in society was largely through the nation's churches. Secular education alone was not enough, according to most of the founding generation. Indeed, George Washington derided as a mere "supposition" the claim that "morality can be maintained without religion," because "whatever may be conceded to the influence of refined education on minds of peculiar structure, religion and experience both forbid us to expect that National morality can prevail in exclusion of religious principle." The upshot of all this was aptly summarized by Vice President John Adams in 1789: "Our Constitution was made only for a moral and religious people. It is wholly inadequate to the government of any other" (Howe 1966, 185).

So while the Constitution nowhere explicitly sanctioned a public role for religion, the logic of the republican system it set up required a de facto public role. Religion was assigned the task of making citizens fit for republican government by inculcating civic morality. Indeed, some regarded the churches as taking on the function of the Roman *censor morum*, the public official in Rome who had the power of regulating the manners and morals of the people. The Reverend John Witherspoon made this point in his *Lectures on Moral Philosophy* at Princeton: "In ancient times, in great states the censorial power was found necessary to their continuance, which inspected the manners of men. It seems probable, that supporting the religious sects in modern times answers this end, for the particular discipline of each sect, is intended for the correction of manners" (Witherspoon 1982, 160–61).[13] James Madison echoed Witherspoon's view to a correspondent in 1823, reporting that in Virginia "[t]he settled opinion . . . is . . . that rival sects, with equal rights, exercise mutual censorships in favor of good morals" (1900–1910, 9:126–27). By regarding religion as the public defender of morality, the founders opened the door for religion to become active in politics on issues involving what nineteenth-century evangelist Lyman Beecher liked to call "great questions of national morality" (Beecher 1824, 25). Admittedly, this was not something most of the founders thought a great deal about, though some of them certainly foresaw it. John Adams during the Revolutionary War had called on ministers to "accommodate their discourses to the times, to preach against such sins as are most prevalent, and recommend such virtues as are most wanted" (Adams 1977–89, 2:266). Nevertheless, the logic of the system created by the founders virtually invited the churches to become the institutional defenders of justice and the moral law in politics, and for much of American history they have done precisely that. From Cherokee removal and slavery in the nineteenth century to abortion and civil rights today, religious groups have played a key—if controversial—role in American public life. At their best, they have sought to remind citizens that republicanism cannot rely on self-interest alone if it is to survive and flourish.

Religion and Controversies over the Constitution

Today the Constitution is revered by Americans with almost religious fervor. Indeed, some scholars have described devotion to the Constitution as America's civil religion (Levinson 1992, 102–5). The view of the Constitution as an almost sacred text of American politics has been cultivated by American politicians from the early days of the republic. In 1792, James Madison even identified the Constitution as one of America's "political scriptures" that should be regarded by citizens "with a holy zeal" (1900–1910, 6:85). For the most part, the religious community in America, along with the rest of the culture, has embraced this view of the Constitution. But there have been notable exceptions.

Religious controversy over the Constitution dates back to the ratification debates, when some opponents of the Constitution attacked the document's lack of a religious test for federal offices. This objection was raised during ratifying conventions in Virginia, Massachusetts, South Carolina, and North Carolina (Bradley 1987, 74). In North Carolina, which voted against ratification, critics complained that Roman Catholics, Jews, Muslims, and pagans could be elected to federal office under the new Constitution (Elliot 1836–59, 4:192, 199, 215). James Iredell, a future justice of the U.S. Supreme Court, responded that religious tests were an engine of religious persecution that violated the underpinnings of Christianity.

"The divine Author of our religion never wished for its support by worldly authority," said Iredell. "Has he not said that the gates of hell shall not prevail against it? It made much greater progress for itself, than when supported by the greatest authority upon earth." Iredell also argued that religious tests would not work because the irreligious would falsely swear to beliefs they did not share just so they could serve in office. He further pointed out that people under the new Constitution were left free to vote for whomever they wished, and "it is never to be supposed that the people of America will trust their dearest rights to persons who have no religion at all, or a religion materially different from their own" (Elliot 1836–59, 4:192–94).

Similar exchanges took place during the Massachusetts ratifying convention. Interestingly, the two clergymen who spoke on the issue both defended the ban on religious tests. Congregationalist minister Phillips Payson argued that "attempts to erect human tribunals for the consciences of men are impious encroachments upon the prerogatives of God. Upon these principles, had there been a religious test as a qualification for office, it would, in my opinion, have been a great blemish upon the instrument" (Elliot 1836–59, 2:147). Baptist clergyman Isaac Backus concurred: "Nothing is more evident, both in reason and the Holy Scriptures, than that religion is ever a matter between God and individuals; and, therefore, no man or men can impose any religious test, without invading the essential prerogatives of our Lord Jesus Christ" (Elliot 1836–59, 2:148).

Religious supporters of the Constitution seemed convinced that, if anything, the new Constitution was designed to promote the glory of God. Some turned the tables on critics by questioning whether the critics were really Christians. In the *Pennsylvania Gazette*, for example, a "minister of the Gospel . . . beg[ged] leave to ask, whether men can be serious in regard to the Christian religion, who object to a government that is calculated to promote the glory of God, by establishing peace, order and justice in our country?" (Jensen 1976–90, 3:186).

During the mid-1800s, religious controversy over the Constitution resurfaced with a vengeance concerning the issue of slavery. Most members of the abolitionist movement were animated at least in part by deep religious convictions, and many were active church members. As abolitionism spread and slavery continued to prosper, many of them wondered whether they could defend a document that legally protected slavery where it existed. Firebrand William Lloyd Garrison publicly burned a copy of the Constitution at a mass meeting in 1854 after savaging it as "an agreement with hell." Upon lighting the document, he cried: "And let the people say Amen" (Noonan 1987, 175). American Christians opposed to slavery struggled with whether to embrace Garrison's view or to find a way to defend the Constitution as anti-slavery. African American Frederick Douglass, active in the African Methodist church, first sided with Garrison, but he eventually came to see that the principles of equality and self-government underlying the Constitution made it an anti-slavery document. "Interpreted as it ought to be interpreted," said Douglass, "the Constitution is a glorious liberty document" (Foner 1950–75, 2:202).[14]

The 1800s also saw the revival of concern over the Constitution's lack of a reference to God, and a political movement eventually developed to amend the Constitution to recognize the authority of Jesus Christ. The inspiration for this crusade derived in large part from groups within the Reformed Presbyterian theological tradition that had decided it was immoral to vote in national elections until the Constitution recognized Christ (Hays 1892, 420–21; Stokes and Pfeffer 1964, 565–66). The movement was spearheaded by the National Reform Association, founded in

1863. "This country was settled by Christian men with Christian ends in view," wrote the Reverend J. M. Foster, an official of the group. "But, strange to say, in setting up this government they ignored the claims of the King of kings. Our Constitution does not contain the name of God. It is silent as the grave respecting the authority and law of the reigning Mediator. . . . Morally, it is a compact of political atheism" (Foster 1890, 234). Proposals for a "Christian Amendment" to the Constitution continued into the twentieth century, with Senator Ralph Flanders of Vermont submitting to Congress in 1953 an amendment that would have the Constitution declare: "This Nation devoutly recognizes the authority and law of Jesus Christ, Saviour and Ruler of Nations through whom are bestowed the blessings of Almighty God" (Stokes and Pfeffer 1964, 567). Like previous proposals, this one went nowhere.

Despite these intermittent controversies implicating the Constitution, the more usual response of religious people to the nation's founding document has been unqualified support. Given the successful history of the Constitution in action, this fact should come as little surprise. By crafting a document that took seriously the fallibility of human nature, the founders created a government that has withstood the political passions that have destroyed so many other regimes throughout human history. By refusing to sanction even the hint of an official state religion in their new Constitution, the founders encouraged the conditions necessary for religion to flourish free from government regulation. Finally, by recognizing the need for civic virtue in order to make their constitutional system work in practice, the founders opened the door for religion to act as a vibrant moral force in American public life.

References

Adair, Douglass. 1974. "'That Politics May Be Reduced to a Science': David Hume, James Madison, and the Tenth Federalist" and "'Experience Must Be Our Only Guide': History, Democratic Theory, and the United States Constitution." In *Fame and the Founding Fathers*, edited by Trevor Colbourn, 93–123. New York: W. W. Norton.

Adair, Douglass, and Marvin Harvey. 1974. "Was Alexander Hamilton a Christian Statesman?" In *Fame and the Founding Fathers*, edited by Trevor Colbourn, 141–59. New York: W. W. Norton.

Adams, John. 1977–89. *Papers of John Adams*. Edited by Robert J. Taylor. Cambridge, Mass.: Harvard University Press, Belknap Press.

Ahlstrom, Sydney. 1972. *A Religious History of the American People*. New Haven: Yale University Press.

Allen, W. B., and Gordon Lloyd. 1985. *The Essential Antifederalist*. New York: University Press of America.

Amos, Gary, and Richard Gardiner. 1998. *Never Before in History: America's Inspired Birth*. Dallas: Haughton.

Baird, Robert. 1856. *Religion in America*. New York: Harper and Brothers.

Barlow, J. Jackson, Leonard W. Levy, and Ken Masugi. 1988. *The American Founding: Essays on the Formation of the Constitution*. New York: Greenwood Press.

Barton, David. 1995. *America's Godly Heritage*. Worcester, Pa.: WallBuilders. Distributed by Vision Video. Videocassette.

Beecher, Lyman. 1824. *The Faith Once Delivered to the Saints*. 2d ed. Boston: Crocker and Brewster.

———. 1852–53. *Beecher's Works*. 3 vols. Boston: Jewett.

Berns, Walter. 1986. "Religion and the Founding Principle." In *The Moral Foundations of the American Republic*, edited by Robert Horwitz, 204–29. 3d ed. Charlottesville: University Press of Virginia.

Boller, Paul F. 1963. *George Washington and Religion*. Dallas: Southern Methodist University Press.

Bouton, Nathaniel. 1828. *The Responsibilities of Rulers*. Concord, Mass.: Henry F. Moore.

Bradford, M. E. 1982. *A Worthy Company: Brief Lives of the Framers of the United States Constitution*. Marlborough, N.H.: Plymouth Rock Foundation.

Bradley, Gerard V. 1987. *Church-State Relationships in America*. New York: Greenwood Press.

Buckley, Thomas. 1977. *Church and State in Revolutionary Virginia, 1776–1787*. Charlottesville: University Press of Virginia.

Budziszewski, J. 1997. *Written on the Heart: The Case for Natural Law*. Downers Grove, Ill.: InterVarsity Press.

Carman. 1998. "America Again." In *Carman: Absolute Best Videos*. Brentwood, Tenn.: Sparrow Communications Group. Videocassette.

Cooke, Phinehas. 1825. *Reciprocal Obligations of Religion and Civil Government*. Concord, Mass.: Jacob B. Moore.

Cousins, Norman, ed. 1958. *"In God We Trust": The Religious Beliefs and Ideas of the American Founding Fathers*. New York: Harper and Brothers.

Cromartie, Michael, ed. 1997. *A Preserving Grace: Protestants, Catholics, and Natural Law*. Grand Rapids: Eerdmans.

Curry, Thomas. 1986. *The First Freedoms: Church and State in America to the Passage of the First Amendment*. New York: Oxford University Press.

Dana, Daniel. 1823. *An Election Sermon*. Concord, Mass.: J. B. Moore.

D'Arusmont, Frances Wright. 1972. *Life, Letters, and Lectures, 1834–1844*. New York: Arno Press.

Dreisbach, Daniel. 1996a. "The Constitution's Forgotten Religion Clause: Reflections on the Article VI Religious Test Ban." *Journal of Church and State* 38 (spring): 261–95.

———. 1996b. "In Search of a Christian Commonwealth: An Examination of Selected Nineteenth-Century Commentaries on References to God and the Christian Religion in the United States Constitution." *Baylor Law Review* 48 (fall): 927–1000.

———, ed. 1996c. *Religion and Politics in the Early Republic: Jaspar Adams and the Church-State Debate*. Lexington: University Press of Kentucky.

Eidsmoe, John. 1987. *Christianity and the Constitution: The Faith of Our Founding Fathers*. Grand Rapids: Baker.

Elliot, Jonathan, ed. 1836–59. *The debates in the several state conventions on the adoption of the federal Constitution, as recommended by the General Convention at Philadelphia in 1787*. Philadelphia: J. B. Lippincott.

Emmons, Nathanael. 1842–50. *The Works of Nathanael Emmons*. Edited by Jacob Ide. 7 vols. Boston: Crocker and Brewster.

Farrand, Max, ed. 1966. *Records of the Federal Convention of 1787*. Rev. ed. 4 vols. New Haven: Yale University Press.

Fitzpatrick, John, ed. 1931–44. *Writings of George Washington*. Washington, D.C.: U.S. George Washington Bicentennial Commission.

Foner, Philip S., ed. 1950–75. *The Life and Writings of Frederick Douglass*. 5 vols. New York: International Publishers.

Foster, J. M. 1890. *Reformation Principles, Stated and Applied*. Chicago: Fleming H. Revell.

Franklin, Benjamin. 1905–7. *Writings of Benjamin Franklin*. Edited by Albert Henry Smyth. 10 vols. New York: Macmillan.

[Frelinghuysen, Theodore ?]. 1838. *An Inquiry into the Moral and Religious Character of the American Government*. New York: Wiley and Putnam.

Gaustad, Edwin. 1987. *Faith of Our Fathers: Religion and the New Nation*. San Francisco: Harper and Row.

Grimké, Thomas S. 1833. *Oration on the Principal Duties of Americans*. Charleston, S.C.: William Estill.

Hall, Mark David. 1997. *The Political and Legal Philosophy of James Wilson, 1742–1798*. Columbia: University of Missouri Press.

Hays, George P. 1892. *Presbyterians*. New York: Hill.

Howe, John R., Jr. 1966. *The Changing Political Thought of John Adams*. Princeton, N.J.: Princeton University Press.

Jensen, Merrill, ed. 1976–90. *The Documentary History of the Ratification of the Constitution*. 16 vols. Madison: State Historical Society of Wisconsin.

Johnson, Richard. 1834. Report of Mr. Johnson (March 4–5). In *American State Papers*, class VII: Post Office Department, I:229–31. Washington, D.C.: Gales and Seaton.

Johnson, William J. 1919. *George Washington the Christian*. New York: Abingdon Press.

Kelly, Alfred, and Winfred Harbison. 1976. *The American Constitution: Its Origins and Development*. 5th ed. New York: W. W. Norton.

Kendal, Samuel. 1804. "Religion the Only Sure Basis of Free Government." In *American Political Writing during the Founding Era, 1760–1805*, edited by Charles S. Hyneman and Donald S. Lutz, 2:1241–63. Indianapolis: Liberty Press, 1983.

King, Jr., Martin Luther. 1991. "Letter from Birmingham City Jail." In *A Testament of Hope: The Essential Writings and Speeches of Martin Luther King Jr.*, edited by James Melvin Washington. San Francisco: Harper.

Kramnick, Isaac, and R. Laurence Moore. 1996. *The Godless Constitution: The Case against Religious Correctness*. New York: Norton.

LaHaye, Tim. 1987. *Faith of Our Founding Fathers*. Brentwood, Tenn.: Wolgemuth and Hyatt.

Levinson, Sanford. 1992. "Constitution as Civil Religion." In *The Encyclopedia of the American Constitution: Supplement I*, edited by Leonard W. Levy, Kenneth Karst, and John G. West Jr. New York: Macmillan.

Levy, Leonard W. 1986. *The Establishment Clause: Religion and the First Amendment*. New York: Macmillan.

Lord, Nathan. 1831. *A Sermon Preached at the Annual Election*. Concord: Hill and Barton.

Lumpkin, Wilson. 1907. *The Removal of the Cherokee Indians from Georgia*. New York: Dodd, Mead.

Lutz, Donald S. 1984. "The Relative Influence of European Writers on Late-Eighteenth-Century American Political Thought." *American Political Science Review* 189:189–97.

Madison, James. 1900–1910. *The Writings of James Madison*. Edited by Galliard Hunt. 9 vols. New York: G. P. Putnam's Sons.

———. 1962–. *Papers*. Edited by William T. Hutchinson and William M. E. Rachal. 17 vols. Chicago: University of Chicago Press.

———. 1987. *Notes of Debates in the Federal Convention of 1787*. New York: W. W. Norton.

Marshall, Peter, and David Manuel. 1977. *The Light and the Glory*. Old Tappan, N.J.: Fleming H. Revell.

———. 1986. *From Sea to Shining Sea*. Old Tappan, N.J.: Fleming H. Revell.

Mason, Ebenezer, ed. 1849. *Complete Works of John M. Mason*. 4 vols. New York: Baker and Scribner.

McLaughlin, Andrew. 1932. *Foundations of American Constitutionalism*. New York: New York University Press.

McMaster, Gilbert. 1832. *The Moral Character of Civil Government, Considered with Reference to the Political Institutions of the United States*. Albany, N.Y.: W. C. Little.

M'Guire, E. C. 1836. *The Religious Opinions and Character of Washington*. New York: Harper and Brothers.

Miller, John C. 1960. *The Federalists, 1789–1801*. New York: Harper and Row.

Miller, Perry, and Thomas H. Johnson, eds. 1963. *The Puritans: A Sourcebook of Their Writings*. Rev. ed. 2 vols. New York: Harper Torchbooks.

Noonan, John T. 1987. *The Believer and the Powers That Are*. New York: Macmillan.

Pangle, Thomas. 1988. *The Spirit of Modern Republicanism: The Moral Vision of the American Founders and the Philosophy of Locke*. Chicago: University of Chicago Press.

Rossiter, Clinton. 1961. *The Federalist Papers*. New York: New American Library.

Schaeffer, Francis A. 1981. *A Christian Manifesto*. Westchester, Ill.: Crossway Books.

Schultz, Jeffrey D., John G. West Jr., and Iain Maclean, eds. 1999. *The Encyclopedia of Religion in American Politics*. Phoenix: Oryx Press.

Stokes, Anson Phelps, and Leo Pfeffer. 1964. *Church and State in the United States*. Westport, Conn.: Greenwood.

Wayland, Francis. 1963. *The Elements of Moral Science*. Edited by Joseph L. Blau. Cambridge, Mass.: Harvard University Press, Belknap Press.

West, John G. 1996. *The Politics of Revelation and Reason*. Lawrence: University Press of Kansas.

Whitehead, John W. 1982. *The Second American Revolution*. Elgin, Ill.: David C. Cook.

Will, George. 1983. *Statecraft as Soulcraft*. New York: Simon and Schuster.

Wilson, James. 1967. *The Works of James Wilson*. Edited by Robert Green McCloskey. Cambridge, Mass.: Harvard University Press, Belknap Press.

Witherspoon, John. 1802. *The Works of the Rev. John Witherspoon*. 2d ed., revised and corrected. 4 vols. Philadelphia: W. W. Woodward.

———. 1982. *Annotated Edition of Lectures on Moral Philosophy*. Edited by Jack Scott. Newark: University of Delaware Press.

Wood, Gordon. 1980. "Evangelical America and Early Mormonism." *New York History* 61 (October): 359–86.

Zahniser, Marvin R. 1967. *Charles Cotesworth Pinckney: Founding Father*. Chapel Hill: University of North Carolina Press.

Teaching Tools

Discussion Questions

1. How did reading this chapter change your understanding of the U.S. Constitution and its relationship to religion?

2. Why do you think many Americans continue to be interested in the religious beliefs of the framers of the Constitution? What relevance do the framers' beliefs have for how we view the Constitution and its authority today?

3. You come across two fellow students engaged in an argument. One declares that "America was founded as a Christian nation, and its Constitution was written by Christians seeking to apply Christian principles to government." The other insists that "most of the Constitution's framers were Deists, and they demanded a separation between church and state because they wanted to keep religion out of the public square." Both students want to know your opinion on the matter. What do you say?

4. Describe how America's federal government might be different today if the Constitution's framers had not believed that human beings are sinful.

5. What are the most important ways that religion influenced the American Constitution?

6. According to the Founding Fathers, how important was religion to the constitutional system they set up? Do you think their reasoning still holds true today? Why or why not?

7. At the time the Constitution was ratified, how did religious people view the Constitution's ban on religious tests for federal office?

8. What is the relationship between federalism and how religion is treated in the original (unamended) Constitution?
9. Why have some religious people been offended by the Constitution at various times in American history?

Topics for Student Research

1. Investigate the religious beliefs of selected Founding Fathers and look at how their beliefs influenced their views of government.
2. Explore the political theory of the Puritans and trace the Puritan influence on the development of American constitutionalism.
3. Examine the development of religious tests for public office and the disagreement among Christians over whether such tests were appropriate.
4. Examine how different parts of the religious community viewed the Constitution during the movement to abolish slavery in the mid–nineteenth century.

Exercises

1. Show students the music video "America Again" by the Christian pop singer Carman (1998). Ask them to discuss how Carman's view of the Founding Fathers compares with the information presented in this chapter.
2. Have students read the U.S. Constitution and compare it to selected Puritan documents, such as the Mayflower Compact, the Fundamental Orders of Connecticut, and the Massachusetts Body of Liberties. Ask them to list the similarities and differences among these documents and to think about how Puritanism may have informed the development of American constitutionalism.
3. Have students visit the Library of Congress's online exhibition, *Religion and the Founding of the American Republic*, at http://lcweb .loc.gov/exhibits/religion/religion.html.

    Direct them to section VI of the exhibition, "Religion and the Federal Government," which includes documents and information relating to the drafting and ratification of the Constitution.

3

Religion and American Political Culture

STACEY HUNTER HECHT

It is clear now that we now live in a hostile culture. Any nation that finds a Bill Clinton more popular after his trial than before is a nation that Alexis de Tocqueville would not recognize. Consequently we are now going to have to examine parallel institutions with which we can win the culture war.

Paul Weyrich, Free Congress Foundation, 1999

Much to the dismay of the politically involved religious people in our community, I have avoided all political activity. No debating. No television talk shows. No marches. No voter registrations. No public comments on politics. Perhaps I have overreacted. My beliefs have not changed. My concern for the moral decline of our country has not changed. What has changed is that I now believe that the way to transform our nation has little to do with politics and everything to do with offering people the gospel.

Ed Dobson, *Blinded by Might*, 1999

For conservative Christians, trends in political participation are clearly changing again. Lamenting the failure of Christian political groups to change American culture, Paul Weyrich, president of the Free Congress Foundation and the person who gave the name "Moral Majority" to Jerry Falwell's political movement, has called for Christians to withdraw from a "hostile culture" and to seek change through nonpolitical institutions. Similarly, Ed Dobson, a former aide to Falwell and currently pastor of a large nondenominational church, has argued that the appropriate means for addressing moral decline lie outside the political arena (Thomas and Dobson 1999). For both Weyrich and Dobson, efforts to elect conservatives to the Congress and presidency have failed to win the "culture wars."

Although Weyrich and Dobson are undoubtedly concerned about American culture broadly construed, their comments can help to orient a discussion of religion and American *political* culture. Perhaps without recognizing it, Weyrich and Dobson neglect the role that political culture can play in affecting political practice. Still, their arguments make some interesting claims about the nature of American political culture and political practice. Weyrich, Dobson, and others believe that political engagement should cause changes in the culture. But since the kind of "cultural" change they worked for did not occur, they have concluded that the American culture was hostile to the policies desired by conservative Christians. In other words, since the culture itself was hostile to conservative Christian political activity, political action could not change that culture. Thus, they have argued that the culture itself must be changed before conservative Christian groups can achieve political success.[1]

Whether or not American culture as a whole is hostile to Christians, do Christians find themselves in a hostile *political* culture? Weyrich, in effect, makes this claim when he argues that Alexis de Tocqueville would "not recognize" our political culture. Author of the classic *Democracy in America*, the young Frenchman had come to the United States in 1831 to discover why the aftermath of the American Revolution differed from that of the French Revolution. What he found, to his surprise, was that the strength of religious practice enhanced democratic life in America. In fact, Tocqueville called American churches the first of American political institutions.

Still, American political culture may not have changed dramatically from Tocqueville's day, as American political culture has always contained contradictory features. These contradictions are especially relevant to groups seeking a strong link between religious belief and political practice. Indeed, the evidence suggests that American political culture is not inherently hostile to religion, but that Americans disagree on the way religion should affect both American political culture and public life.

To understand why some religious groups are frustrated by the practice of politics, we must examine the relationship between religion and American political culture. What is political culture? What is the American political culture like? And what role does religion play in forming American political culture? This chapter seeks to illumine how religion and political culture are intertwined and how they interact. To address these questions, we must first define values, political culture, and political practice.

Values, Political Culture, and Political Practice

Through the process of political socialization, people acquire the values and beliefs that guide their political choices, actions, and behavior. Family, school, church, communities, and peers can all be powerful "agents of political socialization," the vehicles through which people acquire their beliefs and values about politics. As we mature, we learn through a variety of messages that certain ideals are important. In school, for example, we may learn that all should be treated equally by the requirement to "bring enough for everyone" when providing treats for a birthday or celebration. From church and hearing stories from the Bible, we learn that we should love one another. These experiences instill values, and, as we share these experiences with others, it is not surprising that some values are held by a sizable portion of the citizenry.

The *political values and beliefs* on which there is a great deal of consensus provide the foundation for the political culture. Powerful forces like songs learned in childhood and family conversations reinforce the political values about which a people feel strongly. Consider the line from one patriotic song, "My country, 'tis of thee, sweet land of liberty, of thee I sing." Clearly, when naming the country, liberty is the value that is most significant. From experiences like this a people develop shared expectations about the values that the political order should support.

These values can lead people to engage in political activities, such as voting, working on a campaign, donating money to a political cause, or contacting an officeholder. Such activities create a set of behaviors called *political practice*. Beliefs concerning what constitutes acceptable political practice differ greatly from one religious group to another. Some believe that people of faith must do all they can to influence government to bring about justice, whether through voting, lobbying, or even holding office. Other religious groups believe that people of faith should

60

remain free from participation in the daily activities of governing, so as to scrutinize and criticize the government without a conflict of interest. Still others think people of faith should avoid any contact with the political process. Clearly, the values derived from religion can affect whether and how one participates in politics.

But values do more than tell people whether or not to vote. They are also the foundation for broader philosophical approaches to public life—for the ideologies that tell people how to act politically—and specify the ends toward which government should work. Perhaps more significant, values are also the building blocks of a political culture, which in turn incorporates different political ideologies. The *political culture* is a set of beliefs, implicit or explicit, about public life and how it should be conducted. The political culture creates the context for political practice by condensing the values on which most members of society agree.

Sociologists James Davison Hunter and Carl Bowman suggest a useful metaphor for understanding how political culture and political practices relate. Hunter and Bowman write that politics, or political practice, is like the weather, whereas political culture is like the climate (1996, 1). The climate records averages, or generalities, about the weather over long periods of time. Similarly, political culture provides broad parameters within which the practice of politics occurs. These parameters are based on observations of political activity, behavior, and opinion over time. Political activity may vary from season to season, but it varies within boundaries, which move very gradually if they move at all.

As an illustration of the relationship between politics and political culture, one might look at patterns of representation in Congress. Virtually all members of Congress are either Democrats or Republicans. While there may be other parties on the ballot, the election of only Democrats and Republicans reflects values and beliefs that most Americans have about political parties. In 1991, however, Vermont elected Bernard Sanders to Congress as an independent. Because the election of independents to the House of Representatives is so infrequent, and since Sanders has voted like most liberal Democrats, we can safely argue that his election marked a change in political practice, but it did not represent a change in the political culture.

Although elections are perhaps the political practice most familiar to Americans, changes in the law are also changes in political practice. Changes in the law, however, do not always result in immediate changes in values or habits, since political culture changes much more slowly. Consider, for example, this lesson from American history. The Fifteenth Amendment, ratified in 1870, states that "the right . . . to vote shall not be . . . abridged by the United States or by any State on account of race, color, or previous condition of servitude." Coupled with the Thirteenth and Fourteenth Amendments, this measure was designed to allow newly freed African American slaves to participate in politics. Despite the change in law, however, many southern whites resisted extending suffrage to African Americans, and southern states created barriers to their participation, such as poll taxes, literacy tests, and simple intimidation. Such barriers remained in place for almost a century, until passage and implementation of the federal Voting Rights Act of 1965. Thus, in this example, the change in political practice—a constitutional amendment—was ahead of the values dominant in the political culture of the South. Because the change in practice preceded a change in the culture, it did not achieve the intended result—the extension of voting rights—until nearly one hundred years later.

In these examples, political culture appears to be a much stronger force than political practice. But we must remember that just as small changes in the weather sustained over time constitute a change in climate, small changes in political practice over time change the political culture. Ultimately, through the efforts of concerned citizens and legislators, African Americans did surmount the barriers to electoral participation and did vote. Their struggle to exercise their rights did eventually challenge and change the existing political culture.

Given this potential for political practice to change political culture, Weyrich's and Dobson's views merit careful scrutiny. Their frustrations may result from trying to change the political culture too quickly. Political practice may well modify the political culture, but only after sustained efforts; perhaps conservative Christians have not been active in politics long enough to expect changes in that culture. Compare their situation with that of the environmental movement. Environmentalists seek to protect the environment by passing statutes, but such laws may not succeed fully without changing Americans' values and habits. Changing laws may be essential, but not sufficient, to accomplish one's goals.

Political culture can certainly hinder political practice or activity in the way Weyrich sees American political culture thwarting success by conservative Christians. As a result, he contends that Christians should turn to strategies designed to change the political culture from the "outside"—that is, through means other than political practice. Because they believe the political culture is too resistant to the changes that they would implement through political practice, conservatives have turned to activities like homeschooling as a means of inculcating their values in at least part of the citizenry.

Although such resistance can be frustrating to religious people who feel a spiritual or moral mandate to alter the political culture, that very resistance may ensure that the will of the majority prevails in our democracy. For example, in the case of abortion, in which conservative Christians perceive a political culture that values the individual and liberty over the putative rights of the unborn, those objectionable values may indeed be held by a majority of citizens. While the political culture can seem like a barrier to the initiatives of certain religious groups at certain times, it may also contribute to stability of the political order, ultimately vital for the religious and nonreligious alike.

An understanding of the differences among values, political culture, and political practice is central to the investigation of the relationship between religion and political culture. A principal tension in the study of religion and political culture is the competition between two alternative approaches. The traditional understanding is that religion functions primarily as *source for the values* that constitute the political culture. An alternative perspective sees religion functioning primarily as an ideology that shapes how people practice politics *within* the political culture. Sociologist Rhys Williams suggests that we keep both alternatives in mind as we seek to understand how religion can serve as a political resource (1996). The following discussion, then, considers these two different understandings of the relationship between religion and political culture in the United States.

Religion and Political Culture

The Traditional Understanding

According to this view, religion shapes political culture by supplying some of the values and beliefs that form that culture. These values and beliefs lead, through the medium of political culture, to certain kinds of behaviors and practices. The classic definition of *political culture* is "attitudes toward the political system and its various parts, and attitudes toward the role of the self in the system" (Almond and Verba 1963, 4). Accordingly, we might think of the relationship among values, political culture, and political practice as linear: values shape the political culture, which in turn influences political practice. In other words, values and beliefs derived from the broader culture, including religious influences, help form the political culture. Once these values and beliefs have been formed into a cohesive set of guidelines or priorities, they are put into practice through the creation of particular institutions and rules of government.

This definition is an accurate depiction of how the American political culture developed. Since the founding, we have subscribed to an

"American creed" that includes political values embodying our most significant national goals. According to some scholars, for many Americans this creed has "the attributes and functions of a church" (Huntington 1981, 158–59). Important values such as liberty, equality, and individuality are deeply embedded in American political culture and practice. For example, the political value of liberty—considered as the greatest freedom possible without harming others—is certainly a part of our political culture. Fully 92 percent of Americans believe that children should be taught that "our founders limited the power of government, so government would not intrude too much into the lives of its citizens" (Hunter and Bowman 1996, 3). Because liberty is a central value in our political culture, our political practices—our institutions and behaviors—are set up to ensure that liberty is given priority. For example, the Bill of Rights specifies that certain spheres of activity are protected from government intrusion, such as freedom of speech, assembly, and religion. There is no doubt that the political value of liberty is embedded in our political culture.

But where did this concern for liberty come from? How did it become a part of the American political culture? Important values like liberty, equality, and individuality undoubtedly emanated, at least in part, from religious belief. Religion affects political culture to the extent that it is compatible with other forces affecting attitudes and beliefs. Scholars have long noted that many values in the American national creed have their roots in religious beliefs. For example, social scientist Seymour Martin Lipset writes that American Protestantism, due to its congregational system of organization, "fostered egalitarian, individualistic, and populist values" (1997, 61).

Even at the local level we find evidence of religion's influence on political culture. Political scientist Daniel Elazar argues that a state's political culture may be determined in part by the religious backgrounds of its early settlers. The Puritans' dominance of New England had a profound effect on that region's development into a *moralistic* political culture, which stresses the use of politics to bring about good in society. This stands in contrast to the *individualistic* political culture in the middle-Atlantic states, which sees government as a limited activity, developed primarily for utilitarian reasons. This view was influenced by Nonconformist and dissenting religious ideas brought by immigrants from England and Protestant Germany (Elazar 1984, 127).

Religion's generation of values and beliefs that affect political culture is not simply an artifact of the past, but continues to the present. Scholars have long studied *American exceptionalism*, the ways Americans differ from citizens of other industrialized democracies (Lipset 1997). This exceptionalism is evident even today, as Americans consistently demonstrate commitment to different political values and exhibit higher levels of religiosity than citizens of other nations. The data in table 3.1 compare the United States with six other industrial democracies on the importance of religion in daily life.

Table 3.1 Religiosity in Seven Industrial Democracies

	Agree that church/ religion has a good influence on nation (%)	Worship once or more a week (%)	Consider self a religious person (%)	Find life meaningful because God exists (%)
United States	73	43	82	59
Canada	61	27	69	34
Spain	48	29	64	33
Mexico	73	43	72	50
U.K.	41	14	55	35
France	39	10	48	27
Germany	24	18	54	25

Sources: Data from Times-Mirror Center for the People and the Press, in "Faith in America," The American Enterprise, September–October 1994, 92; and Inter-University Consortium for Political and Social Research, "World Values Survey, 1990–1993," The Public Perspective, April–May 1995, 25.

Citizens of the United States are indeed distinct in their opinions about religion. Fully 82 percent of Americans consider themselves religious, 10 percent more than citizens of Mexico, the country ranked next closest. Moreover, the United States also stands out as the only country analyzed in which more than half the respondents find life meaningful because God exists. Americans are also most likely, along with Mexicans, to attend a worship service every week (43 percent). Perhaps most telling for a study of religion and political culture, however, is that 73 percent of Americans believe that the church or religion has a good influence on the nation. This stands in stark contrast to France and Germany, where fewer than 40 percent think that religion or the church has similarly good effects. Given these patterns, it would be surprising if religion did not affect American political culture, since Americans place more importance on religious life and on its positive effects on public life than citizens of other nations.

Americans are more religious, but what effects, if any, do religious beliefs and practices have on American political culture? As we can see from table 3.2, Americans may report that religion is important in their lives, but they do not necessarily use that religion as a guiding force in political decisions. The picture that emerges is more complex. Americans are significantly more likely to see some role for religion in public life than the British or (former) West Germans. But, at the same time, Americans are far less likely to endorse an explicit connection between religion and *public* life than to endorse the *personal* significance of religion. For example, in 1991 Americans were far more likely than people in the United Kingdom or West Germany to agree that politicians should believe in God in order to hold public office. Likewise, Americans were much more likely than the British or Germans to believe that their country would be better off if more people with strong religious beliefs held office. But notice that the percentage of Americans who held these beliefs is decidedly smaller than the percentage who reported themselves to be "religious," or who thought that the church or religion had a good effect on the nation (see table 3.1). And, while Americans were more likely than Europeans to believe that religious leaders should try to influence how people vote in elections, most Americans (65 percent) believe that religious leaders should *not* play this role.

Table 3.2 Religion and Public Life in the United States, United Kingdom, and West Germany (percentage who "strongly agree" or "somewhat agree")

	Politicians who do not believe in God are not fit for public office	It would be better for (country) if more people with strong religious beliefs held public office	Religious leaders should not try to influence how people vote in elections
United States	30	39	65
United Kingdom	9	18	74
West Germany	14	20	85

Source: Data from University of Chicago National Opinion Research Center, in "Faith in America," *The American Enterprise,* September–October 1994, 97.

Thus, many Americans share attitudes about the personal importance of religion, as well as about religion's potential effect on politics. These attitudes are strikingly different from those found in other countries. Still, it is also evident that Americans do not agree about what religion's impact on politics should be. This conclusion is reinforced by more recent surveys, which reveal that only 38 percent of Americans report that religious beliefs play a major role in determining their vote on election day. Indeed, 93 percent of Americans report that they have *never* voted for or against a candidate simply because of the candidate's religious beliefs. Moreover, 64 percent report that if conservative Christian leaders supported a candidate, it would not affect their vote one way or the other.[2]

This lack of consensus as to how religion should affect public life in the United States is further revealed in table 3.3. For example, a little more than one-third of the American public (35 percent) believe it is appropriate for religious leaders to talk about their political beliefs as part of their religious activities; only 40 percent think it appropriate for candidates to talk about their religious beliefs during campaigns. In fact, only two out of five Americans (41 percent) think it is appropriate for religious groups to advance their beliefs by being involved in politics and working to affect policy. These data reveal that Americans are a bit squeamish about incorporating religious belief and values into the political culture. They do see some appropriate public involvement; for example, 73 percent of Americans said it was a good idea for religious groups to sponsor community social action groups to address family problems, drugs, and crime. On the other hand, only 19 percent thought that it was a similarly good idea for religious groups to raise money and support candidates whose ideas most closely reflect their beliefs.[3] Clearly, Americans have not reached a consensus on what religion's impact should be on the political culture.

Table 3.3 American Public Opinion on the Appropriate Role of Religion in Public Life

	Religious leaders talk about their political beliefs as part of their religious activities (%)	Religious groups advance their beliefs by being involved in politics and working to affect policy (%)	Political candidates talk about their religious beliefs as part of their campaigns (%)
Appropriate	35	41	40
Not appropriate	61	54	56

Source: Data from Yankelovich Clancy Shulman and NBC News/*Wall Street Journal,* in "Faith in America," *The American Enterprise,* September–October 1994, 93.

Thus, Americans' strong personal religiosity does not lead to a cohesive set of beliefs about our political life. Although we are a religiously active people, we do not share a widespread understanding as to how individual religious commitments should affect political behavior. This reality has lead some scholars to question the traditional understanding of religion as a primary source for the values that in turn undergird the political culture.

An Alternative Understanding

If religion does not supply the values that undergird the entire political culture, perhaps it affects the practice of politics among different segments. In this view, religion functions as a distinct worldview or ideology that may shape the political thought and action of members of distinct religious groups. Those holding this perspective often contend that a political culture cannot be easily captured or depicted through the use of quantitative data on public opinion. "Attitude studies," such as those reported above, separate political culture too much from the practice of politics, and thus miss important clues about how religion may affect political practice. For example, sociologist Mabel Berezin contends that political culture can be understood as a "matrix of meanings embodied in expressive symbols, practices and beliefs that constitute ordinary politics in a bounded collectivity" (1997, 362). In other words, to understand the political culture, we need to examine the practice of politics more closely.

It may be, then, that religion supplies values that affect the day-to-day choices people make about their own political practices, as well as their preferences for the institutions and rules that they want to govern them. To learn about the political culture, one needs to examine closely the relationship between religion and political practice in a more embedded context, to discern what the actions of both people and structures reveal about broad areas of agreement concerning politics. This approach differs from the survey approach, which asks people about the values they think important in public life.

Examining the political practices of Americans to determine how religion affects political culture is a very difficult task. This may be due, in part, to the fact that different understandings of political culture are espoused by different religious groups. Jelen (1995) suggests that three distinct models of political culture lead to conflicting views about the relationship between religion and political practice in the United States—namely, consensus theories, pluralist theories, and dualistic theories. These competing perspectives posit different effects that religion can and should have on political practice and public life in general. The *consensus theory* holds that a shared Judeo-Christian tradition allows our political culture to be built on a common set of rules and understandings. The *pluralist theory* argues that resilient democracies are built so that religious beliefs, as well as other kinds of beliefs, are permitted to enter public discussion and debate. The pluralist vision, however, does not give privileged position to any particular set of beliefs; rather, it emphasizes fair competition among groups. Finally, the *dualist theory* holds that the political culture is up for grabs, ready to be defined

68

either by cultural elites, with a "progressive" outlook, or by the orthodox, who want to maintain traditional values.

The Christian Right provides an example of a group that holds a dualistic theory of political culture. For example, Hunter and Bowman found that 80 percent of Christian Right members say that "the Federal government seems mostly hostile toward religion" compared with only 40 percent of the general American population. Similarly, 77 percent of the Christian Right "have little or no confidence that the people who run our government tell the truth to the public," versus 64 percent of the general population. And, while 25 percent of the Christian Right report having "little confidence" in the federal government, and 47 percent say they have little confidence in the president, the corresponding figures for the general population are 17 percent and 23 percent, respectively (Hunter and Bowman 1996, 9). These views reflect greater overall distrust of political elites among members of the Christian Right than among the general population. If different religious groups adhere to different models of the role of religion as they engage in political practice, the political culture itself may be threatened by deeply held ideological differences born of differing transcendent values.

Culture Wars and Political Culture: Is the Political Culture at Risk?

Recognizing the mounting disagreement in politics that seemed to stem from the effects of religion, sociologist James Davison Hunter labeled this phenomenon "culture wars." Hunter defines this culture war as "political and social hostility rooted in different systems of moral understanding" (1991, 42). This view fits well with Jelen's depiction of the dualistic theory of political culture noted above. When groups advocate their point of view without appealing to some set of values they share with outsiders, compromise may be impossible.

The culture wars, understood this way, have proven to be particularly intractable in American politics. Once again, Americans differ greatly from citizens in other industrial democracies in the types of issues that cause the greatest political rifts. In other countries, economic class forms the major political fault line, but Americans seem much less concerned about such issues. For example, table 3.4 shows how Americans and citizens of the United Kingdom and West Germany differ in their perceptions of the role of government in providing income guarantees and of the likelihood that one can improve his or her standard of living. Unlike their European counterparts, Americans do not believe that government should provide an income guarantee. Fewer than one in four Americans agree with this proposition, versus more than half the citizens in the two other countries. Moreover, Americans are much more likely to envision personal economic mobility than citizens in Britain and Germany.

Table 3.4 Beliefs about Economic Class in the United States, United Kingdom, and West Germany (percentage who "strongly agree" or "agree")

	The government should provide everyone with a guaranteed basic income	The way things are in (country), people like me and my family have a good chance of improving our standard of living
United States	21	72
United Kingdom	61	37
West Germany	56	40

Sources: Data from National Opinion Research Center, Social and Community Planning Research, and Zentrum für Umfragen, Methoden and Analysen, "International Social Survey Program," *The American Enterprise*, March–April 1990, 113, 116.

Thus, any "war" raging in the United States is not so much a war between economic classes as between cultural classes. Issues like abortion, whether to teach creation or evolution in the public schools, and government funding for artistic endeavors are guided not so much by the shared values of the political culture but by individual beliefs about morality. Such conflicts can touch close to the heart, causing some citizens to take stands that strike at the core of other citizens' identities.

Religion plays a big role in the culture wars. For example, among those who say that "religion is very important in my life," only 30 percent believe abortion should be legal under any circumstance. In contrast, among those who say that religion is "somewhat" or "not" important, 76 percent believe that "abortion should be legal under any circumstance" (Yankelovich Partners 1994, 97). In a similar vein, 70 percent of those who consider themselves evangelical Christians favor "making it mandatory for public schools to teach the biblical version of how the world was created as well as the Darwinian evolutionary science" view, while only 52 percent of other Americans agree (Yankelovich Partners 1994, 98). That these differences stem, at least in part, from different religious commitments suggests that for some citizens these issues cannot be resolved through recourse to the shared values of the political culture alone.

Hunter and Bowman are pessimistic about the chances for the United States to retain a shared political culture with the culture wars in full swing. They write that the "orthodox" (broader than, but encompassing, the Christian Right) and the "progressive" (or the social elites) "offer opposing languages of public discourse and more than that two distinct directions by which Americans can resolve the contradictions of political culture" (1996, 13). Without consensus as to how the contradictions in the political culture might be reconciled, these authors ask, "Is this situation sustainable over time?"

On a more hopeful note, sociologist Alan Wolfe suggests that while the culture wars may rage on, they are fought by intellectuals, not ordinary citizens. Conducting an ethnographic, in-depth study of Americans, Wolfe discerned that the public does exhibit a fairly broad consensus; divisions among Americans picked up by polls often overstate the fault lines that create the culture wars. For organizational leaders like Paul Weyrich, the culture wars are real and seemingly irresolvable. But Wolfe's ethnographic research yields a picture of the American middle class in which "traditional ideals and modern realities" combine to foster a set of shared values that are at once "inclusive" and in support of "personal responsibility" (1998, 322).

While Wolfe argues that the culture-wars thesis obscures the critical distinction between elites and the middle class, others claim the thesis also neglects the existence of moderates, centrists, and denominational loyalists among people of faith. Sikkink (1998, 71), in a piece aptly titled "I Just Say I'm a Christian," found that 128 interviewees from the major Protestant traditions were more likely to take a strong position "in favor of civility" than to advance deeply held beliefs concerning religious doctrine. Demerath (1998, 39) similarly argues that, when viewed in a comparative perspective, the United States lacks aspects of a full-blown culture war found in other societies. According to Demerath, our "civil religion," that is, the central values of our political culture, is largely a "bottom-up" phenomena, fed by political institutions that reinforce civility in the practice of politics, rather than the sectarian religions exerting a divisive force (1998, 40).

In addition to those who criticize the accuracy or utility of the culture-wars thesis, some suggest that the very idea of culture wars is flawed from the start, concluding that religiously orthodox people demonstrate insufficient uniformity in their political attitudes or beliefs to warrant "war" metaphors (Davis and Robinson 1997, 57). For Williams (1997, 12), the culture-wars notion is a myth in that it is an inaccurate description of the American political culture, but also in that it symbolizes important truths about American politics. In the latter sense, it is clear that whether or not the culture wars really exist, the discussion about them has affected the way certain disputes are characterized. Whether accurate or not, the short-hand use of "culture war" to denote disputes bearing on American political culture will not soon leave our political discourse.

Conclusion

Whether there is currently a culture war transpiring in America and, if so, whether its existence will erode American political culture, remains to be seen. What is abundantly clear is that, even if our present age is one of "low-tension" politics, the values that some citizens hold most dear do not seem to resonate within the political culture. This fact bears witness to the continuing significance of religion in our political culture—both as an ideology and as a generator of values.

In the end, the culture war may be less a death knell to a shared political culture than a warning of the necessity for political reform. Perhaps measures like recently enacted "charitable-choice" legislation, which allows states to grant public funds to faith-based social service providers, will provide a vehicle through which religious groups can unite their political practice with their most deeply held beliefs. It may be that the culture wars point to a need for such political practices, which allow for the recognition of the real differences—some stemming from religious commitments—that exist in a political culture that has long upheld the freedom of people to espouse conflicting points of view.

References

Almond, Gabriel A., and Sidney Verba. 1963. *The Civic Culture: Political Attitudes and Democracy in Five Nations*. Princeton: Princeton University Press.

Berezin, Mabel. 1997. "Politics and Culture: A Less-Fissured Terrain." *Annual Review of Sociology* 23:361–84.

Davis, Nancy, and Robert Robinson. 1997. "A War for America's Soul? The American Religious Landscape." In *Culture Wars in American Politics: Critical Reviews of a Popular Myth*, edited by Rhys Williams. New York: de Gruyter.

Demerath III, N. J. 1998. "America's Culture Wars in Cross-Cultural Perspective." In *Re-forming the Center: American Protestantism, 1900 to the Present*, edited by Douglas Jacobsen and William Vance Trollinger Jr. Grand Rapids: Eerdmans.

Elazar, Daniel J. 1984. *American Federalism: A View from the States*. 3d ed. New York: Harper & Row.

Hunter, James Davison. 1991. *Culture Wars: The Struggle to Define America*. New York: Basic Books.

Hunter, James Davison, and Carl Bowman. 1996. *The State of Disunion: 1996 Survey of American Political Culture, Executive Summary*. Ivy, Va.: In Media Res Education Foundation.

Huntington, Samuel. 1981. *American Politics: The Promise of Disharmony*. Cambridge: Harvard University Press.

Jacobsen, Douglas, and William Vance Trollinger Jr., eds. 1998. *Re-forming the Center: American Protestantism, 1900 to the Present*. Grand Rapids: Eerdmans.

Jelen, Ted G. 1995. "Religion and the American Political Culture: Alternative Models of Citizenship and Discipleship." *Sociology of Religion* 56, no. 3:271–84.

Lipset, Seymour Martin. 1997. *American Exceptionalism: A Double-Edged Sword*. New York: W. W. Norton.

Sikkink, David. 1998. "'I Just Say I'm a Christian': Symbolic Boundaries and Identity Formation among Church-Going Protestants." In *Re-forming the Center: American Protestantism, 1900 to the Present*, edited by Douglas Jacobsen and William Vance Trollinger Jr. Grand Rapids: Eerdmans.

Skillen, James. 1999. "Driving for Dominance; Fleeing for Purity." *Public Justice Report* 22, no. 2:1, 11.

Thomas, Cal, and Ed Dobson. 1999. *Blinded by Might: Can the "Religious Right" Save America?* Grand Rapids: Zondervan.

Williams, Rhys. 1996. "Religion as Political Resource: Culture or Ideology?" *The Journal for the Scientific Study of Religion* 35, no. 4:368–79.

———, ed. 1997. *Culture Wars in American Politics: Critical Reviews of a Popular Myth*. New York: de Gruyter.

Wolfe, Alan. 1998. *One Nation after All: What Middle-Class Americans Really Think about God, Country, Family, Racism, Welfare, Immigration, Homosexuality, Work, the Right, the Left, and Each Other*. New York: Viking.

Yankelovich Partners. 1994. Survey conducted January 22–25, 1993. Reported in *The Public Perspective* 5, no. 6 (September–October): 97.

Teaching Tools

Discussion Questions

1. Do you think your religious tradition contributes values to the political culture directly, or that it functions primarily as an ideology or as a set of rules for political practice? Why?

2. What values do students at your institution seem to think guide political practice? Do you think that these values are the same as the values shared by the American public as a whole? Why or why not?

3. How much consensus seems to be necessary to sustain a political culture? Do you think religion is a threat to the stability of a political culture? Why or why not?

4. How do the values of the political culture affect your choices of political practice in which to engage?
5. Consider the comparative data on the political culture of the United States and other industrialized democracies. How might the political culture of your geographical area compare to that of the United States as a whole?

Research Questions

1. Studies reveal that students are much more likely to have engaged in volunteer activities, like working at a homeless shelter or tutoring youth, than political activities, like working on a campaign. Construct a survey for students at your institution to investigate whether they feel strongly about the shared values of the American political culture, and whether their commitment (or lack thereof) to these values affects their choice to participate or not participate in political activities. Compare student responses to the responses of the American public by visiting the Institute for Advanced Studies in Culture website, http://www.virginia.edu/iasc/home.html.
2. Investigate differences in understanding the links between values and political practice by interviewing members of a variety of churches or religious traditions. Consider whether some religious groups are more likely to succeed within a particular political culture than others. The Pluralism Project at Harvard University website provides useful information about religions in a pluralistic culture like the United States. Visit http://www.fas.harvard.edu/~pluralsm/.
3. Politicians often sound religious themes in their campaigns. What kinds of values underlie these themes, and how do these themes contribute to or erode the political culture? Collect campaign speeches by presidential candidates in recent elections, and consider how the religious symbols and language interact with the political culture. The C-SPAN website maintains an archive of campaign speeches by presidential candidates at http://www.c-span.org/campaign2000/speeches.asp.

4

Religion and the Bill of Rights

MICHELLE DONALDSON DEARDORFF

One of the primary complaints about American politics is its contentious nature. Certainly when one examines news coverage of American political life, one is often struck by the large number of pitched battles over public policy, executive decisions, and judicial interpretations of existing laws. In fact, the combative nature of politics is often used as a justification for Christians to withdraw from the political and electoral process. The intensity of this conflict seems to heighten when the contested issue centers on the rights of one individual or group versus another. But when the issue centers on rights related to religious freedoms, the debate can become even more intense.

As confusing and overwhelming as this "rights talk" might be, these conflicts are a fundamental aspect of our political process. Our political system was designed not only to accommodate struggle, but to encourage it. James Madison, in Federalist Paper No. 10, recognized that conflict is inherent in any political system, because

> as long as the reason of man continues fallible, and he is at liberty to exercise it, different opinions will be formed. As long as the connection subsists between his reason and his self-love, his opinions and his passions

will have a reciprocal influence on each other; and the former will be objects to which the latter will attach themselves. (Rossiter 1961, 78)

One of the primary fears of the founders was the potential of tyranny. But, as Madison later noted in Federalist 51, tyranny is to be averted by conflict, as "ambition is made to counteract ambition" within the government itself. So the separation of powers, checks and balances, and federalism act to promote conflict and avert tyranny within and between governmental branches and levels.

But we can go further. Within the Bill of Rights itself, basic tensions and conflicts prevent one right from trumping all others. If some privileged rights could supersede all other rights within the Constitution, one might assume it would be the right to free speech or the right to the free exercise of religion, both of which are found within the First Amendment. But these rights are limited in scope. Neither is absolute, as each right is limited by other rights and obligations articulated in the Constitution. Such tensions or conflicts are evident throughout the Bill of Rights, but an analysis of the establishment and free exercise clauses of the First Amendment can illuminate how such conflict can protect the rights of all citizens.

The Free Exercise of Religion on a College Campus

In 1990, several undergraduates at the University of Virginia, including Ronald Rosenberger, formed a new student organization, Wide Awake Productions (WAP). After filing the appropriate paperwork, they were deemed by the university to be a certified student organization. This status allowed them to use university resources (computers and facilities) as well as to apply for funds to help support their functions. At the time, each student at the University of Virginia was assessed a student-activity fee of fourteen dollars, and these funds were then distributed among the recognized groups on campus.

Soon after they were granted official university recognition, WAP applied for student-activity funds to pay for printing *Wide Awake: A Christian Perspective*, a newspaper designed to facilitate discussion among Christian students from different cultural backgrounds. As the publication noted, its mission was "to challenge Christians to live, in word and deed, according to the faith they proclaim and to encourage students to consider what a personal relationship with Jesus Christ means."

76

The University of Virginia guidelines for the student-activity fees, however, directly prohibited the use of university funding for religious or political activities, though such restrictions were "not intended to preclude funding of any otherwise eligible student organization which . . . espouses particular positions or ideological viewpoints, including those that may be unpopular or are not generally accepted." Nevertheless, the committee controlling the student-activity fee found that WAP was seeking funding for a religious activity and was "promot[ing] or manifest[ing] a particular belief in or about a deity or an ultimate reality." As a result, the committee denied funding to WAP, and all subsequent appeals to the University were denied.

Rosenberger and the other *Wide Awake* editors then filed a suit in federal district court alleging that the refusal to fund *Wide Awake* simply on the basis of the publication's religious perspective constituted a violation of their free exercise of religion, as well as their freedoms of speech and press. The federal district court disagreed and ruled that university funding would violate the First and Fourteenth Amendments' barrier against the establishment of religion. Later, a federal court of appeals affirmed the lower court's decision and concluded that the university had a "compelling interest in maintaining strict separation of church and state"—one that superseded the plaintiffs' claim to a right to freely exercise their religion. In response, Rosenberger and WAP then appealed their case to the Supreme Court.

As one can see, Rosenberger and WAP have a clear First Amendment claim. Yet such a claim does not guarantee that they have the right for which they appealed. What competing interests could explain this accepted limitation to the free exercise clause? To address these issues we must look back to the source of conflict—our constitutional structure.

Conflict within the Bill of Rights

One of the reasons people form governments is for protection—whether personal safety or the protection of personal and collective property. To enjoy such protection, individuals may be willing to give up certain freedoms or "rights." Political philosophers call this implicit agreement—the sacrifice of personal freedom in exchange for some form of societal protection—a social contract. To guarantee these protections, governments are given powers such as authority to police and the power to punish. But the granting of these powers to some governmental authority results in a new fear—the fear that, with the formation of government, it could choose to abuse its powers and destroy its citizens, or to eliminate their freedom.

The framers of the U.S. Constitution and the Bill of Rights faced this same dilemma. How do we make a government strong enough to protect the people, without giving it so much power that it could become tyrannical? On the other hand, how do we guarantee freedom and limit governmental authority without rendering the government impotent? How do we provide personal freedom to one individual so that such freedom does not restrict or violate the freedom of others?

Such tensions are pervasive in our political system. For example, Americans believe in the value of personal freedom as well as equality. But these two values can frequently come into conflict. Giving individual freedom priority can lead to greater social inequality, while giving equality greater priority can necessitate placing restrictions on individual freedom. We believe in both concepts. But these two values cannot be perfectly attained simultaneously. Similar tensions or conflicts are also evident within the Constitution and the Bill of Rights.

Two fundamental tensions exist within the Constitution and the Bill of Rights. The first is the tension (or conflict) among the protections and assurances given to the nation's citizens as individuals, and the second is the tension (or conflict) between the limited authority given to the government and the rights granted to the people.

These fundamental conflicts are illustrated by the case of *Rosenberger v. The University of Virginia*. Both the University of Virginia and WAP had legitimate constitutional claims grounded in the Bill of Rights. For Rosenberger and his fellow members of WAP, the free exercise of religion meant that they could practice their religion freely without interference or limitation from the government, and that WAP could not be "discriminated against" based on the group's religious character. For many evangelical Christians, the effort to bring others to Christ is a part of exercising one's religious faith—it is viewed as a fundamental and necessary component of their religious belief and commitment. Not to do so would be to behave sinfully. So when the state—in this case the University of Virginia—did not support WAP in the same manner that it supported other student organizations, WAP asserted that its right to exercise its religion was unconstitutionally restricted.

On the other hand, the state argued that, if it funded this particular religious group, it was thereby moving toward an establishment of religion. To use state tax money as well as student fees to support a campus religious group financially was, in its view, unconstitutional. The First Amendment clearly states that the government cannot establish a religion, and the Fourteenth Amendment has been interpreted to mean that states cannot do so either.

The Free Exercise Clause Meets the Establishment Clause

In *Rosenberger v. University of Virginia*, the conflict is thus between the First Amendment's free exercise and establishment clauses. The free exercise clause protects one's right to worship as one believes, and the establishment clause limits the power of the government to interfere in the citizen's life. The basic principle beneath the free exercise clause is respect for the individual's right of conscience; it prevents the government from coercing individuals either to believe, join, or practice a particular religion or to refrain from believing, joining, or practicing a particular religion. The focus of the establishment clause is different; it grew out of a hostility and fear of a national church. But there is a tension between these two clauses in that "pressing one to its logical limit can lead it into conflict with the other." If nothing else, the establishment clause restricts the free exercise of religion to the extent that such an exercise would create an established religion.

This tension can be seen in other ways as well. The establishment clause could lead a court, if it wished, to interpret the clause to forbid both direct and indirect government assistance to religious schools on the grounds that any financial assistance, direct or indirect, would move toward establishment of religion. On the other hand, parents who wish to send their children to religious schools could argue that having to pay taxes for public schools restricts their right to free exercise. By being forced to pay taxes for public schools, they may be deprived of the money needed to send their children to the religious school of their choice. Such parents can claim that they have been unconstitutionally denied the right to freely exercise their religion (Arthur 1989, 118–19).

In the policy debate surrounding governmental support of religious schools, this tension between the establishment and free exercise clause is particularly visible. For example, during the early 1980s, New York City initiated a program to send public school teachers to private religious schools in order to provide remedial education for underprivileged children. In an attempt to address the constitutionality of the program, the city sent such teachers to mobile classrooms set up adjacent to, but not on, school property—with the city spending approximately six million dollars a year to do so. However, in 1985, the Supreme Court ruled the program unconstitutional. But, in 1997, the Supreme Court reconsidered the issue in *Agostini v. Felton* and partially overruled their earlier decision. With the 1997 decision, public school teachers can now work on the private school property, but only after normal school hours. Thus, the court's ruling seeks to balance the individual's right to exercise one's religion freely (and the student's right to receive a religious education in the parochial school) with the state's interest in ensuring that the student receive a good education in reading, math, and science. The decision also permits state tax dollars to be used to educate students attending private, parochial schools. Thus, in *Agostini*, the Supreme Court appears to be attempting to balance competing constitutional demands—preventing the establishment of religion while avoiding unnecessary restrictions on the free exercise of religion.

The same is true with regard to the "crèche" cases, better known as the "manger-scene conflicts." Many local communities have historically celebrated the Christmas holidays not only by giving city and state employees time off from work, but by decorating city property according to the season. In the 1970s and 1980s, a number of court cases emerged regarding the incorporation of crèches or manger scenes in municipalities' annual Christmas displays. Some citizens, perhaps many, want to demonstrate their religious beliefs and understanding of the significance of Christmas through these displays, while others argue that by doing so the state advances religion. Some communities have attempted to address the issue by displaying the religious symbols of other traditions, for example, a menorah in honor of Hanukkah or an Islamic crescent at the time of Ramadan, but the constitutional issue remains the same.

The Supreme Court in *Lemon v. Kurtzman* (1971) issued a three-prong test to ascertain whether an action moved toward the establishment of religion. In order for an act to pass this test, it had to be judged as (1) neither advancing nor inhibiting religion; (2) having a clearly secular purpose; and (3) not leading to excessive entanglement between religion and government. How then can a religious scene at Christmas be viewed as having a clear secular purpose? The Supreme Court decided in *Lynch v. Donnelly* (1984) that the state could have a secular legislative purpose (and not advance religion) in displaying a crèche scene during the Christmas holidays. To do so helped to advance the commercial interests of Christmas shopping in the city centers in which public squares where generally located. Moreover, such displays could be viewed as representing the history of Christmas, and thus did not constitute a move toward the establishment of some state religion.

Many of these First Amendment religion cases attempt to reconcile the apparent tension between the free exercise and establishment clauses by ruling, as in *Lynch*, that the governmental action or the religious activity has cultural significance—not inherent religious meaning. But, according to Stephen L. Carter (1993), this "solution" also has significant risks in that it "trivializes religion" within our cultural, political, and legal lives.

As can be seen from the discussion thus far, the interests of the state and of the individual can come in conflict over religious clauses in the First Amendment. But this conflict can be a healthy one that strengthens both the religious life of the individual and the political relevance of the state. We do not have to gloss over this conflict; nor do we need to reconcile it falsely, trivializing one or both sides, for our civic community to survive. In a dynamic democracy, we are better off accepting, understanding, and living with these tensions than pretending we have resolved them permanently.

This tension between the free exercise of religion and the right to be free from an established religion is not unique within the Bill of Rights. Many protected rights in the Bill of Rights are in direct conflict, the result being that both sides in a dispute may well possess legitimate constitutional arguments. Yet somehow we have to find a way to mediate these conflicts in a manner that not only protects the rights of both parties but the stability of the entire constitutional system. In the previously mentioned cases of *Rosenberger*, *Agostini*, and *Lynch*, the federal courts served as mediator, hearing the arguments from both sides and negotiating a resolution. Thus, in our increasingly diverse society, the Bill of Rights helps secure the rights of both the religious and irreligious, recognizing that rights may conflict. In addition, the Bill of Rights provides a means of protecting the people not only from each other, but from the federal government, and, more recently, from the state governments as well.

The Bill of Rights as Protection from the Government

In cases involving religion, the Bill of Rights protects us from the federal government, because it prevents the government from favoring one religious group over all others or by legislating an unpopular religious group out of existence. But what happens when mandated governmental objectives (e.g., providing for a common national defense, ensuring domestic tranquillity, or protecting the health and welfare of citizens) come in conflict with our fundamental right to worship as we desire? How do we determine whether one's religious rights or the government's constitutionally mandated duty prevails? In *Rosenberger*, for instance, the members of Wide Awake Productions initially found that their right to express themselves religiously was treated differently from rights of other student organizations. But the government also has an obligation to protect people from being forced to participate in a religion they do not want to support. Does the free exercise of religion, therefore, always win over governmental obligation?

Free Exercise of Religion versus National Defense

Prior to the advent of the volunteer army, the military sustained its ranks through the use of the draft. One question that arose, particularly during international conflict in which the United States was a party and when the need for draftees swelled, was, Who is obligated to serve in the military and to fight in these wars? Traditionally, those who were pacifists for religious purposes were exempted; as the 1940 Universal Military Training and Exemption Act specified, individuals are exempted "who[,] by reason of religious training and belief, [are] conscientiously opposed to participation in war in any form." While some groups, such as Quakers, have long counted pacifism among their basic tenets, the Supreme Court often had to consider the claims of those who were not part of an organized religion. Can a person who does not participate in any visible religious group or institution still be deferred from military service on the basis of his or her "religious" beliefs?

Such a question arose during the Vietnam War in *United States v. Seeger* (1965). Daniel Seeger's objection to participating in the war was not based on formal membership in any organized religious body, but was founded on a well-documented, and long-held, personal and moral belief in pacifism. Although the federal government agreed that Seeger was clearly sincere in his beliefs, it argued that the military draft and its integrity was essential to the survival of the nation. The concern was that if the standard for conscientious objector were broadened, more individuals would qualify for the exemption and fewer people would be eligible for the draft.

The Supreme Court mediated this dispute and found that Seeger's objection to wartime participation was based on a moral and ethical belief and not on a specific understanding of God or religion. But if his beliefs were sincerely held and strong, the court ruled that such beliefs assumed a religious character and received First Amendment protections. Consequently, despite Seeger's lack of formal religious affiliation, his views were granted protection by the First Amendment.

In the wake of the *Seeger* decision, a new legal problem has emerged—how does one discern what constitutes a religious belief or practice if the court has ruled that it merely has to function as a religion to the individual? If one's religion is simply personal, then potentially there are as many religions in American society as individuals, with each individual potentially expressing beliefs and engaging in practices that function as a religion for that person. How does the state discern between what may be "legitimate" religion and what may be patently fraudulent? For example, do three prisoners in a state prison who claim to be adherents of the *XYZ* religious faith, whose sole mandate is that adherents smoke crack as part of their communion ritual, have the right to claim constitutional protection under the free exercise clause? One might think that this example is frivolous, but it does address the problem of discerning what groups and practices are protected under the free exercise clause. Or consider more socially prominent groups that are still difficult to classify. Should transcendental meditation or Scientology be viewed as a religion and enjoy constitutional protection? How do we guarantee religious freedom if every understanding of religion is deserving of constitutional protection (Kmiec and Presser 1998, 128)?

Free Exercise of Religion versus Health and Safety

Does the responsibility of the state to protect the health and safety of children supersede the power of a family to exercise its own religious beliefs, especially when the parents' actions seem illogical to the public? Consider, for example, the case of Ian Lundman. Ian died in 1989 at eleven years of age, after his mother and stepfather, with the assistance of two Christian Science practitioners, attempted to use prayer as the sole means of healing his diabetes. Christian Science relies on direct intervention with God for healing via prayer, and its followers do not believe in the use of medicine. As devout Christian Scientists, Ian's parents exercised their religion and prayed for him when he began complaining of stomach pains. Despite the family's prayers, Ian went into a coma and died. Ian's father sued his ex-wife and her husband for damages from the loss of his son; medical testimony at the trial indicated that the administration of insulin would have saved the boy's life. This state court case (the Supreme Court refused to hear the case in January 1996, thereby allowing the $1.5 million verdict to stand) clearly notes an interest in the life of the child that the religious beliefs of the parent cannot supersede. This was the first time that a well-established and widely recognized religion, in this case Christian Science, was held liable in court for trying, and failing, to heal (Carter 1996). But similar court cases have arisen with some Pentecostal and charismatic Christians, who have been found guilty of negligent homicide by relying solely on the practice of faith healing. Thus it would appear that the free exercise of religion, at least in the form of faith healing, may not necessarily "trump" the state's right to protect the health and safety of children.

Do cities, then, have the power to protect the health and safety of their own populations, either because of particular acts associated with a religion or because of the location where a church or temple seeks to place its center of worship? Can cities zone and regulate religion in order to guarantee a safe living environment for their people? These questions forced the Supreme Court in 1993 to consider the case of the *Church of the Lukumi Babalu Aye v. City of Hialeah*. The members of this church were practitioners of the Santeria religion, which originated with the Yoruba peoples of Africa but whose religious beliefs later merged with those of Catholicism and other religious beliefs and practices in the Caribbean during the time of slavery. The practitioners of Santeria believe that individuals have a unique destiny provided by God, a destiny that can only be discovered through *orishas* or spirits. These *orishas* are represented through the icons of the Catholic saints and require animal sacrifices to survive. The animals are killed by the quick, ritualized severing of the carotid arteries in the neck and are subsequently cooked and eaten. Today there are approximately fifty thousand practitioners of Santeria in southern Florida, particularly in and around the city of Hialeah.

In 1987, a Santerian church was established in Hialeah after it had received the necessary city approvals. But the growth of this religion concerned many city officials. Consequently, Hialeah passed six ordinances that banned ritual animal sacrifices, while exempting the killing of animals in commercial slaughterhouses or done for nonreligious reasons such as fishing or vermin extermination. The ordinance defined an illegal sacrifice "as to unnecessarily kill, torment, or mutilate an animal in a public or private ritual or ceremony not for the primary purpose of food consumption."[1] Hialeah argued that such sacrifices were a health threat because of the number of number of animals being sacrificed. Not only was there a health risk associated with the necessary disposal of such a large quantity of carcasses, but there was also the potential of increased vermin and disease. Finally, the city of Hialeah also noted its intent to stop the inhumane treatment of the animals that occurred prior to and during the ritual of sacrifice.

After the lower federal courts heard and decided this case, the Supreme Court accepted it on final appeal. In its ruling, the Supreme Court noted that, while the city had valid concerns, it did not seek with its ordinances to isolate health and tranquillity concerns, but instead targeted Santeria as a religion. As one wag noted, "In Hialeah, you can kill a dog in your front yard if you want, you just can't chant over it." As a result, the court upheld the right of Santerias to practice their faith and suggested that the city of Hialeah was more concerned with the destruction of the Santerias than any health risk.

Governmental regulation of religion through the use of zoning powers increasingly confronts churches in America today. On the one hand, municipalities may want to maintain the integrity of neighborhoods and protect their tax base. On the other hand, churches (and mosques, synagogues, temples) argue that they should have the right to build and grow where there is an interested congregation, in a convenient location for those who may wish to attend. Certainly, communities have legitimate concerns about where churches build, particularly with regard to increased traffic and commensurate parking difficulties. But communities may also be concerned simply with the fiscal reality of losing taxes. When a church assumes a lease as a tax-exempt entity, the city no longer has the option of a commercial tax-paying business filling that space. When a church buys a large parcel of land (e.g., several acres on which to build a megachurch complex) in a developing neighborhood with very expensive homes, the local government loses potential tax revenues as well. Whatever the reasons, cities and municipalities have increasingly used zoning powers in recent years to limit the growth of religious entities. Still, the constitutional question remains: Under what circumstances and to what extent can the state prevent the free exercise of religion by means of its legitimate power to zone?

Free Exercise of Religion versus the War on Drugs

Since the 1980s, a major concern of the federal government has been the reduction and ultimate elimination of the illegal drug trade. This "War on Drugs" has been viewed by most Americans as a legitimate extension of the domestic powers of the three branches of the federal government. What happens when the effort to eliminate illegal drug use conflicts with one's right to the free exercise of religion?

Such a conflict occurred in 1990 in the case of *Employment Division, Department of Human Resources of Oregon v. Smith*. Alfred Smith and Galin Black were members of the Native American Church who, as part of the church's religious rituals, ingest peyote—a hallucinogen created by regional cactus plants. In fact, twenty-three states have recognized the "spiritual nature" of peyote within the Native American Church, and the federal government even exempted the religious use of peyote from drug-enforcement laws. While peyote is not a widely abused drug (it often causes nausea and vomiting), it is nevertheless a controlled substance under Oregon law. Both Smith and Black were employed as counselors at a private drug rehabilitation center, but they were fired because of their use of peyote during a religious sacrament within the Native American Church. After they had been fired, the two applied for unem-

85

ployment benefits, but, because they had been fired for "misconduct," the state of Oregon denied them benefits.

The *Smith* case is probably best known for providing a new legal test to determine when the government may legitimately infringe on the free exercise of religion. What is intriguing for our purposes here is the tension between legitimate government concerns—specifically, the war on drugs and the fair distribution of governmental benefits on the one hand, with the right to exercise one's religion without excessive governmental interference on the other. While this case was initially examined by the Oregon state courts, the U.S. Supreme Court was the ultimate arbitrator. In its ruling, the Supreme Court recognized the importance of religious exercise and the necessity of protecting religious beliefs, but it found in favor of the state of Oregon. Basically, the court ruled that infringements on the free exercise of religion can be constitutional (1) when the government pursues a legitimate governmental objective by regulations; (2) under conditions that constitute the least intrusive means possible; and (3) when any resultant infringement on the free exercise of religion is accidental, and not deliberate. The court clearly stated, "We have never held that an individual's religious beliefs excuse him from compliance with an otherwise valid law prohibiting conduct that the State is free to regulate." Thus, in this instance, the court has held that, while free exercise of religion is a fundamental right, there may be times when governmental goals and objectives may be deemed to be more important.

The Bill of Rights as Mediator between Competing Rights of Citizens

Not only does the Bill of Rights protect citizens from the government, it also protects citizens from harming each other. While the Fourteenth Amendment does not provide this protection directly, the courts have interpreted this amendment as prohibiting private acts of discrimination against other individuals. The Bill of Rights recognizes that those in the majority are capable of discriminating against minority groups simply by limiting their rights or by guaranteeing that the rights of the majority always triumph. In a democracy, citizens are in a very real sense the government. The line between the power that the majority of people possess and the power of the government can thereby become blurred. In *Rosenberger*, for instance, one issue was whether money from those who pay taxes to the state of Virginia[2] should go to a specific religious group. Students at the University of Virginia could argue that they did not want their student-activity fee to go to groups actively trying to convert them to another belief system. On the other hand, Rosenberger and others could say that the majority has no right to silence them by denying them the very tax and student-activity dollars that other groups receive, whether or not such groups advance more popular, or unpopular, agendas.

The Right to Proselytize versus the Right to Be Left Alone

An essential element of many religions is the need to proselytize (i.e., to attempt to convert others to their viewpoint) or to raise money for their activities. For many religious people, this requirement exists not only because they believe their religious perspective to be the correct one, but because their religious faith mandates them to do so. But for people outside these religious communities, such attempts may mean being intruded upon in streets, in airports, or at home. Not only may such actions be irritating and make a person uncomfortable, they could also be viewed as a violation of one's privacy. Even worse, some people can use the free exercise of religion to conceal or protect their own fraudulent activities. How then can the government protect one's right to freely exercise one's religion, while simultaneously ensuring that other individuals' privacy and pocketbook are protected?

This question was addressed by the Supreme Court in the 1940 case of *Cantwell v. Connecticut*. The state of Connecticut decided to address the problem of street solicitation through legislation that required a state license before money could be solicited for any cause. The Connecticut State Secretary of Public Welfare then had to determine whether the applicant represented either a religion or legitimate charity. If so, they received the permit; if not, the permit was withheld. Newton Cantwell and his sons were Jehovah's Witnesses living in New Haven, Connecticut. As part of their religious activities, they would stand in a public street in a predominantly Catholic area, playing records and distributing pamphlets to passersby. Two individuals who received this literature found it to be anti-Catholic, and they had the police arrest the Cantwells for soliciting money without a license. The Cantwells argued that, although the law was neutral (it applied to all religions and to the nonreligious alike), it deprived them of the ability to freely exercise their religion.

In their decision, the Supreme Court found both sets of competing interests important and legitimate, but they were concerned with the manner by which Connecticut refereed those rights. In fact, Justice Roberts's majority opinion clearly states that, at times,

[e]ven the free exercise of religion may be at some slight inconvenience in order that the state may protect its citizens from injury. . . . But to condition the solicitation of and for the perpetuation of religious views or systems upon a license, the grant of which rests in the exercise of a determination by state authority as to what is a religious cause, is to lay a forbidden burden upon the exercise of liberty protected by the Constitution. . . .

In this instance, Justice Roberts ruled that it is better to be inconvenienced personally than to damage or heavily burden the exercise of religion. Once again, the court recognized the legitimacy of competing interests and attempted to find a balance between and among the interests of free exercise, privacy, and domestic protection of people as individuals, the public as a whole, and the state.

The Right to Protest Abortion Clinics versus the Right to Exercise Abortion Rights

For some individuals, certain types of political activity and social activism are a natural outcome of their religious faith—in fact, for many, their religion makes these a demand. Many people explain their involvement in the civil rights movement, for example, as a moral imperative of their religious belief. Likewise, many people attest that their involvement in the abortion issue results from their religious beliefs, since much of the pro-life/anti-abortion activity is fueled by Catholics and Evangelical/Fundamentalist Protestants who believe that abortion is murder. For these individuals, not to challenge or attempt to prevent such abortions would be to commit a sin. Therefore, the free exercise of their religion moves them to be politically engaged in the pro-life movement. Yet, at the same time, abortions are legal in the United States and have been ruled a constitutional guarantee by the courts. How then can these two constitutional rights coexist?

This very issue confronted the Supreme Court in 1994 in *Madsen v. Women's Health Center, Inc*. The directors of the Aware Woman Center for Choice in Melbourne, Florida, sought a court injunction to stop anti-abortion protesters from picketing on the clinic's driveway and surrounding street and from confronting the women and doctors entering the center. Judy Madsen and other leaders of Operation Rescue countered that this injunction would hinder their free speech under the First Amendment. In this instance, then, the right to free speech and the right to the free exercise of religion became entangled.

A state trial judge tried to negotiate this conflict through compromise. The judge ruled in favor of a buffer zone that (1) prohibited demonstrators from coming within thirty-six feet of the clinic; (2) banned contact between protesters and clients or doctors of the clinic; (3) constrained protests outside the private homes of clinic employees to three hundred feet; and (4) prevented chanting and bullhorn usage during surgery and recovery hours.

The Florida State Supreme Court agreed that most of the lower-court decision was constitutional, but the court found the compromise infringed too much on the protesters' constitutional rights. While the U.S. Supreme Court later found the compromise constitutional in its buffer zone, it did not find other aspects of the compromise constitutional. The court's decision sought to balance competing constitutional rights, ensuring that both sides could exercise their beliefs as fully as possible without infringing on the rights of other groups. It is likely that neither side, whether protesters or the pro-choice advocates, was satisfied with these results.

The Right Not to Fund Causes versus the Freedom of Speech

The students at the University of Wisconsin–Madison had a system for funding student activities similar to the University of Virginia's system, tested in the *Rosenberger* decision. In 2000, the Supreme Court in *Board of Regents of the University of Wisconsin v. Southworth* decided a case quite different from Wide Awake Production's lawsuit. Along with several other students, Wisconsin student Scott Harold Southworth, a graduate of both the undergraduate university and the law school, sued the university. All seven plaintiffs described themselves as conservative Christians; they decided to sue because they objected to the university's reliance on mandatory student fees to finance campus groups that supported political and ideological causes. In particular, the plaintiffs named the funding of groups such as the Campus Women's Center; the Lesbian, Gay, Bisexual, and Transgender Campus Center; UW Greens; and the International Socialist Organization as violations of their First Amendment rights. Such funding, they argued, forced them to fund advocacy groups that they personally opposed. Southworth claimed, "Every student has the right to say, 'I don't want to fund that organization'" (Schmidt 1999, A31).

The university advocates for the existing fee structure argued that the system employed a neutral political process and provided support for any student groups that applied. They noted that the First Amendment protects free speech and that it fosters the development of ideas, especially on college campuses. The chair of the student government council, Adam A. Klaus, stated that the breadth of the student-activity fee "helps the university be a place where students can really solidify their beliefs. This is part of the educational mission of the university: to encourage democratic engagement by students outside of classroom walls" (Schmidt 1999, A34). The court found that the First Amendment allows the use of a mandatory activity fee to fund and support extracurricular student speech, as long as the program maintains neutrality of viewpoint. While this legal conflict was decided by the Supreme Court, the conflicting values and rights that undergird the debate will continue to be evident even after the court's decision.

Reconciliation of Constitutional Conflicts

As the above cases demonstrate, many conflicts are difficult to resolve due to legitimate constitutional claims bolstering each position. If, as contended, this is the design of the Constitution, how are these tensions resolved? As evident from this chapter, resolutions frequently emerge through the judicial process. Such resolutions do not necessarily settle the dispute to the mutual satisfaction of the conflicting parties, but the dispute is resolved simply because the appellate process has been exhausted and a final court, the Supreme Court, has spoken. But what happens after the Supreme Court has spoken? Is this the end of the process? Do we ever see reconciliation of these tensions?

Consider the earlier case of *Smith v. Employment Services of Oregon*. Remember in the *Smith* case that the court upheld the denial of unemployment benefits to two individuals who had been fired from their drug-counseling positions for ingesting peyote as part of their religious practices. But the Supreme Court's ruling did not end the controversy over when legitimate governmental objectives can, and should, constitutionally supersede free exercise rights.

In response to the *Smith* decision, Congress passed the Religious Freedom Restoration Act (RFRA) of 1993.[3] RFRA was an attempt by Congress to make it more difficult for the government to infringe on the free exercise of religion. RFRA stated that the free exercise of religion could not be denied simply by neutral application of some legitimate governmental objective, but that the law must meet the higher constitutional test—that of a "compelling governmental interest" such as the protection of public health or safety. However, in 1997, the Supreme Court found RFRA unconstitutional in *City of Boerne v. Flores*. In its majority opinion, written by Justice Kennedy, the court said that the Congress does not have the power to interpret the Constitution, nor may Congress "enforce a constitutional right by changing what the right is."

In response, Congress began to discuss what options they had to challenge the court's interpretation of the First Amendment. Given the constitutional provision of separation of powers, coupled with its system of checks and balances, Congress still had several options remaining. It could seek to limit the court's jurisdiction in these matters; it could craft a new act that might be more narrow in scope and pass the court's review; or, it could pass a constitutional amendment that would strengthen the First Amendment's free exercise clause (Carney 1997). In the summer of 1999, Congress began the process of passing a new law, the Religious Liberty Protection Act, which attempts to meet the goals of the RFRA while answering the concerns of the court in *Boerne* (Whitten 1999). Simultaneously, several states have addressed this issue. For example, Florida passed the Florida Religious Freedom Restoration Act of 1998, which guarantees federal religious protections at the state level.

Thus, the Supreme Court does not necessarily have the last word on these issues. Our government is designed to have power check power. As a result, there is constitutional conflict not only between and among the different branches of government (e.g., Congress and the courts) but between the different levels of government as well (e.g., the federal government and the state governments). The system is designed to balance different interests and rights, while at the same time seeking to prevent particular groups from engaging in mob rule or the government from becoming tyrannical.

Conclusion

The Bill of Rights has served our country well. Not only has it specified political rights to be protected, it has allowed us to mediate between conflicting constitutional interests. Efforts to mediate between these conflicting constitutional interests frequently shift between the legislature and judicial branches, though with regard to particularly emotional issues neither branch may be willing to become involved. Nevertheless, over time, some issues become resolved and new issues emerge.

A more recent player in these disputes has been the states. The passage of the Fourteenth Amendment and the developing theory of selective incorporation now mean that states are obligated to protect the rights of citizens from the state itself. Since the states are closest to the people, they are able to regulate and hinder the exercise of a person's rights more directly. Hence, the protection of individual rights from actions of state governments becomes more essential.

The Bill of Rights is a means of mediating between competing legitimate interests—that is, interests that are constitutionally recognized and protected but which cannot be protected simultaneously to an equal degree. In our legal and political system these rights are pitted against each other and may compete for favored status. But it is this process that helps to assure the continuation of our rights as well as to work out some balance between these rights.

Social and economic change lead to political change. As our political climate changes, the rights or groups that tend to be favored over other rights or groups may change as well. While our system is constructed to allow for and encourage conflict, not all conflict is legitimate. Sometimes, even in some of the earlier examples, groups may try to use the Constitution as a club to destroy the rights of groups they distrust, fear, or dislike. Judicial attempts to resolve conflict over constitutional rights seek to ensure that minority and unpopular groups are provided basic protections from governmental threat as well as from majoritarian power. Ideally, this system will seek to encourage dissent while ensuring, in the long run, that we have no perpetual constitutional losers. The cost of this constitutional conflict is, at times, public dissatisfaction with the constant conflict evident in American political life and with the seeming lack of resolution to political issues. But such conflict preserves our rights and freedoms while working to establish balance between different, but legitimate, ends that stand in tension or conflict. With such conflict, there is ambiguity and passionate debate. Is this ambiguity and conflict a price that America, in its third century, is willing to pay?

References

Arthur, John. 1989. *The Unfinished Constitution: Philosophy and Constitutional Practice*. Belmont, Calif.: Wadsworth.

Carney, Dan. 1997. "Religious Freedom Act Overturned, Curbing Congress' Power." *Congressional Quarterly* 55 (28 June): 1526–27.

Carter, Stephen. 1993. *The Culture of Disbelief: How American Law and Politics Trivialize Religious Devotion*. New York: Basic Books.

———. 1996. "The Power of Prayer, Denied." *New York Times*, 31 January 31, A1.

Kmiec, Douglas, and Stephen Presser. 1998. *Individual Rights and the American Constitution*. Cincinnati: Anderson.

Rossiter, Clinton, ed. 1961. *The Federalist Papers*. New York: New American Library.

Schmidt, Peter. 1999. "Student Court Showdown over Student Speech: Do Mandatory Fees at Public Colleges Buttress or Trample the First Amendment?" *The Chronicle of Higher Education* 45 (12 November): A31.

Whitten, Kristian. 1999. "Religious Liberty Protection Act Would Violate Establishment Clause." *Legal Times* (26 July): 17.

Teaching Tools

Discussion Questions

1. How do we in the United States define the concept of *minority* in a representative democracy? Why is the scope of this definition significant?

2. How do we, as a country, ensure that groups who are currently disfavored remain protected?

3. Is it in the best interest of the majority that minority groups have protection? Why or why not?

4. Decide if you agree or disagree with the following thesis and what support you can provide for your position. Within any large representative political system, especially one with as diverse a population as the United States, the question of the political protection of the minority is essential. The principles of democracy guarantee that majority rule is the cornerstone of decision making, but also create a critical concern for the preservation of views that cannot command a large portion of the population's support. Confirming that protection of minority beliefs and unpopular viewpoints is an essential aspect of American political culture, this concern is reflected in the First Amendment.

5. America is considered a representative democracy in which the majority makes primary decisions regarding governance. But in a heterogeneous society such as ours, there will be a tremendous number of factions and smaller minority groups. What protections exist to prevent these minority groups from being destroyed or having their civil rights and liberties trampled? What protections exist to guarantee that the majority still rules and that one small fragment of society cannot dictate public policy? Does our system work adequately to protect minority groups, majority groups, and the individual? Examine specific policy issues or current policy debates in constructing your answer.

6. Why do you believe that we are so uncomfortable with debate and conflict? What are the costs of resolving real disagreements artificially?

Class Simulation

The following are the facts and background information surrounding a case decided by the Supreme Court in 1992. In this case there is concern about the state, represented by the local school board, establishing religion by allowing prayer at public school commencement exercises. Some parents and members of the school board, however, believe that by denying this prayer they are preventing free exercise of religious beliefs. There are many different rights and arguments articulated. What are they? How would you reconcile this tension? Can you find out how the Supreme Court resolved this case?

Lee v. Weisman (505 U.S. 577 [1992])

Each June, the Nathan Bishop Middle School, a public school in Providence, Rhode Island, holds formal graduation exercises on school grounds. Attendance is voluntary. For years, it has been the practice of the school district to allow principals to invite local clergy to give invocations and benedictions at the middle school and high school graduation exercises. Typically, school principals contact members of the clergy and ask them to give an invocation or benediction; if the clergy agree, principals give them a copy of the pamphlet entitled "Guidelines for Civic Occasions." Prepared by the National Conference of Christians and Jews, the guidelines stress "inclusiveness and sensitivity" in writing nonsectarian prayers. For the June 1989 graduation, Principal Robert E. Lee contacted Rabbi Leslie Gutterman and, once the rabbi had agreed to give the invocation and benediction, Lee gave him a copy of the guidelines. Lee also advised Rabbi Gutterman that prayers should be nonsectarian.

Daniel Weisman, whose daughter, Deborah, was in the graduating class, challenged as a violation of the First Amendment the school's allowing invocations and benedictions at graduation exercises.

Question: Is the state violating the establishment clause by providing prayer at a public school commencement exercise for high school and middle school students?

Rabbi Gutterman, Invocation:

God of the Free, Hope of the Brave:

For the legacy of America where diversity is celebrated and the rights of minorities are protected, we thank You. May these young men and women grow up to enrich it.

For the liberty of America, we thank You. May these new graduates grow up to guard it.

For the political process of America in which all its citizens may participate, for its court system where all may seek justice, we thank You. May those we honor this morning always turn to it in trust.

For the destiny of America, we thank You. May the graduates of Nathan Bishop Middle School so live that they might help to share it.

May our aspirations for our country and for these young people, who are our hope for the future, be richly fulfilled. Amen.

Benediction:

O God, we are grateful to You for having endowed us with the capacity for learning which we have celebrated on this joyous commencement.

Happy families give thanks for seeing their children achieve an important milestone. Send Your blessings upon the teachers and administrators who helped prepare them.

The graduates now need strength and guidance for the future. Help them to understand that we are not complete with academic knowledge alone.

We must each strive to fulfill what You require from all of us: To do justly, to love mercy, to walk humbly.

We give thanks to You, Lord, for keeping us alive, sustaining us and allowing us to reach this special, happy occasion. Amen.

Class Exercise

The class is divided into three groups—one group represents the Providence school board and sympathetic parents, one group represents Daniel and Deborah Weisman, and one group is the court hearing this case. Each group meets separately to wrestle with the facts and to find evidence defending its position and its interpretation of the Constitution. After suitable deliberations, the school board (Lee) and Weisman groups have five to seven minutes to present their arguments before the court. The court is allowed to question the panels after their presentations, to assist them in formulating their decision. The court meets briefly after the oral presentations, votes, and then reports to the class its majority and minority (dissenting) opinions. Have the class discuss the process and whether it believes the issue was suitably resolved. What would be their next step in changing the court's resolution?

5

Religion and American Public Opinion

Corwin E. Smidt

Religious faith addresses ultimate questions about the meaning of life. But it is more than that. It also addresses practical issues about daily life— what is right and wrong behavior, what should be valued, and how people should relate to one another. Since political life in democratic societies concerns how people choose to arrange their lives together, including the policies, goals, and values that people wish promoted, it is inevitable that religion and politics will intersect. Religious values are likely to shape political values, and religious beliefs will likely inform, and affect, political views. While a political system may choose constitutionally to mandate an institutional separation of church and state, such an arrangement cannot thereby separate religion from politics. At the individual level, one's religious beliefs and values (or one's rejection of them) are likely to shape and color the way(s) one approaches political life.

The role that religion may play in shaping stands on political issues is likely to vary, since religion is likely to be more relevant to some issues than others. For some issues, there may be differences in political opinion between two or more religious groups, though these differences may not be due to variation in religious factors per se, but reflect variation in the social and economic makeup of the two groups.

This chapter addresses the role religion plays in shaping the political attitudes and opinions expressed by the American electorate. It seeks to ascertain, in relatively broad fashion, the ways in which religion shapes public opinion and the extent to which it does so. At the same time, it examines how Americans approach political life and how such factors color the ways in which religion shapes political life in the United States. Finally, this chapter addresses why Christians, who share a particular religious faith, find it difficult to act in concert within the political arena—or even why those who share the same high level of religious commitment within a specific Christian religious tradition may not agree politically.

Public Opinion, Religion, and Democratic Government

Democratic Theory

Classical theory contends that various requirements must be met in order for democratic government to exist and function properly. For example, this notion of democratic government generally embodies representative democracy. But certain constitutional features are required to enable representative governments to be viewed as democratic. Elections must be held periodically to determine who should serve as the representatives of the people. Elections alone are not sufficient; such elections need to provide voters with some meaningful choice of candidates. Generally speaking, universal suffrage must also be practiced, as no particular group should be excluded from participating in elections because of race, religion, gender, or class. Finally, decisions must be made on the basis of majority rule, provided that the basic rights of people, including those in the minority, are not violated.

However, such constitutional provisions are not sufficient to ensure that a democratic form of government will function properly. Classical democratic theory also specifies certain requirements for individual citizens—for example, that citizens be concerned about and take an interest in political matters. Similarly, citizens must exhibit an adequate level of knowledge about political matters; uninformed voters undermine the quality of political decisions and democratic life. And citizens should participate in political life, at least voting periodically in elections.

Finally, classical theories of democracy generally specify that representatives of the people should base their decisions on the public interest. It should be noted, however, that basing decisions on the public interest is not necessarily basing decisions on public opinion. Still, representative governments rest on the consent of the governed, and the laws and public policies passed by the duly elected representatives should reflect, though not necessarily mirror perfectly, the desires of the people. While representatives who function as trustees rather than as delegates[1] may choose to make decisions based on their personal knowledge, expertise, and conscience, they nevertheless are expected to hear and reflect upon the voices of their constituents. Thus, the "voice of the people" is to be taken seriously, even revered.[2]

Religion and Democratic Theory

Where does religion fit within democratic theory, and what role does democratic theory assign to religion in political life? Different political philosophers have given different answers to these questions. Still, generalizations can be drawn and observations made with regard to this issue. Some ways in which religion may shape democratic life and government are viewed as legitimate, and other ways as illegitimate.

First, democratic theory values the voice of the people. Accordingly, there is no "court of morality" that can veto policies simply because they violate a particular moral code. Democratic governments seek to reflect the views of the majority of the people. Policies achieved through democratic procedures are no less democratic simply because they violate some religious moral code; they may be wrong morally, but they are not thereby undemocratic in nature.

There are "legitimate" means by which religion can help shape democratic political life. First, religion can function *as conventional morality* within democratic societies. All policies embody particular moral values, and, in this sense, all governments, and all policies, "legislate morality." Every individual holds particular moral values—even the position that all values are socially constructed and are therefore equal in social standing, with none "truer" or better than another. For many individuals, religion serves as the primary, though not exclusive, basis for their moral values. Whether or not they are derived from a particular religious faith, one's values affect the way one views the ends and purposes of government, the policy goals it should pursue, and the kinds of procedures to be employed. In this sense, religious values, like all other values, help to shape democratic political life.

There is a second related, though conceptually distinct, way in which religion can legitimately affect democratic life—*as associational activity*. Churches are by far the most prevalent form of voluntary association in American society, and religious involvement is linked with other forms of civic engagement. Through these associational activities, religion helps to shape and color civic life, which, in turn, undergirds political life—whether it entails attending church with others, volunteering in a faith-based soup kitchen, or learning organizational and negotiating skills through participation in congregational committee structures. There is a growing recognition among scholars that, while much of associational life may not be explicitly political in nature, "nonpolitical" civic associations have important political consequences, for example, the role civic associations may play in promoting civic education, fostering civic skills, and bridging social cleavages.[3] Certainly, Tocqueville, the Frenchman who wrote his observations of American life in the early 1800s in *Democracy in America*, saw religious life and institutions as central components of American civil society, with crucial importance for American political life. But Tocqueville was not alone. Other scholars, for example, have contended that rational self-interest is not a sufficient basis for social order and that religion serves as that basis. Accordingly, it is religious life, located within civil society, that enables public moral choices and fosters basic forms of civility and social restraint.

Third, religion can legitimately affect democratic life *as a social group*, through the political activities of citizens who are religious in faith and practice. Religious people possess the same rights as other citizens. And religious people belong to social groups that may seek to mobilize their members politically—advancing a political agenda, promoting solutions, and supporting candidates.

Finally, religion can legitimately operate within democratic political systems *as a "voice."* Many religious traditions call adherents to engage in "prophetic politics"—to speak out against evil in all its forms, including its political forms, and to live out models of social life that better reflect the kingdom of God. In addition, the U.S. Constitution in the First Amendment protects the expression of religious thoughts and values by allowing for freedom of speech and the free exercise of religion.

American Public Opinion

Opinion Formation

How are political opinions and attitudes formed and shaped? Though personality may influence the political views one expresses, most political views are thought to be learned or acquired through experience and exposure to others (Corbett 1991, chaps. 9–12). Some may be learned through childhood socialization, and scholars of political socialization tend to place great emphasis on early learning. Two fundamental principles characterize early learning: (1) the *primacy principle*—what is learned early is learned best or retained; and (2) the *structuring principle*—what is learned first structures later learning (Janda, Berry, and Goldman 1997, 147). Because most individuals learn first within the context of their family, the family is viewed as an important, if not the most important, agent in early socialization. Moreover, the family frequently chooses other socializing agents (e.g., the church) that may reinforce the values and norms taught within the family.

Other political attitudes and opinions may be learned through group interaction or through exposure to media of mass communication. Political socialization continues throughout life, though the primary agents of socialization may change. Exposure to the socializing influences of parents and school wanes as individuals move into adulthood, and peer groups begin to assume greater importance. Peer groups can involve friendship groups, neighbors, coworkers, or fellow associational members. Likewise, because many adults learn about political events through mass media, the media also serve as important agents of socialization. But regardless of the major means by which political opinions and attitudes are formed, they are generally learned from one's environment and are not a function of one's genetic makeup.

Characteristics of American Public Opinion

Low interest in politics. Americans tend to be relatively uninterested in politics and public affairs. For example, Bennett (1986), in his extensive study of American political apathy, estimated that 30 to 45 percent of Americans were politically interested, 25 to 35 percent apathetic, and the remainder, 20 to 45 percent, were not very interested.

Why is this the case? Perhaps it is due to the fact that political issues are frequently complex, with the information surrounding an issue ambiguous, and the ramifications of policies uncertain. In addition, many matters of public policy are rather remote and do not necessarily affect a citizen's personal life directly. Americans tend to be much more interested in their private, day-to-day concerns related to their jobs, family, health, recreation, and personal relationships. Not only do these concerns affect their daily lives more directly and immediately, but they understand them better and may have more control over them.

Low political knowledge. Given that Americans express a relatively modest interest in politics, it is not surprising that they also exhibit a low level of knowledge about politics. Many American voters cannot identify who represents them politically, articulate how their government is organized, or explain basic political terminology. This lack of basic political information has been documented repeatedly over the past several decades. Voters identify some political figures more readily than others. For example, in 1987, 78 percent of those surveyed could provide the name of the governor of their state, but only 36 percent could specify the name of their U.S. representative (Corbett 1991, 8). Even fewer can identify who serves as Secretary of State or Secretary of Defense. Few can name the three branches of government. Nor can many specify what the first ten amendments to the U.S. Constitution are called, let alone indicate their content. The same is true on matters of public policy. Members of the American electorate generally possess little information about proposed legislation.

While analysts can debate whether such basic political information truly reflects the kind of knowledge that voters need to make informed decisions, such findings do raise important questions about the quality of democratic decision making. For example, how can members of government be held accountable when so few people are able to identify who serves them—let alone how these representatives may have voted on a particular bill?

Low attitudinal constraint. The notion of attitudinal constraint refers to the expectation that the position one adopts on a political issue should affect, or be related to, the position that one expresses on a second, but related, issue. More generally, attitudinal constraint refers to the expectation that an individual will exhibit some form of ideological consistency in expressing his or her positions on different issues.

Attitudinal consistency is largely absent among voters, as the positions they adopt on one issue do little to constrain the positions they adopt on other, even related, issues. Rather than approaching political issues through some philosophical framework by which to derive positions, voters generally forge positions on an issue-by-issue basis. When a new issue emerges on the American political scene, voters gather information on that issue, usually in isolation from information they may possess on other issues. Thus, the American public's response to the 1999 crisis in Kosovo was likely made largely in response to that particular, unique crisis, and not as part of some general approach to foreign policy or U.S. intervention abroad. Many voters do not consider how their position on one issue (for example, whether to intervene in the Kosovo crisis) may relate to positions on a related issue (for example, whether to intervene in the Middle East to stop the displacement of Palestinian refugees).

Perhaps this lack of issue constraint is to be expected, given that the American public is relatively uninterested in politics and possesses relatively little information about the content of proposed public policies. Greater issue constraint is likely when a particular issue domain (e.g., issues related to abortion or the environment) is highly salient to an individual. In addition, those more knowledgeable about politics are more likely to exhibit attitudinal constraint, both within and across issue domains.

Consequences. Several important consequences flow from these characteristics of American public opinion. First, public opinion exhibits a great deal of instability. When people possess little information about an issue, the acquisition of additional information is likely to have a disproportionate impact on their position (e.g., being for or against a proposed piece of legislation). Stated differently, when people possess a great deal of information on an issue, it is unlikely that the acquisition of additional information will change their position. This is why advocacy groups frequently engage in information campaigns. It also explains why political advertising by one candidate for public office can help shift important segments of the vote when the opposing candidate is unable to mount an advertising campaign to counter such claims. When voters possess little information, any piece of information, however small or inconsequential, may be used to make a decision.

A second consequence flows from the general apathy and political ignorance of voters. Since voters are often uninterested in politics and do not wish to invest a great deal of time to become informed, they frequently employ "informational shortcuts" by which to derive "relatively informed" political positions. One reason political party identification plays such an important role in predicting voters' electoral decisions is that, when voters possess little information about a candidate except his or her party affiliation, party label provides a relatively reliable guide to that candidate's likely policy positions and voting patterns. In other words, a great deal of informational "bang" can be derived from the simple "buck" of party identification.

In a similar fashion, voters frequently use the "social representation" of different groups to assess political matters. People generally derive only a small fraction of their knowledge about others from direct social interaction (e.g., our knowledge and perception of Muslims are not likely to have been forged primarily by interaction with them). Instead, much of our knowledge about others is supplied though verbal and visual images that create "social representations" of these collectivities. These social representations embody "ideas, thoughts, images and knowledge that members of a collectivity share" (Glynn et al. 1999, 163).

However, there are important perception effects tied to the classification of people into categories—namely, increased perceptions of differences between the groups and decreased perceptions of differences within each of the groups (Glynn et al. 1999, 165). Thus, whether one chooses to categorize oneself (e.g., as an environmentalist) or chooses to label others (e.g., as part of the "radical Christian Right"), such classification serves as an informational device that helps the individual evaluate others and the ideas they may promote.

Finally, as a response to these characteristics of American public opinion, public officials pay greater attention to what might be labeled "issue publics" than to American public opinion as a whole. Issue publics comprise individuals for whom the particular issue is highly salient and for whom the issue constitutes the primary basis for making the voting decision. Thus, for example, even though a majority of Americans may favor a legislative proposal, such as increased handgun control or greater environmental protection, representatives may not vote for the bill if there is a *minority*, substantial in number, for whom the issue is highly salient and who will make electoral choices on the basis of that issue. While members of an issue public are likely to vote based on one particular bill, the majority of Americans are likely to consider a broader range of issues (e.g., abortion, the environment, welfare reform, or Social Security) in making their electoral decisions.

Religion and American Public Opinion

Belief, Belonging, and Behavior

American religion is a multifaceted phenomenon, a mosaic that combines beliefs, affiliations, and practices—the "three Bs" of believing, belonging, and behavior. While religious beliefs are likely to shape religious affiliations, religious affiliations also help forge religious beliefs. Religious beliefs and religious affiliations, in turn, influence religious behavior.

When considering the relationship between religion and public opinion, one needs to determine what facet of religion to analyze. Given the constraints of this chapter, attention will be given predominantly to only one facet—religious belonging as evidenced by affiliation with a particular religious tradition.[4]

Religion and Issue Positions

Table 5.1 presents the positions on fourteen different issues as expressed by Americans during the 1996 presidential election, according to the particular religious tradition with which they are affiliated.[5] The six religious traditions analyzed are Evangelical Protestants, Mainline Protestants, Black Protestants, Roman Catholics, Jews, and "seculars." While these six religious traditions do not reflect the religious tradition of all Americans,[6] they do include the overwhelming majority; the six traditions incorporated 93 percent of the 4,037 respondents in the survey.

103

Several patterns should be observed with regard to the relationship between issue positions and religious affiliation. First, there are important differences in the positions expressed by members of the six religious traditions. On almost all the issues analyzed, the minimum percentage difference across the different religious traditions is 15 percent or more. The one exception is whether or not to cut defense spending "sharply" in the wake of the Cold War. But, even on this issue, there is a 10 percent difference between Roman Catholics and "seculars." Thus, religious traditions seem to shape positions on political issues.

Second, these differences do not always pit those who are "religious" against those who are "secular" in their religious orientations. Those who are classified as "secular" do not always stand in polar opposition to members of the other five religious traditions. In fact, there are many instances in which "seculars" express political attitudes that mirror those expressed by members of other traditions. In this sense, if there is any "culture war" within American politics today (Hunter 1991), it cannot be a simple division that pits those who are not religiously affiliated against those who are. Nevertheless, seculars generally tend to fall closest to Jews, rather than to any of the four Christian traditions, with one major exception—on the question of whether the United States should back Israel over the Arabs in the Middle East.

Third, there are some issues in which members of one religious tradition stand in stark contrast to those in the remaining five traditions. For example, it is clear that those affiliated with the Black Protestant tradition are much more likely to agree with the statement that "minorities need governmental assistance to obtain their rightful place in American society" than are those in the other traditions. The same is true with regard to the issue of Israel. Not surprisingly, Jews stand in stark contrast to other traditions over their level of support for Israel.

Table 5.1 Position on Various Political Issues by Religious Tradition (percentage who agree with statement)

	Evangelical Protestant N=1058	Mainline Protestant N=710	Black Protestant N=322	Roman Catholic N=890	Jews N=87	Seculars N=690
Minorities need assistance	32	36	69	39	39	34
Need Equal Rights Amendment to ensure women's rights	55	64	82	67	62	65

	Evangelical Protestant N=1058	Mainline Protestant N=710	Black Protestant N=322	Roman Catholic N=890	Jews N=87	Seculars N=690
Gays should have same rights as other Americans	45	56	65	64	86	63
Parents need more school choice	66	54	64	63	51	54
U.S. needs comprehensive health insurance [even if it means fewer choices for patients]	38	44	51	46	54	49
Must spend more on hunger	47	45	68	52	63	55
Need to protect American jobs	49	56	61	55	45	51
Need strict laws to protect environment	52	57	41	56	63	60
Need to balance federal budget	32	36	69	39	39	34
Cut defense spending sharply	32	31	37	31	40	41
Must reduce number of legal immigrants	58	67	63	63	52	61
U.S. should back Israel over Arabs	40	29	27	30	82	25
U.S. should not send troops to keep the peace [in places like Bosnia and Haiti]	47	44	52	45	36	43
Abortion should be solely up to woman	28	49	37	37	76	56

Finally, with regard to abortion, one can see considerable variation in the belief that an abortion "should be solely up to the woman." Only about one-quarter (28 percent) of Evangelical Protestants expressed such a position in 1996. But, nearly four out of every ten Roman Catholics and Black Protestants did so (37 percent), versus nearly one-half of Mainline Protestants (49 percent). On the other hand, a majority of seculars (56 percent) and an overwhelming majority of Jews (76 percent) expressed support for such a position.

Religion, Group Evaluations, and Ideological Orientations

Political issues can be very complex, causing many to express ambivalence. In addition, the amount of public attention given to particular issues can vary considerably. As a result, people may be better able and more willing to evaluate particular groups tied to different political agendas than they may be to express an opinion on particular issues tied to such groups. In other words, voters may respond more to political groups than to political issues.

Table 5.2 examines the relative "distance" that members of different religious traditions expressed toward certain groups in society—including the American Civil Liberties Union (ACLU), an organization devoted to protecting civil liberties; feminist groups; the National Rifle Association (NRA); pro-life groups; environmental groups; gay-rights groups; and groups associated with the Christian Right. Again, members of religious traditions differ considerably in their assessments of the distance they feel toward members of these groups. In fact, if anything, table 5.2 reveals greater variation across religious traditions than table 5.1. For example, if one examines whether respondents felt "far" from a particular group, one finds that differences always exceed 30 percent (the only exception relates to feelings about environmental groups).

Second, there are some groups about which members of religious traditions express almost universal agreement. For example, Evangelical Protestants overwhelmingly express distance from the ACLU and from gay-rights groups. Likewise, Jews are almost unanimous in feeling far from the NRA, pro-life groups, and groups associated with the Christian Right. Mainline Protestants and seculars also express relatively similar, and overwhelming, assessments of the distance they feel from pro-life groups.

Third, table 5.2 reveals the need to differentiate, in assessing group evaluations, between the policy positions adopted by a particular political group and the political tactics employed by that group. For exam-

Table 5.2 Distance Expressed toward Certain Groups and Ideological Self-Identification by Religious Tradition (by percentage)

	Evangelical Protestant	Mainline Protestant	Black Protestant	Roman Catholic	Jews	Seculars
ACLU						
Close	10	20	29	16	29	23
Far	61	55	44	46	35	47
Feminists						
Close	15	19	30	22	34	24
Far	56	44	39	42	26	42
National Rifle Association						
Close	33	23	23	26	8	33
Far	39	48	57	49	76	44
Pro-life Groups						
Close	30	12	25	25	7	11
Far	52	67	51	52	84	70
Christian Right						
Close	55	30	56	30	0	14
Far	20	38	22	36	82	57
Environmental Groups						
Close	43	50	46	56	60	54
Far	26	17	30	16	17	19
Gay-Rights Groups						
Close	9	12	21	17	31	19
Far	69	55	53	47	24	48
Ideological Self-Identification						
Very liberal	4	6	10	8	4	9
Liberal	17	23	32	26	46	27
Moderate	16	19	21	18	18	23
Conservative	39	42	29	37	25	34
Very conservative	24	10	9	11	7	7

ple, in table 5.1, members of the Evangelical Protestant tradition were the least willing of the six religious traditions to express the strong pro-choice position that "abortion should be solely up to the woman to decide." Thus, Evangelical Protestants can generally be labeled as "pro-life" with regard to their stand on abortion. Yet, no less than 52 percent of Evangelical Protestants said they felt "far" from pro-life groups, while only 30 percent indicated that they felt "close" to such groups. Thus, whereas many Evangelical Protestants may support the policy positions of pro-life groups, they may object to the political tactics that some pro-life groups employ (e.g., blocking abortion clinics or other physical efforts to prevent abortions).[7]

Fourth, while Evangelical Protestants may be more supportive of the Christian Right than members of other religious traditions, they are far from unanimous in that support. Frequently, the media treat Evangelical Protestants as if they were a unified whole and, at times, as synonymous with the Christian Right. But table 5.2 reveals that such assessments are far from accurate. A majority of those in the Evangelical Protestant tradition felt "close" to the Christian Right (55 percent), but one in five (20 percent) expressed considerable distance from the Christian Right.[8]

Finally, table 5.2 presents the ideological self-classifications of those within the six religious traditions. Again, members of these religious traditions vary in their orientations. Evangelical Protestants tend, as a whole, to be more conservative in their ideological self-identifications. More than 60 percent of Evangelical Protestants classify themselves as either conservative or very conservative ideologically, while 50 percent of Jews and 42 percent of Black Protestants label themselves as either liberal or very liberal.

Religion, Political Knowledge, and Attitudinal Constraint

Earlier it was noted that American voters often use "informational shortcuts" in making political decisions. Are ideological orientations more closely tied to evaluations of particular groups in society or to the policy positions taken by such groups? Table 5.3 addresses this question by examining the strength of the relationship between ideological self-identifications and positions on issues, in comparison to the strength of the relationship between ideological self-classifications and evaluation of related groups in society. Since the survey did not analyze corresponding groups for each of the issues examined in table 5.1, the analysis in table 5.3 is limited to those issues with corresponding groups. These relationships are measured by correlation coefficients, with higher values indicating a stronger relationship. These correlation coefficients are presented for Americans as a whole and for each of three major Christian traditions.[9]

Table 5.3 shows that correlation coefficients are greater between ideological self-classification and evaluation of a particular group than between ideological self-classification and the positions those groups adopt. The only exception to this pattern relates to abortion, in which the correlation coefficient between one's ideological self-identification and one's position on the issue is greater than the corresponding correlation between one's ideological self-identification and feelings about pro-life groups. However, this particular exception may be due to the fact that many individuals label themselves ideologically simply on the basis of their position on abortion.

These patterns are evident within each major religious tradition examined in table 5.3, whether Evangelical Protestants, Mainline Protestants, or Roman Catholics. Again, the only exception to this pattern relates to abortion.

Overall, such patterns suggest that members of each religious tradition, as well as Americans as a whole, react to these high-profile groups largely as symbols. As symbols, these groups receive a mixture of evaluations related to the specific policy positions they advance, the particular political agendas they promote, and/or the kinds of tactics they employ. But, as symbols, they also serve as convenient tools by which voters define themselves politically in relationship to others. As a result, ideological self-classification is more strongly related to the evaluation of particular groups in society than to positions on issues.

Table 5.3 also breaks these correlations down to reveal the coefficients that result when one compares those relatively low in political knowledge with those relatively high in political knowledge.[10] Generally, the correlation between one's ideological orientation and one's positions on political issues should be greater for those who are more knowledgeable politically. This expectation is confirmed in thirty-nine of the forty comparisons (the sole exception was among Mainline Protestants on the Equal Rights Amendment).

In addition, table 5.3 reveals that—even among those who are more knowledgeable politically—group assessments correlate more strongly with ideological self-identity than with one's positions on related political issues. There are a couple of exceptions. This pattern does not hold with regard to the issue of abortion; nor does this pattern hold for knowledgeable Mainline Protestants, for whom support for environmental issues has a slightly stronger correlation with ideological orientation than closeness to environmental groups. Despite these exceptions, group assessments generally relate more strongly to how one chooses to define oneself politically (at least in terms of ideological self-classification) than the positions one adopts on issues, even among the politically knowledgeable.

While Americans may not necessarily exhibit a high level of constraint in the political attitudes they express, their attitudes are not

Table 5.3 Correlations between Ideological Self-Identification and Positions on Selected Issues and Distance toward Corresponding Groups

	All	Evangelical Protestant	Mainline Protestant	Roman Catholic
Favor equal rights amendment to ensure women's rights	.22	.20	.26	.20
Low political knowledge	.16	.19	.36	.10
High political knowledge	.31	.26	.25	.28
Feminist Groups	.29	.28	.36	.28
Low political knowledge	.17	.23	.36	.18
High political knowledge	.42	.39	.38	.33
Favor homosexuals having same rights as other Americans	.23	.21	.26	.18
Low political knowledge	.18	.20	.26	.09
High political knowledge	.36	.28	.29	.29
Gay-Rights Groups	.29	.27	.29	.30
Low political knowledge	.19	.20	.16	.28
High political knowledge	.44	.39	.42	.34
Favor strict rules to protect the environment	.16	.18	.16	.08
Low political knowledge	.03	.14	.08	.20
High political knowledge	.27	.20	.35	.14
Environmental Groups	.21	.21	.23	.20
Low political knowledge	.07	.06	.19	.03
High political knowledge	.30	.26	.33	.22

	All	Evangelical Protestant	Mainline Protestant	Roman Catholic
Favor laws reflecting religious values of majority	.17	.12	.15	.16
Low political knowledge	.07	.00	.10	.06
High political knowledge	.26	.27	.22	.23
American Civil Liberties Union	.28	.23	.36	.22
Low political knowledge	.22	.22	.29	.21
High political knowledge	.39	.31	.38	.28
Favor fewer restrictions on abortion	.21	.27	.21	.18
Low political knowledge	.11	.25	.14	.00
High political knowledge	.30	.28	.28	.31
Pro-life Groups	.16	.20	.19	.04
Low political knowledge	.11	.19	.12	.04
High political knowledge	.25	.22	.25	.14

random. Their political attitudes may be shaped in reaction to group evaluations or changing political events. But political positions are also shaped by sociological dynamics (e.g., friendship patterns and patterns of social interaction with others who may express similar points of view) and, in part, by other beliefs and attitudes a person may hold. There is great variation in the political positions adopted by major social groups, even among those who fall within the major religious traditions.

The political importance of religious groups is shaped by a variety of factors.[11] Both the size of a group and the level of cohesion (unity) it exhibits contribute to its potential importance politically. However, there is usually an inverse relationship between the size of a group and the cohesion it exhibits with regard to political attitudes and voting behavior. The larger the group, the greater the likelihood that there will be greater diversity (or less uniformity) in its political expression.

Religion and Issue Cohesion

Given the diversity within each of the religious traditions, can members ever exhibit sufficient cohesion in the political positions they adopt to have an impact politically? Segments of such large groups can exhibit greater (or less) uniformity in political expression as various sociological factors or cognitive factors come into play. This reality is illustrated in table 5.4, which examines the extent to which Evangelical Protestants express pro-life attitudes on abortion—based on different sociological and cognitive factors.

In the table, we start with Evangelical Protestants, defined broadly by their pattern of religious affiliation; so defined, Evangelical Protes-

Table 5.4 Attitude toward Abortion among Evangelical Protestants: Assessing How Additional Characteristics Enhance Cohesion

Characteristic of Evangelical Protestants	Percentage of Evangelicals Who Are Pro-Life[a]	Total Number of Evangelicals Who Meet Characteristics Specified
All Evangelical Protestants	59	$N=1081$
Condition 1		
Evangelical Protestants who believe the Bible to be the inspired Word of God and to be true in all its details	65	$N=837$
Condition 2		
Evangelical Protestants who meet condition 1 and who attend church one or more times a week	75	$N=533$
Condition 3		
Evangelical Protestants who meet condition 2 and whose close friends (about one-half or more) belong to the same congregation they attend	80	$N=311$
Condition 4		
Evangelical Protestants who meet condition 3 and who agree that there are clear and absolute standards for right and wrong	83	$N=282$

[a]Respondents were classified as "pro-life" if they responded that abortion should not be legal or that abortion should be legal in only a few circumstances, such as to save the life of the mother.

tants constitute a fairly sizable segment of the American electorate—about 25 percent of all voters. While Evangelical Protestants are, as a whole, fairly pro-life, there is still considerable diversity within their ranks—only 59 percent express positions that might be labeled pro-life. However, when one further specifies that such Evangelical Protestants express a "high view" of biblical authority, the resultant percentage of evangelicals who hold pro-life positions rises to 65 percent. When one adds the condition that these Evangelical Protestants not only hold a high view of scriptural authority but also attend church on a weekly basis, the percentage expressing pro-life positions rises to 75 percent. Similarly, further specifying that these Evangelical Protestants not only hold a high view of Scripture and attend church on a weekly basis, but also have half of their close friends attend the same congregation that they do, raises the percentage expressing a pro-life position to 80 percent. Thus, as certain sociological and cognitive factors come into play, greater uniformity in political expression is evident.

But this greater uniformity is also linked to a declining number of respondents; as additional conditions are specified, the number of people who meet such conditions declines. Thus, there is frequently a "political trade-off" between size and political cohesion when talking about the political potential of groups, whether or not they are religious in nature. Generally speaking, larger numbers are coupled with greater diversity, whereas smaller numbers can be tied to greater uniformity.

Religion, Social Theologies, and Public Opinion

Finally, members of a religious tradition exhibit different social theologies,[12] by which they interpret the particular religious doctrines associated with their religious tradition. Religious doctrines are not directly political in nature—though they have political implications. Rather, such political implications must be drawn inferentially, and, as a result, are subject to differences in interpretation.

As an example of one's social theology, consider expressions of agreement or disagreement to the statement, "If enough people are brought to Christ, social problems would take care of themselves." According to Christian theology, humanity's sinful nature leads to social problems. But even among Evangelical Protestants, who historically have had an emphasis on witnessing to their faith and bringing nonbelievers to Christ, there is still disagreement about whether social problems are *totally* due to humankind's fallen nature. As one sometimes reads on bumper stickers, "Christians are not perfect, just forgiven"; neither are

113

church congregations immune to disagreement and conflict. Thus, even recognizing humankind's fallen nature, it is possible for Christians to disagree about the extent to which social problems would be eliminated, even with sufficient numbers of Christian conversions.

Table 5.5 The Relationship between Social Theology and Attitude toward Abortion, Controlling for Religious Tradition (by percentage)

Attitude toward Abortion	Evangelical Protestants		Mainline Protestants		Roman Catholics	
	Individ-ualist	Com-muni-tarian	Individ-ualist	Com-muni-tarian	Individ-ualist	Com-muni-tarian
Legal, up to the woman	25	34	43	57	31	45
Legal, available in wide variety of circumstances	12	16	14	21	11	17
Legal, available in a few circumstances	45	40	35	19	40	32
Should not be legal	18	9	8	4	18	6

In table 5.5, members of religious traditions who indicated that they agreed with the statement, "If enough people are brought to Christ, social problems would take care of themselves," were classified as "individualists," while those who disagreed were classified as "communitarians." The positions on abortion among those who express an "individualist" social theology are compared with those who express a "communitarian" social theology, while controlling for the three largest religious traditions. As seen from the table, and as was shown earlier, religious traditions matter. For example, the percentage of Evangelical Protestants who indicated that abortions should not be legal, regardless of their particular social theology, exceeded the percentage of Mainline Protestants who expressed such a position, regardless of their social theology. Yet social theologies also matter. Within each religious tradition, individualists differ from communitarians in being more pro-life.

Conclusion

Several conclusions can be drawn from this analysis. First, membership within different religious traditions serves as a major, though not the only, factor shaping American public opinion. Other factors (e.g., gender, age, race, and educational attainment) also help to shape the opinions expressed by Americans. Nevertheless, the impact that religious variables have on political attitudes and opinions cannot be reduced to variation in other sociological factors, such as differences in educational attainment evident across the different religious traditions. Religion has a unique and important impact on opinions about issues; religion matters politically.

Second, while religion may be important politically, the attitudinal formation of religiously committed Americans is, at the same time, affected by the same social and cognitive processes that shape and color the attitudes of those not so religiously committed. For example, both members of religious traditions as well as those who might be labeled "secular" develop political opinions through similar processes (e.g., socialization processes) and constraints (e.g., a limited amount of time available for politics, prompting the use of informational shortcuts).

Third, religious groups can be involved in political processes through a variety of legal, and constitutionally protected, means, and religious groups frequently have political significance. In fact, religious groups frequently become building blocks of political coalitions. Nevertheless, the political significance of a religious group depends on a variety of factors—including size, unity on issues, politicization, and cohesion in voting. There tends to be an inverse relationship between the size of a group and the unity the group exhibits on a spectrum of political issues. Finally, members of religious groups tend to exhibit more or less unity depending on the issue analyzed and the social theology they express.

References

Bennett, Stephen Earl. 1986. *Apathy in America, 1960–1984*. Dobbs Ferry, N.Y.: Transnational.

Corbett, Michael. 1991. *American Public Opinion: Trends, Processes, and Patterns*. White Plains, N.Y.: Longman.

Glynn, Carroll, et al. 1999. *Public Opinion*. Boulder, Colo.: Westview Press.

Guth, James, et al. 1998. *The Bully Pulpit: The Politics of Protestant Clergy*. Lawrence: University Press of Kansas.

Hunter, James Davison. 1991. *Culture Wars: The Struggle to Define America*. New York: Basic Books.

Janda, Kenneth, Jeffrey Berry, and Jerry Goldman. 1997. *The Challenge of Democracy: Government in America*. 5th ed. Boston: Houghton Mifflin.

Ladd, Everett C. 1996. "The Data Just Don't Show Erosion of America's 'Social Capital.'" *The Public Perspective* 1:5–6.

Putnam, Robert. 1995. "Bowling Alone: America's Declining Social Capital." *Journal of Democracy* 6 (January): 65–78.

Zaller, John. 1992. *The Nature and Origins of Mass Opinion*. New York: Cambridge University Press.

Teaching Tools

Discussion Questions

1. Why is the separation of church and state possible, while the separation of religion and politics is much more difficult, if not impossible, to attain?

2. Why does the impact of religion on political thought and action vary among American citizens? Assume that citizen *A* is a devout Christian. Why does the impact of religion on citizen *A*'s political thought and action vary among political issues? Why is it also true that the impact of religion on citizen *A*'s stance on issue *X* might vary from one time to another?

3. In what ways can religion legitimately shape democratic life?

4. What factors help to explain why Americans exhibit low attitudinal constraint, that is, that the positions they adopt on one issue do little to constrain the positions they adopt on other, even related, issues?

5. How do members from different religious traditions view politics differently? What religious factors among these religious traditions help account for such differences politically? What social and economic variation within religious traditions might also help account for political differences across religious traditions?

6. Why may Americans be more willing and able to evaluate social groups advancing distinct political agendas than to articulate a particular position on issues related to those agendas?

7. What factors make it difficult for members of a religious tradition to exhibit cohesion on a public-policy issue, even an issue that might be directly related to the faith of that tradition?

Topics for Student Research

1. Locate the major listing of denominational websites at http://www.forministry.com/denomination/. Analyze the "social presentation" of these websites. How do denominations seek to present themselves to the public? To what extent do these denominational web-

sites indicate where they stand on matters of social thought and action?

2. Locate the American Religion Data Archive, an Internet-based archive for the study of American religion at http://www.arda.tm/. This site allows you to search data from major studies on American religion and to locate topics of major interest quickly, including political topics. As an exercise, log on to the site.

   1. Click on "Data File Directory."
   2. Click on "Surveys of the General Population: A. National Surveys."
   3. Click on survey 1 "96KOHUT: Religion and Politics Survey, 1996."
   4. Read the description.
   5. Click on "Analyze" from the menu to the left of the study description.
   6. Select variable 117, "VOTE92," and click on the "Analyze!" button.

The program will analyze the data automatically and provide the frequency distribution of the respondents who voted for different presidential candidates in the 1992 election. It will also provide cross-tabulations of how such respondents voted relative to their (*a*) sex; (*b*) religion—Christian, Jew, other, none; (*c*) age—18–29, 30–49, 50 and over; (*d*) marital status; (*e*) education; (*f*) race; (*g*) income; and (*h*) region.

There are a large number of religious as well as political variables available for analysis, as well as a host of other studies to analyze.

3. Assess the relative influence of different facets of religion (e.g., religious affiliation, church attendance, and religious beliefs) in shaping attitudes toward a particular political issue (e.g., abortion, the environment, support for Israel) or support for a particular candidate (e.g., voting for Bush or Gore in the 2000 presidential election). Why do such religious factors vary in relative importance in the instance chosen? Assess the relative influence of religious factors against other social and economic factors (e.g., gender differences, educational difference, income differences). How important are religious differences in relationship to other social and economic differences in the case chosen?

6

Religious Lobbying and American Politics

Religious Faith Meets the Real World of Politics

Daniel J. B. Hofrenning

Imagine that you are a newly elected member of Congress. On the day you are to be sworn in, you walk down the marbled halls and into the hushed Senate chamber. Looking at the ornate surroundings, you ponder the great debates that have taken place here: the struggles over slavery, the declarations of war, momentous civil rights legislation. You feel a sense of awe. In your office later that afternoon, a man introduces himself as a lobbyist for a high-tech corporation. You cannot help but notice the impeccable way that he carries himself, the gold cufflinks, the pressed shirt, and the rich leather shoes. You are also startled by the friendly way in which he carries on. He asks about your family, your home, your hobbies. Then he asks if you want tickets to the Kennedy Center later that month. Later that week, his company is hosting a lavish dinner at a posh hotel in town. He can have a driver pick you up if you wish.

Not surprisingly, you will ultimately have to vote on legislation that affects his company. A committee to which you have been assigned will write the legislation. Through the months ahead, he almost becomes a friend, and he provides lots of important and helpful information. He is always both collegial and sharp; he knows his subject. He also offers campaign contributions for your next election and pledges to find others who will give to your campaign. The legislation that affects his company is quite obscure and technical; few of your constituents care about it. He never talks about buying your vote or twisting your arm, but the soft sell is powerful.

You also get to know another lobbyist. He is not as carefully dressed. He is affable, but there is a twinge of judgment in his voice. He tells you that he represents a religious denomination that has many members in your district. While he has no tickets or campaign contributions to give, he speaks with a resolve in his voice, and he too wants some legislation passed. His pitch is not as technical as other lobbyists. You are impressed by the steely resolve in his eyes. He wants major changes in both the health care and foreign policy of the nation. You do not recall those issues being mentioned in the churches that he purports to represent, but you rethink when you get lots of phone calls and letters.

Throughout American history, religious groups have tried to influence public officials. Before the Civil War, religious groups worked hard to end slavery. Religious groups also contributed mightily to the populist and progressive movements, which were responses to industrial capitalism. The Prohibition movement was essentially a religious movement. And, were it not for the religious leaders who protested, were arrested, and lobbied Congress, major civil rights legislation in the 1960s would not have passed. Likewise, the debate over American foreign policy toward Central America during the 1980s was informed and shaped by the input of religious groups. And, the struggle over abortion today includes religious activists working and lobbying on both sides of the issue, particularly on the pro-life side.

Lobbying[1] involves a group representative trying to persuade government officials to adopt specific types of public policy. It is a political activity that religious groups can choose; even if they choose not to lobby government directly, religious interest groups can still engage in other forms of political behavior. They can seek to influence the political views of their members, or they can form political committees that provide volunteers to work in election campaigns. However, since forming a political committee legally necessitates giving up tax-exempt status as a religious organization, few religious groups choose to do this. Not surprisingly, therefore, the electoral activities of religious groups are largely limited by the legal requirements for maintaining one's tax-exempt status.

119

Some lobbying organizations actually stretch the limits of those laws and become quite active in elections. For example, some African American churches collect money and organize for political candidates; in fact, some observers refer to African American churches as surrogate precincts (Hertzke 1993, 129–32). On the right, groups like the Christian Coalition pass out millions of voter guides in the weeks prior to an election. Virtually all of these voter guides conclude that Republican candidates are superior. But beyond these exceptions, few religious groups are so engaged. Instead, most religious groups file as nonprofit organizations. As such, they are not permitted to endorse candidates or to get involved in campaigns, though they are permitted to lobby public officials between elections. And many choose to do so.

Religious lobbyists are increasing in number and are part of what has been labeled an "advocacy explosion." Overall, the number of lobbyists and interest groups has skyrocketed in recent decades, especially in the 1960s and 1970s (Baumgartner and Leech 1998, 100–101).[2] But religious lobbyists differ from their nonreligious counterparts, in part because they lobby differently than their nonreligious colleagues. To be sure, religious lobbyists are shaped by the same milieu of American politics, and many of their tactics conform to the norms of Washington lobbying. However, religious lobbyists have a distinctive style. Compared to other lobbyists, they avoid the compromising and dealing that most lobbyists practice. Not satisfied with minute incremental change, they seek instead to transform society.

To understand better the role that religious interest groups play in American politics, this chapter first assesses why there are relatively few religious lobbyists within the American interest-group system. The second section examines the diverse range of religious lobbyists within American politics. The chapter then turns to the unique nature of religious lobbying, particularly the strategies that religious lobbyists use to live out their faith. Finally, the chapter concludes with an assessment of religious interest groups within American politics.

A Religious Nation, but Few Religious Lobbyists

A dazzling variety of religions have bloomed on American soil. Liturgical Catholic churches grow side by side with more freewheeling Pentecostal churches. Fundamentalist Christian churches flourish amid Jewish synagogues and Islamic mosques. While most European countries currently count only 5 to 20 percent of their citizens as active members of religious bodies, fully 70 percent of American citizens belong to a church, synagogue, or other religious organization (Greeley 1995; American Jewish Congress and Gallup International Institute 1996). Indeed, religious organizations claim more citizens as members than any other type of organization—more than labor unions and business. Because of their numbers, religious groups are potentially the most powerful interest group in America.

Looking at the throng of lobbyists in our nation's capital, one notices that religious representatives do not make up 70 percent of lobbyists. Recent studies estimate that religious lobbyists constitute only between 1 and 5 percent of the total (Hofrenning 1995, 73; Baumgartner and Leech 1998, 109). Most lobbyists in Washington represent business— between 50 and 70 percent—with much smaller numbers representing unions or educational organizations (Schlozman and Tierney 1986, 70; Baumgartner and Leech 1998, 106ff.). When the number of lobbyists is compared to the number of the groups' members, religious interests are underrepresented. The lobbying presence of American religious life is meager, considering that religious groups represent more than half of the American citizenry.

Religious ambivalence about politics helps to explain this low presence. The religious understandings of many citizens direct their gaze beyond the politics of this world. They see the corruption of politics as anathema to the purity of faith, so much so that they retreat from its presence. They join religious organizations for religious, not political, reasons. In fact, many members of churches and synagogues are unaware that they even have lobbyists working on their behalf. Moreover, many religious organizations employ only part-time lobbyists, and bigger denominations devote only a small portion of their overall resources to lobbying. When religious organizations avoid lobbying and other forms of politics, they are responding, in part, to a membership that is wary of politics.

In recent years, some prominent religious organizations of differing theological persuasions have curtailed their political involvement. In the 1980s, the more liberal National Council of Churches (NCC) was criticized for its extensive political involvement. While neither abandoning nor refraining from political involvement, the leadership of the NCC reemphasized the spiritual dimensions of the organization (Briggs 1984). More recently, Paul Weyrich, a prominent leader of the Christian Right, called on Christian conservatives to withdraw from politics. Seeing the tepid condemnation of President Clinton that occurred in the wake of the Monica Lewinsky revelations, Weyrich concluded that American culture was becoming an "ever-widening sewer." He argued, in response, that politics was hopeless and that true Christians should withdraw from the political realm (Andersen 1999; Niebuhr and Berke

1999, 1). To effect change, Weyrich suggested activities such as home-schooling and alternative radio as viable alternatives to the futility of lobbying and other forms of politics.

To other religious citizens, political activity such as lobbying is the inevitable and intrinsic part of their faith. A recent poll by the Pew Center found that 54 percent of citizens believed that "churches should express views on social and political matters" (Pew Research Center for the People and the Press 1996). In 1968, only 40 percent of Americans felt the same way—which suggests that American citizens increasingly want their churches and synagogues to be more political. To activists who see legalized abortion as an offense against God, joining an organization that lobbies for the abolition of abortion is an inevitable act of faith. To citizens who treasure the biblical condemnations of wealth and Scripture's clarion call to care for the poor, political advocacy for more compassionate social welfare policies is a spiritual practice just as integral to their spiritual lives as prayer and worship. And to those who see war as inimical to their faith in the Prince of Peace, joining a peace movement is nothing less than devotion to their God.

The Quandary of Representing Religious Interest

Because different religious lobbies work for strikingly diverse policies, one might conclude that there is no coherent religious interest. In contrast, other interest groups may not, at first glance, appear quite so disparate. Virtually all business lobbyists work for lower taxes and a more favorable regulatory climate. Organized labor lobbies for collective-bargaining rights and minimum-wage increases. There are disagreements in each of these communities, but such differences seem to pale in comparison to those within the religious community. Religious lobbyists work for both abortion rights and a right to life. Some religious advocates see school prayer as the key to a national recovery; others view it as a threat to religious liberty. Some faith-based lobbyists see universal health care as caring for what Jesus called "the least of those among us"; others see the same issue as the growth of an overbearing and secular government.

Disagreement about religion and politics is not new. During the American Revolution, most clergy supported the war and often used their pulpits to call citizens to its support. Yet many priests in the American branch of the Church of England supported the Crown (Reichley 1985, 97). During the Civil War, both the North and the South used religious reasons to support their cause. In his famous Second Inaugural Address,

Abraham Lincoln noted that both sides "read the same Bible and pray to the same God, and each invokes His aid against the other." Noting the strangeness of invoking God's aid for assistance in war, Lincoln (quoted in Ratvich 1991) adds that the "prayers of both could not be answered. That of neither has been answered fully. The Almighty has His own purposes."

Other organized interests have internal struggles similar to those of organized religious groups. For example, women make up at least half the population, but lobbyists for women's organizations do not make up half of lobbyists. Moreover, some women feel that their political interests can be represented in organizations not characterized as women's organizations. Even among women who are politically active, there is much disagreement. While most women's groups (such as the National Organization for Women) are fairly liberal, there are also several conservative organizations such as Concerned Women for America. Compounding these political disagreements over policy direction, some women also call for less political activity by women,[3] while other observers suggest that women and men should organize politically for a distinctive women's agenda. Without a women's lobby, issues such as comparable worth, equal rights, and abortion could be downplayed. Furthermore, since issues of war and economics affect women differently that they do men, women's political organizations are necessary.[4]

Despite the numerous religious citizens who negate the political aspects of their faith, enough see a distinctively religious aspect to politics. They are the citizens and leaders who organize groups and lobby government. David Truman, a leading interest-group scholar, calls the tendency to lobby the "inevitable gravitation to government" (1951, 104–5). Religious groups offer a fascinating story. Often they have played crucial roles in American politics. Despite a small lobbying presence, religious groups are sometimes very influential. Because of the scope of their membership and the fervent convictions of their advocates, it is important that we study them.

The Range of Religious Interest Groups

Religious interest groups can be classified by religious tradition or political ideology. Classified as broadly constructed religious traditions, there are Protestant, Catholic, and Jewish groups represented in Washington. A small, yet growing, Muslim population also finds some representation. Since Protestants are the largest group in the United States, it is not surprising that there are more Protestant interest groups on Capitol Hill than

123

any other religious category. And there are a number of ecumenical groups that make no reference to a particular religious tradition.

In an earlier era, most analysts simply divided American religion into three categories: Protestants, Catholics, and Jews (e.g., Herberg 1955). Now, however, such a simple tripartite division is not helpful as a means to understand our more complex religious world. More nuanced classifications have to be used. Important distinctions can be made between and among Mainline Protestants, Evangelical Protestants, "peace" Protestants, and African American Protestants. Although the evangelical community is diverse, most scholars have contended that Evangelical Protestants adhere to central religious tenets, including (1) a more literalistic view of Scripture, (2) an emphasis on an adult born-again experience that marks a dramatic turning to faith in Jesus Christ, and (3) an emphasis on bringing others to Christ. In contrast, Mainline Protestants accept (1) a historical-critical view of Scripture, (2) the priority of infant baptism into faith in Jesus Christ, and (3) a less aggressive approach to bringing in new members. In addition to Evangelical and Mainline Protestants, most observers see African American Protestants as another distinctive religious tradition. African Americans hold many evangelical theological beliefs, but their political priorities are usually more liberal than those of other Evangelical Protestants. Finally, "peace" Protestants are often a separate category. Mennonites, Quakers, and Church of the Brethren distinguish themselves with a strong religious commitment to pacifism that many other Protestants do not share.

In ideology, most observers divide religious groups into liberal and conservative categories; however, some religious political activists protest those divisions. Jim Wallis, leader of the religious movement A Call for Renewal, contends that religious groups should (1) provide an alternative to the polarized partisans who seemingly dominate our political process and (2) offer a message that transcends the conventional categories of left and right (Wallis and Sterling 1995). These protests notwithstanding, ideological labels do tell us something. Liberal groups focus primarily on questions of economic justice and a less militaristic foreign policy. They draw their inspirations from Old Testament prophets, who call people of faith to "beat their swords into plowshares, . . . their spears into pruning hooks" (Isa. 2:4), and to "let justice roll on like a river" (Amos 5:24). Looking to the New Testament, they are enlivened by Jesus' words in Luke, "The Spirit of the Lord is on me, because he has anointed me to preach good news to the poor . . . to release the oppressed" (4:18). Such passages serve as the basis for liberal lobbyists to make caring for the poor and working for peace their central concerns.

In contrast, conservative lobbyists avoid economic concerns and focus on other moral issues. They draw much of their biblical inspiration from

Pauline letters, especially the injunctions to individual holiness and purity. In recent years, their issue priorities have been school prayer, making abortion illegal, and opposing gay rights. Sometimes leaders of the Christian Right have focused on foreign policy and economics, but social issues such as abortion and school prayer remain their main priorities.

Conservative religious interest groups are fewer in number than liberal religious interest groups; however, their active membership base is larger. Among conservative religious interest groups, the Christian Coalition is the largest in membership. Formed in the late 1980s, following the collapse of Pat Robertson's presidential campaign, the Christian Coalition was initially led by Robertson and Ralph Reed. Reed was a conservative political activist who, despite his youth, had considerable political experience along with academic credentials (a Ph.D. in history) and media savvy.

Robertson and Reed began a grassroots strategy that focused on state and local elections—not the White House. Building on an extensive grassroots base, the Christian Coalition lobbied at the national level of American government. Every year it focused on a range of issues, rated members of Congress, and urged its multimillion membership to call or write their member of Congress. Over time, the numbers of Senators and Representatives with high Christian Coalition ratings have increased. For example, in 1992–93, 30 percent of the House and 26 percent of the Senate had Christian Coalition scores over 80 percent, where a score of 80 percent indicated that the legislator had voted the Christian Coalition position 80 percent of the time on the organization's selected key pieces of legislation. But in the 1996–97 Congress, 43 percent of members of Congress received ratings of 80 percent or higher.[5] One cannot claim that the Christian Coalition alone caused these changes toward a more conservative tone, but it surely played a role.

The Christian Coalition is not the only major conservative religious interest group. Other conservative organizations include the Family Research Council, led by Gary Bauer, a former Reagan administration official and a Republican presidential candidate during the early part of the 2000 campaign. The Family Research Council lobbies primarily on a variety of issues related to protecting the traditional family. Concerned Women for America, another conservative Christian organization, reaches out to conservative women and works on a range of "family" issues, particularly abortion. While these three groups are the largest and most active of the conservative religious organizations on Capitol Hill, there are a variety of other conservative organizations—for example, the National Association of Evangelicals, an umbrella organization of more moderate evangelicals, some single-issue anti-abortion groups, and denominational groups such as the Lutheran Church–Missouri Synod and organizations within the Southern Baptist Convention.

The liberal side consists of a larger number of religious groups than the conservative side, though the membership within these particular liberal groups tends to be smaller than within the conservative religious groups. Mainline Protestant denominations including the United Methodist Church, the Presbyterian Church (USA), the Evangelical Lutheran Church in America, American Baptists, and the United Church of Christ have lobbying offices in Washington. So does the Roman Catholic church through its lobbying office within the United States Conference of Bishops. Endowed with ample resources, this latter office analyzes issues and lobbies Congress and the White House on behalf of the Conference of Bishops. Jews are represented by several lobbies, including the American-Israel Political Action Committee (AIPAC), which most observers view as a powerful and effective lobby for aid to Israel; the American Jewish Congress; the American Jewish Committee; and the Union of American Hebrew Congregations. Finally, liberal groups include a number of ecumenical coalitions such as the National Council of Churches, representatives of African American denominations, and membership organizations such as Bread for the World, an antihunger group, and NETWORK, a membership organization of activist lay Catholics. By and large, all of these Jewish, Catholic, and Mainline Protestant groups share a liberal agenda. All lobby for increased aid to the poor; most lobby for a less militaristic foreign policy.

There are, of course, exceptions to this unanimity among religious liberals. Jewish organizations are basically alone in their support of aid to Israel, but the Christian Coalition, the Southern Baptist Convention, and other conservative Christian organizations support American foreign aid to Israel. Roman Catholic groups lobby for a range of economic issues with a broad liberal alliance, but their work against legalized abortion puts them, at times, in the conservative coalition of religious groups. Other liberal groups are pro-choice, but abortion is not an important issue to them. Exceptions to this pro-choice passivity are the Religious Coalition for Abortion Rights and Catholics for a Free Choice. Other than these two issues related to Israel and abortion, there is a fair amount of common ground among the liberal groups; they work together in broad coalitions on most issues.

Occasionally, however, liberal and conservative groups work together on issues of general concern. If the tax status of churches and synagogues is threatened, the ranks of these diverse religious groups will converge. But such cooperation is not limited to issues of economic self-interest. For example, during the 1980s, Congress considered the Equal Access Act, which guaranteed religious groups access to public school facilities for after-school activities on an equal basis with nonreligious groups. Evangelical Protestants, Catholics, and most Mainline Protestants lobbied for its passage. While there was opposition among Jewish organizations and some Mainline Protestants, the bill enjoyed an unusual alliance of liberals and conservatives and was passed.[6]

In the 1990s, an even broader coalition supported the Religious Freedom Restoration Act (RFRA). The bill was drafted in response to the Supreme Court's decision in *Employment Division, Department of Human Resources of Oregon v. Smith*. As previously mentioned (see chapter 4), the case concerned the petition of two Native Americans, who lost their jobs at a drug-rehabilitation clinic because they had ingested peyote during an Indian ceremony. Because they violated Oregon drug laws, the two were deemed ineligible to receive unemployment benefits. The claimants, however, contended that the law and the court's subsequent decision interfered with their First Amendment right to practice their religion, because peyote was used for sacramental purposes. The court, however, ruled that unless a law is expressly designed to limit religion, it is constitutional—even if a limit on religion is a consequence of the law. This decision enraged the religious community, because it was largely viewed as a change from a long-standing legal principle that prohibited state interference with religious practices, unless the state could demonstrate a "compelling interest." In response to the Supreme Court decision, Congress drafted the Religious Freedom Restoration Act, which stated that "governments should not substantially burden religious exercise without a compelling interest." Virtually the entire religious community—liberal and conservative, Protestant, Catholic, and Jewish—lobbied vigorously in support of the bill, which passed on nearly unanimous votes in Congress (Steinfels 1993, A18).

In a subsequent clash with Congress, the Supreme Court struck down the Religious Freedom Restoration Act. Congress then responded with another piece of legislation, crafted to meet the court's objections. Like the 1993 law, the new piece of legislation passed by huge margins in Congress and enjoyed the support of a diverse coalition of legislators. According to the *Christian Century* ("Religious Freedom—Take Two" 1998):

> Liberal and conservative Christian, Jewish, Muslim, Buddhist, America Indian, Sikh, Unitarian Universalist and other faith groups are among the more than 80 religious organizations backing the measure. They include the National Association of Evangelicals, the National Council of Churches, the U.S. Catholic Conference, the Southern Baptist Convention, the Church of Jesus Christ of Latter-day Saints, James Dobson's Focus on the Family, the Religious Action Center of Reform Judaism and the American Mus-

lim Council. Several civil liberties groups and church-state watchdog organizations also support the bill. They include Americans United for Separation of Church and State, Americans for Democratic Action and the NAACP. The limited opposition toward RLPA [Religious Liberty Protection Act] expressed so far has come from some Religious Right groups that object to the measure's legal reliance on interstate commerce and federal funding and what they see as its inherent approval of expanded federal powers.

Tactics, Strategies, and Effectiveness

Political scientists usually divide the tactics of lobbyists into two categories: insider lobbying and outsider lobbying (Gais and Walker 1991; Kollman 1998; Schlozman and Tierney 1986, chaps. 8 and 11). *Insider lobbying*, as its name suggests, takes place inside the halls of government, usually in the Capitol and White House in Washington, D.C. Insider activities focus primarily on shaping the language of legislation and its implementation. Successful insider lobbying requires access; therefore, lobbyists must cultivate a long-term relationship with government officials. This often occurs in social settings—on the golf course, in restaurants, and at cocktail parties. Two writers for the *New Republic* (Grann and Niedowski 1997, 21) provide this example of insider influence:

> In February, the man leading the House investigation into the Clinton fund-raising practices, Indiana Congressman Dan Burton, took a break from his do-good work and flew to Pebble Beach, California, to play golf in an AT&T-sponsored tournament with the company's chairman, Robert Allen. As it happens, AT&T is competing with Sprint and MCI for a government telephone contract worth up to $10 billion. As it also happens, Burton's Government Reform and Oversight Committee will oversee the awarding of that contract.

Often the insider lobbyists themselves are former members of Congress or the executive branch. In these cases, lobbyists simply maintain the relationships they forged during years in government to assist their insider lobbying. Birch Bayh, Tom Foley, and Toby Moffett were all Democratic members of Congress; now they are lobbyists. Similarly, on the Republican side, Michael Deaver left the Reagan administration to lobby government and ignited a scandal stemming from the use of his government contacts. Beyond these high-profile individuals, the more frequent transitions involve congressional staffers.

[A]n influential Hill staffer may be well-known among members of Congress and—even more important—among other Hill staffers, but obscure to the press and the public. . . . Most issues that concern businesses and foreign governments—a military contract, a tax loophole, a specific trade provision— . . . can be of major importance to a senator on a certain committee or a House member with a particular company in her district. . . . So congressional aides routinely switch sides and go to work as lobbyists, or "legislative counsels," or "legislative specialists." (Pasley 1987, 22)

In contrast, *outsider lobbying* occurs when lobbyists try to shape public opinion and generate grassroots pressure. The quintessential outsider tactics are mobilizing members to write letters to government officials and engaging in demonstrations. These activities involve activities outside of government—often at the grassroots—and not within the clubby and cozy atmosphere of government. When a key piece of legislation comes up, an organization will get the word to its members so they can write their representatives. Ideally, these petitions will literally flood Washington and influence legislative outcomes.

This type of lobbying was particularly effective in the 1980s in affecting the Reagan administration's policy toward Central America. President Reagan favored military assistance to the Nicaraguan contras, who were trying to overthrow the Sandinista-led government of Nicaragua, which he viewed as communist. Liberal religious lobbies organized demonstrations in Washington and initiated many letter-writing campaigns to oppose this pro-contra policy, and despite Reagan's tremendous national popularity and a national television appeal, his aid proposals were defeated on several key congressional votes. Following one vote, Assistant Secretary of State Langhorne Motley said, "Taking on the churches is really tough. . . . They are really formidable" (quoted in Ferber 1985, 12). And various national correspondents, including Cokie Roberts, observed that the religious lobbies were the most important opponent of the president's proposal (Hertzke 1988, 234–35).

Intense grassroots lobbying also occurred in 1984 when the Senate was considering constitutional amendments concerning abortion and school prayer. At critical moments, lobbyists for fundamentalist Christians flooded Capitol Hill with letters and phone calls. When the school-prayer amendment was on the agenda, Senator Pete Wilson (R, Calif.) received two thousand phone calls over a two-week period—ten times the usual number ("Famous Faces Fighting Hard" 1984). As a result, a proposal to make school prayer legal again received majority support in the Senate, but with less than the two-thirds vote necessary to approve a constitutional amendment. At the same time, a coalition of four Jewish and ten Protestant groups actively opposed the school-prayer proposal and lobbied for its defeat ("Prayer Issue Engulfs Congress" 1984; Moen 1989).

Religious lobbyists, for several reasons, generally favor outsider tactics more than their secular counterparts. First, they tend to be more principled and less willing to compromise. If the foundation of one's policy positions are principles derived from religious faith, then making deals, negotiating, and bargaining can chip away at the core of that faith. Moreover, the religious faith of some lobbyists moves them to seek the creation of a new "kingdom of God on earth." As a result, they are more inclined to seek fundamental change and not simply to negotiate shifts in the minutiae of policy. Second, religious lobbyists are more inclined to criticize the Washington establishment. They style themselves as prophets, bedraggled clarions of truth pounding on the doors and hearts of the powerful. In many ways, religious lobbyists expect the stubborn resistance of the rulers and maintain their own purity by standing apart.

In the early 1990s, when Gary Bauer served as president of the Family Research Council, he gave a speech to his members extolling their values, saying, "How superior your values are to the decadent elite of this city" (quoted in People for the American Way 1993, 1). Other conservative leaders from Jerry Falwell to Pat Robertson have echoed this criticism of contemporary American moral values. Falwell was motivated by what he termed "the moral decay of America" when he chose to enter activist politics, listing legalized abortion, gay rights, and the loss of school prayer as the evils being promulgated by elected officials. Pat Robertson has also spoken repeatedly about the decline of America, writing in a letter to his members: "By standing together, we can turn America back from its headlong plunge into moral chaos. . . . I am sending you this [Congressional] scorecard because I need your help to stop (or at least slow down) the anti-family train of destruction coming down our tracks" (quoted in Watson 1997, 104).

While running against Washington is a broadly popular tactic, religious lobbyists frame their criticisms of government in unique ways. Conservative religious lobbyists repeatedly contend that a secular elite is in control—an elite that will neither protect the life of the unborn nor recognize the value of the family. Interestingly, most religious liberals also see an elitist cabal in control, but an elite of a different nature. Liberals rage against what they perceive to be a wealthy corporate elite that siphons resources away from the needy. A veteran liberal lobbyist stated:

> Money talks and Congress listens. We try to represent the poor, the disadvantaged, both here and in other countries. They're vastly underrepresented, whereas people with money hire the high-priced lawyers. They make all the contacts on the hill and are way ahead. (Quoted in Hofrenning 1995, 98)

Other liberal lobbyists echo this concern for the poor. Interviews with a range of liberal lobbyists repeatedly reveal a belief that they provide representation, rarely found in Washington, for the poor and needy.[7]

To challenge the dominant elite, religious lobbyists use outsider tactics more than other lobbyists. To be sure, virtually all lobbyists use outsider tactics, but religious lobbyists do so more frequently and exclusively (see table 6.1).

Table 6.1 Tactics Used by Organizational Type (percentage of organizations citing tactic used frequently)

	Religious Organizations	Unions	Citizens' Groups	Trade Associations	Corporations
Entering into coalitions	50	7	17	24	30
Talking with people from the press and media	9	0	26	9	4
Inspiring letter-writing campaigns	34	20	9	12	2
Sending letters to members of your organization	66	13	9	18	6
Shaping the government's agenda by raising new issues	19	33	27	24	11
Mounting grassroots lobbying efforts	34	53	44	18	22
Engaging in protests or demonstrations	0	7	0	0	0
Running advertisements in the media	0	0	0	0	0

Source: Hofrenning 1995, 136.

Compared to other groups, religious lobbyists spend more time writing letters to their members, encouraging their members to contact government officials, and forming coalitions with other organizations. With these emphases, religious organizations look like unions and citizens' groups in their choice of tactics. Perhaps this suggests that outside strategies are favored by resource-poor organizations. After examining a range of interest groups, Gais and Walker (1991) concluded that groups that possess fewer monetary resources, but a broader membership base, do indeed tend to use outsider tactics. On the other hand, corporations and trade associations are better equipped for the campaign contributions, gifts, and close relationships that are part of the insider game. The most valuable resource that religious organizations possess is their mass membership base, not their financial resources. As a result, outsider strategies play to their organizational strengths as well as their religious beliefs.

The prior experience of religious lobbyists also reveals their outsider status. A majority of lobbyists have had some prior experience in government (Schlozman and Tierney 1986; Salisbury 1986; Milbrath 1963), while less than 10 percent of religious lobbyists have such experience. Though religious organizations could hire former government officials to represent them, they almost never do. For example, a Mainline Protestant church could hire a member of its denomination—someone who has served as a governmental official—but instead it hires individuals within its organization, such as former pastors, bureaucrats, or teachers from seminaries (Zwier 1988; Hofrenning 1995, 114). In so doing, religious interest groups are missing a chance to play the insider game, but most such organizations would have it no other way.

Diminished legislative success is a consequence of rejecting an insider strategy. Despite occasional victories, religious lobbyists usually lose. Nevertheless, they maintain this strategy because they hold to a different definition of success. Defying a narrow focus on winning or losing, religious lobbyists choose to be faithful. Such principled attitudes are reflected when they say, "We are called by God to act . . . to act boldly for justice and compassion whatever the odds." Some lobbyists have talked about the need to tolerate short-term failure and even embarrassment given their unwavering convictions. In the long run, religious lobbyists have faith that the world will change. Sometimes it does.

Enhancing the Insider Game

While most religious lobbyists prefer an outsider strategy, there are exceptions. Many observers contend that Jewish lobbyists have been especially astute in cultivating insider contacts (Fowler and Hertzke 1995, 58). Other religious lobbyists report success in influencing the language of specific amendments and laws. Bread for the World, an antihunger lobby, routinely gets involved in writing food-stamps and WIC (Women,

Infants, and Children program) legislation, while conservative lobbyists have offered hosts of amendments on issues including antipornography and civil rights laws. As a result, Hertzke concludes that religious lobbyists achieve "episodic effectiveness" at the insider game (1988, 79ff.).

During the 1990s, the Christian Coalition attempted to develop an effective insider strategy. It cultivated working relationships with congressional leadership, particularly among the leadership of the Republican Party. The foundation for this insider strategy had been laid a decade earlier by the Moral Majority, a Christian Right organization led by the Reverend Jerry Falwell, a Baptist minister. The Moral Majority was actively involved in the 1980 presidential campaign, when it favored Ronald Reagan over Jimmy Carter, despite the fact that Carter was a devout evangelical Christian. Unlike Carter, Reagan vigorously supported Christian conservatives on a range of social issues including school prayer, abortion, gay rights, and the Equal Rights Amendment. When Reagan won the 1980 election, Christian conservatives gained the possibility of insider access to the White House. Because they seemed to play a crucial role in getting Reagan elected president, Christian conservatives gained unprecedented access to the White House. Ed Dobson, then an aide to Jerry Falwell, acknowledged the thrill:

> Ronald Reagan and others recognized that we had made a difference so we were invited to the table for the first time. . . . It meant we were somebody, that we mattered . . . that all of the years in the back woods of the culture were over. We had come home, and the home was the White House. (Martin 1996, 225–26)

In some cases, such access may have had its price. In 1981, President Reagan nominated Sandra Day O'Connor to serve as a justice on the Supreme Court. Because she had favored legalized abortion as an Arizona legislator, many Christian conservatives were enraged. For example, Connie Marsher, a prominent Christian conservative leader, said, "With this nomination, the [Reagan] administration effectively said, 'Good-bye, we don't need you.' [President Reagan] had not consulted with his allies, had not checked with his conservative friends. They got a phone call saying, 'This is who it's going to be,' but. . . . no care had been paid to the fact that she had a pro-abortion voting record in Arizona" (quoted in Martin 1996, 229). In contrast, however, Jerry Falwell, at President Reagan's request, agreed not to comment on the nomination. His only public comment was, "I do not believe [Reagan] would intentionally appoint someone who supports abortion" (quoted in Martin 1996, 228). In so doing, some leaders in the Christian Right contended that Falwell had traded his prophetic mantle for a role as presidential adviser.

The disillusionment continued as the Reagan administration focused on economic issues, rather than the core priorities of Christian conservatives. In the late 1980s, the Moral Majority and other prominent organizations folded. But after his unsuccessful presidential campaign in 1988, Pat Robertson started a new organization, the Christian Coalition. While this organization ultimately sought to develop an insider strategy, it began with a decidedly outsider emphasis. Moreover, the Christian Coalition initially shifted its focus away from presidential politics and focused more on state and local elections. Its headquarters were first located in Chesapeake, Virginia, rather than the nation's capital. As Ralph Reed stated: "We tried to change Washington when we should have been focusing on the states." Still, a national focus remained strong, as leaders realized that developing a grassroots base at the state and local level was a prerequisite to attaining national success.

The Christian Coalition grew quickly and did become a national political force. In 1990, it claimed a membership of 25,000. By 1995, it claimed 1.6 million members in all fifty states. While many contend that these membership claims are exaggerations, the Christian Coalition was developing a broad membership base. Reed was doing a number of things to broaden the base of the coalition. Building on his outsider strategies, he also aggressively played the insider game. He worked to gain status in the inner circle of conservative, primarily Republican, activism. Claiming credit for the Republican sweep of Congress in 1994, he demanded and got a seat at the Republican table.

Gaining insider access included changing the style of religious lobbying. Gone were the days of criticizing a secular Washington elite; instead, Reed suggested that the Christian Coalition was a lobbying group existing side by side with representatives of business, labor, or the environment. "We really see ourselves as a kind of faith-based Chamber of Commerce, a kind of League of Women Voters, if you will, for people of faith" (quoted in Judis 1994, 24). Second, the Christian Coalition gave up on the demand for a constitutional amendment banning virtually all abortions in favor of an incremental approach focused on banning only late-term (or partial birth) abortions. At Reed's direction, the organization also supported some pro-choice Republicans. Third, Reed also began advocating the economic agenda of mainstream Republicans, including tax cuts, free trade, and a balanced budget. Finally, in 1996, the Christian Coalition backed Bob Dole for president instead of Patrick Buchanan, who shared a stronger issue affinity with the Christian Right's agenda. In sum, Reed was trying to move the Christian Coalition away from the fringes of the Republican Party.

Many within the Christian Right movement, however, criticized Reed. At a 1996 convention, Alan Keyes, a former Senate and presidential candidate, criticized Reed using one of Reed's favorite images. "Do we cling to our place in the game and our seat at the table? Or do we cling to the words of almighty God?" Keyes (1996) told Christian Coalition members that it was honorable to lose an election for the sake of a righteous cause, but if you lose, "having compromised what you believe because you thought someone would win[,] and when they lose, what do you have left?" Dole lost the presidential election of 1996 and Republicans in Congress did poorly in 1998. The Christian Coalition seemed to fade as it experienced membership losses and financial problems. According to some observers, "Many former Christian Coalition donors just kept their money or sent it to other organizations that had not been so visibly 'Doled' in 1996" (Watson 1999, 189). Amid this growing disarray, Reed left the Christian Coalition.

Reed's successor, Donald Hodel, showed signs of moving the Christian Coalition back to the outsider strategy of its early days. Hodel said, "A group like ours may in fact have greater impact if it is not visible. One of the strengths of a grass-roots campaign is that it doesn't show up on a radar screen" (quoted in Hallow 1998). At this point, the future strength of the Christian Coalition is unclear. Some Christian conservative leaders are urging a renewed outsider approach. For example, Richard Land, an official in the Southern Baptist Convention, said, "This go-along, get-along strategy is dead" (quoted in Goodstein 1998). Some Christian conservatives have even spoken of leaving the Republican coalition (Watson 1998, 194ff.), while other voices (e.g., Thomas and Dobson 1999) have called for a much more realistic assessment of what politics can accomplish, suggesting that too much attention has been given to politics by many Christian conservatives.

Conclusion

Proving the influence of interest groups is difficult. Most research in political science suggests that interest groups have little, or at best marginal, influence (Bauer, Poole, and Dexter 1963; Hanson 1991; Rothenberg 1992). While the media seem fixated on the pernicious influence of lobbyists, political scientists are more circumspect, as they see policy decisions more as a function of a number of factors—including personal ideology, party, constituents' opinion, *and* interest-group pressure. Moreover, from a methodological standpoint, it is hard to demonstrate how the outcome would have changed without the presence of a particular group.

Most observers contend that religious groups have played significant roles in shaping the outcomes of a range of issues over time—abolishing slavery, prohibiting or restricting the consumption of alcohol, securing civil rights legislation, shaping foreign policy toward Central America, and affecting the outcome of the 1994 election. In each of these cases, it seems clear that religious groups led the coalitions on the winning side. At a minimum, religious groups clearly influenced the nature of the debate.

However, on a range of other issues, religious groups have experienced frustration. For the Christian Right, abortion is still legal, school prayer has not been reinstated, and gay rights in recent years have expanded. For Christian liberals, none of their economic-policy proposals seems close to passage. The cries for justice on a range of issues including health care and welfare seem to fall on deaf ears. Many religious lobbyists among Christian liberals hardly seem concerned whether they win or lose, as they see their political involvement as an effort to remain true to their faith. Faithfulness to a higher power, rather than success per se, serves as their criterion of evaluation.

In the future, religious citizens will undoubtedly continue to support political action. Similarly, religious lobbyists will undoubtedly continue to be active participants in the policy process. If history sheds light on the future, it is likely that religious groups will emphasize an outsider strategy. Though they may not totally avoid an insider game, the bulk of their efforts will be spent mobilizing grassroots support on selected issues and causes.

References

American Jewish Congress and Gallup International Institute. 1996. "The American Jewish Committee Religious Right Survey, 1996." American Religious Data Archive. http://www.arda.tm/archive/AJCRR96.html

Andersen, M. J. 1999. "What's Eating Paul Weyrich?" *Knight-Ridder/Tribune News Service*, 14 April, p. K0115.

Bauer, Raymond, Ithiel de Sola Pool, and Lewis Anthony Dexter. 1963. *American Business and Public Policy: The Politics of Foreign Trade*. New York: Atherton Press.

Baumgartner, Frank R., and Beth L. Leech. 1998. *Basic Interests: The Importance of Groups in Politics and Political Science*. Princeton: Princeton University Press.

Briggs, Kenneth A. 1984. "Bishop Hopes to Bring New Spirituality to Council of Churches." *The New York Times*, 20 February, 7(N), A8.

"Famous Faces Fighting Hard for School Prayer." 1984. *Congressional Quarterly Weekly Report*, 3 March, 490.

Ferber, Michael. 1985. "Religious Revival on the Left." *The Nation* 241, no. 1:9–13.

Fowler, Robert Booth, and Allen D. Hertzke. 1995. *Religion and Politics in America: Faith, Culture, and Strategic Choices*. Boulder, Colo.: Westview Press.

Gais, Thomas L., and Jack L. Walker Jr. 1991. "Pathways to Influence in American Politics." In *Mobilizing Interest Groups in America: Patrons, Professions, and Social Movements*, by Jack L. Walker Jr. Ann Arbor: University of Michigan Press.

Goodstein, Lauri. 1998. "Religious Right, Frustrated, Trying New Tactic on G.O.P." *New York Times*, 23 March, A1.

Grann, David, and Erika Niedowski. 1997. "The Dirty Hill: The Sleaze That Dare Not Speak Its Name." *The New Republic* 261, no. 14 (7 April): 21–25.

Greeley, Andrew. 1995. "The Persistence of Religion." *Cross Currents* (spring): 24.

Hallow, Ralph. 1998. "Christian Coalition Goes Back to Core Principles." *Washington Times*, 7 January, A1

Hanson, John Mark. 1991. *Gaining Access: Congress and the Farm Lobby*. Chicago: University of Chicago Press.

Herberg, Will. 1955. *Protestant, Catholic, and Jew*. New York: Doubleday.

Hertzke, Allen D. 1988. *Representing God in Washington: The Role of Religious Lobbies in the American Polity*. Knoxville: University of Tennessee Press.

———. 1993. *Echoes of Discontent: Jesse Jackson, Pat Robertson, and the Resurgence of Populism*. Washington, D.C.: Congressional Quarterly Press.

Hofrenning, Daniel J. B. 1995. *In Washington but Not of It: The Prophetic Politics of Religious Lobbyists*. Philadelphia: Temple University Press.

Judis, John. 1994. "Crosses to Bear: The Many Faces of the Religious Right." *The New Republic* 211 (12 September): 21–26.

Keyes, Alan. 1996. "America's Yearning for Spiritual Renewal." Speech at the sixth annual Christian Coalition "Road to Victory" Conference, Washington, D.C.

Kollman, Ken. 1998. *Outside Lobbying: Public Opinion and Interest Group Strategies*. Princeton: Princeton University Press.

Leo, John. 1992. "The Trouble with Feminism." *U.S. News & World Report* 112 (10 February): 19.

Martin, William. 1996. *With God on Our Side: The Rise of the Religious Right in America*. New York: Broadway Books.

Milbrath, Lester W. 1963. *The Washington Lobbyists*. Chicago: Rand McNally.

Moen, Matthew. 1989. *The Christian Right and Congress*. Tuscaloosa: University of Alabama Press.

———. 1993. *The Transformation of the Christian Right*. Tuscaloosa: University of Alabama Press.

Niebuhr, Gustav, and Richard L. Berke. 1999. "Unity Is Elusive as Religious Right Ponders 2000 Vote; No Candidate Satisfies; Some Leaders Suggest Leaving the Political Arena to Focus on Moral Persuasion." *The New York Times*, 7 March, sec. 1, p. 1.

Pasley, Jeffrey L. 1987. "The Aides Virus: The Hill's Influence-Peddling Epidemic." *The New Republic* 194:22–25.

People for the American Way. 1993. *Right-Wing Watch* 4 (October).

Pew Research Center for the People and the Press. 1996. "The Diminishing Divide . . . American Churches, American Politics." National survey, 31 May–9 June, 1996. http://www.people-press.org/relgtab.htm

"Prayer Issue Engulfs Congress as Senate Embarks on Debate." 1984. *Congressional Quarterly Weekly Report*, 10 March, 538.

Ratvich, Diane, ed. 1991. *The American Reader: Words That Moved a Nation*. New York: HarperCollins.

Reichley, A. James. 1985. *Religion in American Public Life*. Washington, D.C.: Brookings Institution.

"Religious Freedom—Take Two." 1998. *Christian Century* 115 (1 July): 639.

Rothenberg, Lawrence. 1992. *Linking Citizens to Government*. Cambridge: Cambridge University Press.

Salisbury, Robert H. 1986. "Washington Lobbyists: A Collective Portrait." In *Interest Group Politics*. 2d ed. Washington, D.C.: Congressional Quarterly Press.

Sapiro, Virginia. 1981. "Research Frontier Essay: When Are Interests Interesting? The Problem of Political Representation of Women." *American Political Science Review* 75:701–16.

Schlozman, Kay Lehman, and John T. Tierney. 1986. *Organized Interests and American Democracy*. New York: Harper & Row.

Seib, Gerald F. 1993. "Christian Coalition Hopes to Expand by Taking Stands on Taxes, Crime, Health Care, and NAFTA [North American Free Trade Agreement]." *The Wall Street Journal*, 7 September, A16(W), A18(E).

Steinfels, Peter. 1993. "Clinton Signs Law Protecting Religious Practices." *The New York Times*, 17 November, A18.

Thomas, Cal, and Ed Dobson. 1999. *Blinded by Might: Can the "Religious Right" Save America?* Grand Rapids: Zondervan.

Truman, David. 1951. *The Governmental Process: Political Interests and Public Opinion*. New York: Alfred A. Knopf.

Walker, Jack L. 1991. *Mobilizing Interest Groups in America: Patrons, Professions, and Social Movements*. Ann Arbor: University of Michigan Press.

Wallis, Jim, and Diane Sterling, eds. 1995. *The Soul of Politics: Beyond "Religious Right" and "Secular Left."* New York: Harvest Books.

Watson, Justin. 1997. *The Christian Coalition: Dreams of Restoration, Demands for Recognition*. New York: St. Martin's Press.

Zwier, Robert. 1988. "The World and Worldview of Religious Lobbyists." Paper presented at the 1988 convention of the Midwest Political Science Association, Chicago, Ill.

Teaching Tools

Discussion Questions

1. Is adopting an "outsider" strategy a good strategic decision? Which tactic, insider or outsider, is more effective?
2. How influential are religious lobbyists? What evidence is necessary to estimate the influence of religious lobbyists?
3. If a religious lobbying organization called you for advice about increasing its influence, what would you tell them?
4. Many people are unaware that the churches and synagogues to which they belong are represented by lobbyists. What is the significance of this ignorance?

5. Does religious lobbying violate the separation of church and state? What are the dangers of religious lobbying?
6. How might a religious leader respond to the religious citizen who argues that religious lobbying undermines religion?

Topics for Student Research

1. Regarding discussion-question 2 above, many observers have recently suggested that the Christian Coalition is a very influential group. What evidence can you gather to test this claim?
2. Examine the literature in political science on issue networks and iron triangles. Are religious lobbyists part of any networks? A good place to start your research would be the following articles: Hugh Heclo, "Issue Networks and the Executive Establishment," in *The New American Political System*, ed. Anthony King (Washington, D.C.: American Enterprise Institute, 1978), 87–124; James Thurber, "Dynamics of Policy Subsystems in American Politics," in *Interest Group Politics*, ed. Allan J. Cigler and Burdett A. Loomis, 3d ed. (Washington, D.C.: Congressional Quarterly Press, 1990).
3. Hofrenning suggests that religious lobbyists do not usually work on technical issues. Can you find any evidence that counters that claim? (You may want to start with some of the websites listed below.)

Exercises

1. Go to the websites of as many religious lobbying organizations as possible and catalog their positions on issues. Which groups would you classify as liberal or conservative? Do any groups, such as those listed below, transcend those ideological labels?

   — A Mainline Protestant group such as the Presbyterian Church (www.pcusa.org/pcusa/nmd/wo/)
   — A coalition of liberal Protestant groups such as the National Council of Churches (www.ncccusa.org/)
   — A group funded partly by liberal churches to lobby on a specific issue, such as the Washington Office on Africa (www.woaafrica.org/) or the Religious Coalition for Reproductive Choice (www.rcrc.org/)
   — A pacifist church such as the Friends Committee on National Legislation (www.fcnl.org/)
   — A conservative group such as Concerned Women for America (www.cwfa.org/) or the Family Research Council (www.frc.org/)

2. Compare some religious lobbying groups to nonreligious groups. What differences do you notice? Begin by comparing the following groups:

— Christian Coalition, a conservative religious group (www.cc.org/)
— The Interfaith Alliance, an ecumenical organization formed primarily to oppose the Christian Coalition (www .interfaithalliance.org/)
— American Conservative Union, a conservative nonreligious group (www.conservative.org/)
— United Methodist Church, General Board of Church and Society, a liberal mainline group (www.umc-gbcs.org/adissue .htm)
— Americans for Democratic Action, a liberal nonreligious group (www.adaction.org/)
— Common Cause, a nonpartisan citizens' group (www .commoncause.org/)
— Bread for the World, a moderate to liberal membership group that focuses on hunger issues (www.bread.org/)
— American Israel Public Affairs Committee, a Jewish organization (www.aipac.org/)
— AFL-CIO, major labor organization (www.aflcio.org/front/wfa.htm)
— The Business Roundtable, preeminent business lobbyists (www.brtable.org/)
— American Medical Association in Washington, representative for major organization of American doctors (www.ama-assn .org/ama/basic/category/0,1060,165,00.html)

3. The Christian Coalition has been in legal trouble for engaging in political action prohibited by its nonprofit tax status (501-c-4). Go to the library and search for articles on this suit. What is the essence of claims against the Christian Coalition? What political activities are permitted and prohibited by the tax status of the Christian Coalition?

Start with the following generally available articles:

Carney, Eliza Newlin. 1996. "Rites Fight: 'God's Laws' v. the IRS's (Political Activity of Churches Makes Them Eligible for Taxation)." *National Journal* 28 (15 June): 1324–27.

"The Clue in the Letter (Evidence That Christian Coalition Contributed to Bush Campaign Contained in Letter to Coalition Founder Pat Robinson from Tycoon J. W. Wolfe)." 1996. *Newsweek* 128 (12 August): 49.

Foerstel, Karen. 1998. "Legal Maneuvers over Issue Ads Steal Spotlight from Congress' Ongoing Campaign Finance Debate." *Congressional Quarterly Weekly Report* 56, no. 2 (18 July): 1930.

"Nonpartisan or Not So Nonpartisan? (Federal Election Commission Investigation of the Christian Coalition)." 1996. *U.S. News & World Report* 121 (12 August): 8.

Salent, Jonathan. 1996. "FEC Files Disclosure Lawsuit against Christian Coalition." *Congressional Quarterly Weekly Report* 54 (3 August): 221.

4. Look for testimony of religious leaders before Congress. How often do religious leaders testify before Congress? On what types of issues do they generally testify? Do you think that their testimony is influential? Why or why not?

7

Religion and American Political Parties

DOUG KOOPMAN

Different religious traditions define differently the best relationship between faith and politics. Religions vary in how they obtain religious truth, how much they embrace modernity, how concerned and involved they are with this world, and what behaviors they think are appropriate.[1] The United States has seen its share of religious individuals, movements, and churches seeking to affect government, politics, and elections. Whereas political involvement is anathema to many faith traditions, other strains of the American religious community have frequently tangled with party politics. In fact, religious interaction with political parties and elections in America is extensive and continuous, beginning at the founding and continuing to the present.[2]

Evangelical Protestant Christianity has been the most politically active religious tradition in America, often urging politicians and government to implement a policy or set of policies that it thinks is required of the nation. Until approximately 1920, theologically orthodox Protestantism dominated religious influences on political parties, mostly through those parties (Federalist, Whig, and Republican) that saw themselves as custodians of traditional moral virtues. Protestant dominance was possible because the bulk of the politically involved citizenry held to one or another culturally conservative denomination within the broad Protestant faith.

Since the early twentieth century, however, Protestantism has been divided into a "two-party system" (Marty 1970), and the rest of American religion has diversified to include many non-Christian faiths as well as a whole spectrum of people attached to no particular religion. During the past century, more theologically and politically liberal Protestants have been a smaller, but nonetheless key, part of a liberal coalition, with partisan influence mostly on the Democratic side.

Thus throughout American history most types of Protestantism, as well as Catholicism, Judaism, and other religions, have entangled themselves in political partisanship. Sometimes these voices have been liberal or progressive, at other times they have been conservative or reactionary, but all have exhibited similar dynamics in the interaction between religion and partisanship.

Religion and political parties in the United States can be, and often have been, good for each other. The historical record suggests, however, that religion may be more helpful for the healthy functioning of American political parties system than party politics is for religion. Before we address this issue, we must first review the functions parties perform in American politics. Then we examine briefly a few incidents in which religion has mixed with partisanship, in order to provide a clearer picture of the nature of their interaction in American history. Finally, this review provides a context for making some critical judgments about the ways religion and party politics interact in American political life.

What Political Parties Do

Partisan activity is usually seen as the clearest form of politics, as either its "highest" or "lowest" form, depending on one's view. Many Christians who willingly influence government in other ways shy away from the high stakes of partisan conflict, and "partisanship" is widely decried by the media and the American public generally. Why are political parties so despised?

Most political science textbooks provide fairly similar definitions of political parties as well as a similar listing of what they do. A political party is usually defined as *a group of individuals with some ideological agreement, who want to win elections, operate government, and determine public policy*.

Parties compete for power—competition and power-seeking being two activities which many religious traditions disavow. Healthy political parties are, however, necessary to a well-functioning democratic political system. On behalf of that larger system, political parties carry out many key activities. They stimulate interest in politics and publicize political issues. Healthy parties socialize the citizenry: they encourage grassroots activity, integrate new members of the electorate, engage in public discussion of political issues, and seek a peaceful resolution of public problems. Second, healthy parties recruit candidates and organize campaigns. They look for good persons to run for office and provide legal and strategic advice and financial help to candidates. Third, largely by scrutinizing the campaign activity of their opponents, parties help maintain honesty in elections and campaigns.

Parties are vital to a well-functioning government and peaceful societal change. Perhaps most important for government, parties operate the "machinery" of government (or, in the case of parties out of power, provide an organized opposition). In the United States, operating government involves the difficult tasks of coordinating policy across the local, state, and national levels in our federalized system, and across the separate branches of government one finds at almost all levels. Perhaps most important to society, healthy political parties reduce social and class tensions. They mobilize mass numbers of average citizens to constrain the elites at the top, help to lessen societal conflict by managing conflicts within a party, and contribute to intersectional and interclass consensus by maintaining broad geographic and demographic support under one party banner.

Parties regularly appeal to the public. A healthy majority party has a good grasp of the public's concerns and views; that is why it is the majority. Minority parties "get healthy" by reaching out to present and potential voters with new issues. Parties battle to gain and keep majority status, raise new issues, and enfold new voters into the system, helping it to keep going.

The potential for broad-based religiously inspired social movements to invigorate a political party makes religious causes and movements prime prospects for "bidding wars" among the major political parties, in order to incorporate that movement into their party and the ongoing party system. Often the results of these battles change political alignments and initiate new party "eras."

The history of American politics is usually divided into five or six of these party "eras." In each era, one party and one set of issues dominate. Eras change through social crises that produce rapid changes in voting patterns, resulting in either a new national majority party or a new agenda that enables a party to keep majority support. The dividing

144

lines between eras are often associated with temporary third parties, steep voting declines or increases, or other evidence of voter disenchantment with prior partisan arrangements.

Compared to parties in other nations, American political parties are decidedly pragmatic, factional, and ideologically flexible. They have these characteristics almost necessarily in that they must carry out the primary, necessary, but arduous task of coordinating policy in our federal and separated governmental system. Unifying policy across branches and levels of government is a constant and consuming preoccupation—both in time and energy. American parties expend so much energy and power trying to coordinate policy among nominal party adherents that, in fact, they often lose their ideological unity and sense of purpose. This potential for disintegration makes them ripe for renewal by more ideologically coherent factions from within, or outside, the existing party structure. In American history, religion has often played that role.

Historical Overview of Religion and American Partisan Politics

Although the interaction between religion and political parties in America has been constant since the founding of the nation, different historical periods reveal much about the strengths and weaknesses of this interaction. This section briefly reviews this relationship in several different eras.[3]

Religion and Party Politics in the First Half of the Nineteenth Century

The role of religion in helping make the case for American independence from Britain in 1776 is well documented. Religious leaders and churches also helped make the argument for ratifying the new American Constitution of 1789. Less well known is religion's recurring role since then in bringing new issues into public debate and realigning the American party system.

Religion played an important role in the political disintegration of the 1840s and 1850s, which led to the realignment of the early 1860s, marked by the ascendance of the Republican Party. The first half of the nineteenth century was a period of great social ferment in America. Westward expansion through the Plains, early industrialism with its urbanization and new labor concentrations, and mass European immi-

145

gration into the cities all contributed to the rise of new social tensions and political issues. Religious groups became active in responding to the new crises of the cities, forming voluntary associations to combat urban poverty, poor health conditions, growing crime, and increasing alcohol abuse. It was an era largely modeling Alexis de Tocqueville's description of America: a nation that forms private voluntary associations to address social ills that people of other nations generally leave to government to solve.

The empowerment of the masses extended to politics, as changes in the election and nomination processes mobilized turnout in national elections from one million in 1828 to three million in 1852. It was a time in which Whigs usually battled Democrats for national prominence, and this "second" party era (the first being Federalists vs. Anti-Federalists) was actually the first era marked by mass political participation or identification. It was also an era in which the two parties were relatively competitive, though the Democrats generally captured the presidency because frequent divisions among the Whigs made victory difficult. Struggles over the continuation of Sunday mail delivery, the sustained effort to open public assemblies with prayers, Jackson's refusal in 1832 to designate a national day of fasting and prayer—on these and many related issues, party differences were distinct, passionate, and enduring (Dreisbach 1996). Many of the "devotionalist" Protestant groups (e.g., New School Calvinists, Old School Presbyterians, Free Will Baptists, Quakers, and others) tended to cooperate in the Whig efforts at "national redemption." On the other hand, those who supported Jackson, an alliance of "confessional" bodies (e.g., Roman Catholics, German Lutherans, Dutch "True" Calvinists, Old School Presbyterians, Antimissional Baptists, and small organizations of "free thinkers"), advanced the old Jeffersonian stance of complete separation of church and state and the promotion of religious liberty (Howe 1979, 176).

But as slavery increasingly overwhelmed all other issues, Whigs could not sustain party unity nationally. They often split, and third parties multiplied. After several multiparty elections in the late 1840s and 1850s in which Democrats usually won, the Republican Party came quickly to prominence and won the White House in 1860, ushering in a new, third, political-party era.

Religious persons and movements had much to do with the tumultuous social and political change in this period. The constitutional separation of church and state allowed most churches to be very aggressive in direct and open evangelism. Churches also created a large network of social service and fraternal organizations to meet growing needs in these areas. A large proportion of new immigrants were European and nominally Catholic, both increasing the tension between

146

Catholicism and the various Protestant denominations as well as spurring the latter to "covert" the newcomers. Baptists and Methodists worked heavily on the frontier, seeking converts among immigrants as well as those restless Americans pushing the nation west.

Evangelical Protestantism was an early leader in the noble cause of abolition, but also in the less commendable anti-Catholic movement. As before the revolution, a preceding religious revival helped shape the evangelical approach to politics and these issues. The Second Great Awakening, launched in the early 1800s, helped bring both newcomers and long-time citizens to the Protestants' view of Christianity, and its key leaders put at least some burning issues on the political agenda. Evangelical Protestantism "got the ball rolling" on slavery as a political issue, as the revivalists of the 1830s and 1840s helped make it a political issue that Congress could not avoid. Revivalist Charles Finney transferred his revivalist methods and rhetoric to his crusade against slavery. Abolitionists Lyman Beecher, Theodore Weld, and William Lloyd Garrison continued and expanded these tactics, sometimes including attacks on intemperance as well.

As revivalism tends to demand immediate perfection, abolitionist pastors usually called for the immediate end of slavery, expressing impatience with both Whigs and Democrats in their more accommodating and incremental approach that is characteristic of peaceful democratic politics. In a political sense, this high religious fervor pushed the parties both too hard and too soon to sustain unity across an increasingly divided nation. The Whig party was the first to collapse.

The collapse of the Whig party in the early 1850s provided an opening for a new opposition party to the Democrats. The first attempt was a pure anti-slavery party called the Liberty Party, which supported immediate abolition. It had strong evangelical support, but failed to gain enough adherents to maintain itself. The Free-Soil Party, opposed to expanding slavery beyond the old South, unsuccessfully ran former president Martin Van Buren as its candidate in 1848. Late in the next decade, the anti-slavery Republican Party finally succeeded in establishing itself as the major opposition. Its anti-slavery position cemented most northern Protestants to it, especially in more established urban areas and the emerging suburban areas, for more than a century.

There is, however, a darker side to this era's Evangelical Protestant politics. The second quarter of the nineteenth century saw the rise of anti-immigrant sentiment, and because immigrants were often Catholic, anti-Catholicism emerged as a political force. The dominant Protestant establishment reacted against, among other things, requests by Catholics for government support of their own schools to counter the Protestantism taught in the "public" schools of the day. Protestants insisted on maintaining their monopoly over the largely Protestant "American system," and used party politics to that end. Anti-Catholicism enjoyed a brief, but influential, heyday in party history. The anti-immigrant, anti-Catholic "Know-Nothing" movement worked first within the Whig Party, and later organized the American Party, which gained power in a few New England and northern Atlantic states in mid-1850s elections. The Know-Nothings/American movement was soon swallowed up by the Republicans, which fortunately made anti-slavery their primary organizing principle.

But anti-Catholic sentiment remained a legacy within local Republican organizations in many areas of the nation. The religious divide is especially apparent in voting statistics of the late 1800s: one observer notes that denominational allegiance, combined with ethnic ties, was the best predictor of national voting behavior throughout the period (Noll 1992, 243). This century-old split has only recently been overcome as politically conservative Catholics finally came over to the GOP in the 1980s and 1990s.

Religion and Party Politics in the Second Half of the Nineteenth Century

Historians focusing on the third electoral system that emerged in the aftermath of the Civil War have frequently advanced ethnocultural interpretations of the political cleavages evident during that era (e.g., Jensen 1971; Kleppner 1970 and 1979). Such historians have emphasized cultural conflict in popular voting, contending that difference in voting patterns within the electorate tended to reflect cultural, rather than economic, forces.

During the third electoral system, the Republican coalition was composed largely of voters drawn from religious groups whose members were pietistic in their religious perspectives. Such people were drawn largely from denominations that had religious cultures shaped by the revivalist ethos and its injunction to purge the world of sin (Kleppner 1982, 45). Pietists emphasized a personal, heartfelt faith in a holy and transcendent God. While pietists saw the world as a sinful, or fallen, order, they believed it could be partially, if not completely, changed through bringing others to Christ. Moreover, godliness for pietists required righteous behavior. Through such changed lives, pietists sought to reduce, if not purge, the presence of sin in the world (Kleppner 1970, 73).

On the other hand, the Democratic coalition was largely composed of voters who were liturgical, or ritualistic, in their religious perspectives—for example, Catholics, German Lutherans, and native-stock Calvinists. Those who held a liturgical perspective emphasized right

148

belief and the "intellectual assent to prescribed doctrine" and rejected the religious emotionalism generally associated with the pietistic perspective. Instead of emphasizing religious feelings and experiences, ritualists emphasized the maintenance of doctrinal purity, the willing assent to formal creed and confessions. Liturgicals also saw the world as a sinful, or fallen, order, but they tended to emphasize resignation to the situation and the differentiation between the religious and the secular spheres of life (Kleppner 1970, 73).

However, by the latter half of the nineteenth century, American society began to experience the full blossoming of urban problems, combined with wider economic problems that were perceived to be caused by the concentration of private wealth and political power. The sociopolitical world responded with the populist movement. Populism was a radical social and political philosophy and grassroots-action movement that developed during this period, largely within agricultural areas of the South, West, and Midwest. It favored government ownership of utilities and key modes of transportation to counter the power of private monopolies, and it favored a range of financial changes to benefit borrowers, small farmers and businesses, and the poor.

Churches and religious organizations also responded to the urban and economic crises by expanding their voluntaristic activities during the antebellum era. The 1870s and 1880s saw the rise of the Salvation Army, YMCA, and YWCA as effective nationwide organizations seeking to address the rising problems of the day.

Populism divided Protestant denominations between the better-off establishment, which was mostly Republican, and the lower-status upstarts, who already harbored Democratic sympathies. The movement also united the socially minded religious (and nonreligious) with most Catholics, who tended to vote Democratic.

This populist "Christian coalition" had majority influence within the Democratic Party, but constituted a minority of all voters. The capture of the Democratic Party by the populists, and the religious nature of this capture, are evidenced in the 1896, 1900, and 1908 presidential nominations of the fundamentalist William Jennings Bryan. Bryan's campaigns and the religious rhetoric surrounding them are evidence both of the power of religion in shaping the emerging fourth party era and of the sectarian bases lining up within each major party. Even as a repeatedly unsuccessful Democratic nominee, Bryan enticed many Protestant religious populists—small farmers and tradesmen especially in the Midwest and Plains—to make a lasting home in the party. Reinforcing the antebellum voting patterns with a new range of issues, Republicans became even more so the party of the Protestant establishment, and Democrats of Catholics, lower-class Protestants, and new Americans.

149

The religious community also responded to the challenges of this era with calls for temperance and prohibition, as the abuse of alcohol was seen as a major cause of, or at least associated with, the social problems of the day. Prohibition had actually begun as a politically relevant movement in the Second Great Awakening of the 1830s and was beginning to enjoy legislative successes before the disruption of the Civil War. Its power grew after the war with a number of individual states outlawing many kinds of alcoholic production or use. While many advocates of temperance were housed in the Republican Party, the movement nevertheless spawned a Prohibition Party in 1872, and the party has had a presidential candidate every election since. The voter appeal of the party peaked in the 1892 election at 2 percent, and has never won more than one-fourth of 1 percent of the vote since 1924. Even though unsuccessful as a separate political party, Prohibition was a highly successful political movement. Its ability to enact the Eighteenth Amendment in 1919, even though it was overturned by the Twenty-first Amendment fourteen years later, illustrated that moral issues could be legislated at the national level.

Religion and Party Politics in the First Half of the Twentieth Century

The lesson of the Prohibition movement was not lost on religious liberals concerned about social issues. But the unity of prohibition efforts fell apart in the debate over emphasizing personal morality versus social justice. Early in the twentieth century, and long before Franklin Roosevelt's New Deal, the "Social Gospel" movement began to propose government agendas to attack social and economic ills, seeking to advance a "kingdom of God on earth" through formal government action. The Social Gospel helped to split the Protestant faiths, and the embarrassment of the Scopes trial reinforced the division.[4] This split between conservatives and liberals sounded the death knell for Protestant hegemony.

Prohibition had provided the practical success that translated over time into theoretical justification for Christian political action. As the Prohibition movement made headway in the political system, many theological and practical arguments against religiously motivated political action had to be discarded or revised. As such, the Social Gospel movement merely took advantage of revised principles and applied them to a new issue, one with which its more conservative brethren disagreed but had little intellectual resources to fight.

The alliance between liberal theology and more liberal politics was direct, intentional, and intellectually similar; early in the twentieth century "both liberal theology and liberal political ideology began to change the generally accepted views of their controlling documents, the Bible and the Constitution, respectively" (Dunn 1984, 47). As Dunn argues, "loose" interpretation of both these "sacred texts" led in the same direction. In the political world came the nationalization of government programs, as the "strict constructionist" interpretations of federalism and separation of powers were swept aside. Theologically, liberal social action arose as the political dimensions of the biblical exodus and "promised land" and Jesus' life and teaching were read into American events of the early 1900s.

Salvation became, at least partly, this-worldly, and the national government became the prime saving agent. Progressives and then New Deal Democrats willingly built on this religious imagery. The alliance of biblical imagery and Social Gospel politics helped draw Catholic and Jewish immigrants, some African Americans, and lower-class whites even closer to the Democratic Party, though none were friendly to the theologically and politically conservative Protestant establishment. In political terms, Hoover's Depression and the Democratic New Deal activism cemented a new and almost insurmountable majority coalition of pro-government liberal elites and their beneficiaries. Religiously, the New Deal coalition consisted of politically liberal Protestant elites, most Catholics, some lower-status Christian religious conservatives, and the smaller non-Christian religious traditions.

Religion and Party Politics in the Second Half of the Twentieth Century

In political terms the 1960s began the era of partisan "dealignment," a time when party allegiances weakened and shifted. Partisan change was far slower in this era than in other eras, and political distrust and apathy were at historically high levels. This period was also marked by polarized debate on three key issues that had significant religious impact—civil rights, trust in government, and government support for traditional moral values.

The civil rights movement created a dynamic that in the short term enhanced the majority position of the Democratic Party nationwide, by cementing the liberal religious community to the party on this key social issue. Second, the party increased its general appeal to most religious persons by championing the proposition that all persons, whatever their color, are fully human and deserve respect. While many Republicans supported civil rights, clearly the Democratic Party was the more supportive party and deservedly obtained most of the credit for the progress made.

But the identification of the Democratic Party with civil rights also harmed it. It disturbed lower-status whites who had happily voted Democratic since the time of Jefferson. These voters were soon wooed by Richard Nixon, who as president developed a "southern strategy" based on toughness on crime and slowness on civil rights to draw this faction to his party, first at the presidential level and (hopefully) later further down the ballot. The long-range electoral success of the southern strategy for the GOP is hard to dispute. In the South today, the Democratic Party is rooted in the African American community, joined by upper-class liberal whites.[5] Republicans now dominate southern congressional elections, and even some local races, obtaining majority status in the U.S. House of Representatives in 1994 largely from the switch in southern white sentiment to the GOP.

Distrust of government has hurt both parties. Vietnam generally exacerbated the social cleavages begun in civil rights, as antiwar sentiment within the Democratic Party fanned by religious liberal elites further turned off patriotic southern whites. Watergate, in turn, harmed GOP credibility. The overall effect of these two events weakened public attachment to government, politics, and both major political parties, and fostered a disengagement from politics and parties that was as evident within the religious community as in the public at large.

Finally, the insertion of moral issues such as abortion, school prayer, and homosexual rights into electoral politics served to sever Democratic ties for nearly all lower-status whites with religious commitments. At the same time, it provided new energy for the most religiously committed and politically conservative groups to re-engage in politics. The divide between lower-status whites and the rest of the Democratic coalition that started with Vietnam became a chasm under the Republican's strategy and the Supreme Court's liberal social policy decisions. With Republicans attacking the Burger and Warren courts for liberal decisions on prayer, crime, and abortion, conservatives of all stripes began associating with the GOP or at least moving away from the Democrats. And liberals more supportive of these decisions gravitated to the Democratic side.

The American party system now appears to be undergoing simultaneously a realignment toward Republicans and dealignment away from party involvement, even as some religious commentators see a "culture war" dividing the larger society (e.g., Hunter 1991). People describing themselves as politically conservative and deeply religious are now the bedrock of Republicanism in all parts of the nation. Economically conservative secularists are mostly Republican, but less so than their religious allies. These latter conservatives seem wary of the national Republican strategy of marrying social conservatism to traditional economic conservatism, and seem ready to bolt to candidates such as Ross Perot, who focus only on economic liberty. Highly religious liberals are vociferously *not* Republican, but frequently claim no strong partisan allegiance to provide psychological distance between them and Democratic politicians whose secularism makes them uncomfortable. Only highly secular liberals seem fully comfortable with Democrats, at least in the early 1990s. Some commentators had gone so far as to say that the Democratic Party in the early 1990s was an anti-religious party, while Republicans at least allowed moral discussions within their ranks. While that characterization went too far, the most interesting trend within the Democratic Party today is the conscious movement by some individual Democrats and some party leaders to use more explicitly religious language and symbolism as a means to overcome the notion of Democratic hostility to religion.

At the turn of the millennium, America's mixture of religion and partisanship has three interesting features. The first is the continuing influence within the Republican Party of a deeply religious politically conservative caucus that remains relatively cohesive despite some internal conflict. Evangelical Protestant Christianity is this faction's major religious tradition, although there are many Catholics, a few Jews and Mainline Protestants, and a smattering of other adherents willing to be identified with this group. The faction is also strongest in the South, both because of its numbers in the region and because this region has given the GOP its greatest electoral gains. Religious conservatives are also prominent in some parts of the Midwest and West, and only in the Northeast is this faction a clear junior partner of the GOP coalition. Within the religious caucus itself there is some disagreement over how loyal it should be to the party and how principled it should be in its policy positions. And the party as a whole, while clearly dependent on deeply religious conservatives for its core support, remains concerned that it must not become too closely identified with the Religious Right if it hopes regularly to gain national majority status.

The second interesting phenomenon is the more recent attempt by national Democrats again to mix religion and politics in order to neutralize the religious advantage enjoyed by Republicans in the 1980s and 1990s. This has been exhibited in at least three areas: frequent use of religious language, symbolism, and backdrops by leading Democrats; greater openness to policies such as "charitable choice," which mix faith and government action; and active support for overtly religious movements countering the Republican activism of politically conservative religious adherents.

The third phenomenon is the decline within the deeply religious community of support for the two-party system. This is exhibited in two related movements, the move away from party involvement toward parachurch movements, and a smaller movement to establish religiously based third parties. Christians and non-Christian religious groups, conservatives and liberals, have increasingly developed parachurch move-

153

ments and policy organizations that, at other times in American history, would have been eager to engage in partisan politics and would have been ripe for recruitment by political parties seeking to regain their health. Mass organizations such as Promise Keepers, aspiring mass movements such as the more liberal Call to Renewal network, and more narrowly focused activist groups such as the African American separatist Nation of Islam have most of the elements required for partisan engagement. But because they are infected with the same anti-party attitude of the public at large, they keep their distance from the parties. Issue-oriented groups such as Focus on the Family and the leadership of Call to Renewal have avoided public cooperation with leaders of either party, although they have felt free to lobby on selected public issues and generally fall in the Republican and Democratic camps, respectively.

The continuing presence of religiously grounded third parties reflects the same aversion to the traditional two-party system. The most prominent is the U.S. Taxpayers Party, which has quietly developed a national party organization. Its platform is committed to restoring the United States to the biblical principles on which it was founded, and to electing to office only citizens who understand and sympathize with this view of the nation's founding (Napolitano 1994).

Assessment of Religion and Partisan Politics

Partisan involvement by religious groups reflects a willingness to enter a competitive arena of power wielding and power sharing to achieve certain policy objectives. Not all religions support such engagement, even in the United States with its open political system and historical support for religious expression.

For those faiths that do support political engagement, at least three options are available. The first option is to enter the fray after the electoral process is over, and to lobby appointed and elected officials selected by others to serve in government. Many American faiths and Christian denominations have chosen this route; indeed, Washington, D.C., is full of religious lobbies and lobbyists connected to a specific denomination or broad faith tradition (Hertzke 1988).

The second option is to engage in electoral politics, but as an interest group aligned with one of the two major political parties. The most obvious contemporary example of that strategy is the Christian Coalition, which in most areas of the nation has worked in and with the Republican Party.

The third option is to strike out on one's own as a separate, religiously based political party. This option has been attempted at least a few times

154

in the past and always has some adherents. While certainly an option to be seriously considered, such a strategy has several drawbacks. This can best be elaborated by referring again to the definition and functions of a political party. A political party is *a group of persons with some ideological agreement who want to win elections, operate government, and determine public policy*.

Parties stimulate interest, recruit candidates, organize and execute campaigns, maintain the honesty of elections, operate government, mobilize the masses, and help to lessen societal conflict. Parties compete with other entities—mostly interest groups, the media, and voluntary associations—in performing most of these duties. The only unique tasks parties perform is to organize campaigns and coordinate government. These are important activities, but it is difficult to see how religious persons might contribute special insight to either of these functions (especially based on their track record in politics).

The arguments against identified religious political parties are many. First, given the pragmatic nature of our present two parties, these institutions have every incentive to absorb prominent, religiously inspired ideas and followers in pursuit of the party's strategy to gain majority support. Second, the "us-versus-them" divisiveness of practical politics requires that a successful religious party will label all other parties "anti-religious." Getting away with this is difficult to imagine in our nation with its history of religious pluralism and vitality. Third, humility about human wisdom and efficacy are key tenets of most religious traditions, yet political parties almost by nature must state their views with great certainty. Many religious traditions, not to mention the secular public, are not likely to support a religious party that is certain about how government should be run. At the same time, a hesitant political party is unlikely to draw much public support. And if a religious party begins with principled opposition to historic elements of the American system, it will be less effective and attractive within that system, and would certainly look revolutionary and threatening.

Denominational fragmentation, which would very likely be duplicated in politics, is a fourth reason not to form a Christian political party. In all likelihood there would not be one religious, or even Christian, party but many, at least one each from the "left" and "right" of political discussion, and more likely several. Fifth, initial success would be difficult. Victorious religious candidates supported by either a religious right or left almost never come from the movements themselves—but rather from the two main parties, suggesting that explicitly religious backgrounds have limited public appeal. Sixth, the American electoral system of single-member districts and winner-take-all elections makes all third-party efforts extremely difficult to sustain. And, finally, the track record of religiously grounded political parties in the United States is very poor. Such parties have almost always been short-lived. Those that lasted more than a few election cycles have never been effective. Many have also been ideologically narrow and socially paranoid, dooming any chance to gain power and to influence policy, the key functions of parties.

The most effective strategy for the preservation and enrichment of both religion and political parties may be to promote a number of Christian, or more broadly religious, "caucuses." With at least one such group within each of the major parties, working within the parties but also engaging in dialogue with each other, a fuller debate about the wisdom of intermingling religion and partisanship, and strategies over how to do so, could be more fully explored.

In theory, religion and partisanship can have a wide range of positive and negative influences on each other. Certainly there are some *potentially positive* influences of partisan involvement on religion. It can increase the relevance of a faith tradition to real issues and concerns and create at least the potential for improving society. It can also engage a religion with the wider culture and its practical problems and possible solutions, providing worldly maturity that can be employed to strengthen the particular faith tradition.

There are also some potentially positive influences on parties and the party system from religious involvement in partisan politics. Such activity can help a party recover or revise its foundational principles, countering the inevitable tendency to dilute or forget those principles. Involvement can also help parties gain new members by raising new issues that mobilize citizens. Religious involvement can help the entire party system by spurring a rejuvenating realignment, accomplished by raising new issues or looking at issues in new way so that real social problems get addressed by politics. Finally, religious influence in party politics can *potentially* increase the civility of both intra- and interparty struggle by reminding all participants to see opponents as equals in the image of God and equally limited by the realities of the human condition.

On the opposite side, there are a number of *potentially negative* influences on religion from its involvement in party politics. Such involvement can provide new causes for division among adherents of a faith or of different faiths. Conflicts over agendas, tactics, and strategy increase the division among groups claiming special knowledge of ultimate things, harming all "witness" to the nonreligious community. Also, political involvement can make religious persons and groups too interested in worldly tactics and less interested in proclaiming basic eternal truths. Finally, political involvement can lend credence to the view that ultimate salvation comes through mere human and secular action, a heresy not uncommon in most religious traditions.

Last, there are at least two potentially negative consequences on parties from religious involvement in their midst. First, such involvement can take parties away from the primary goals of winning elections and governing, which involve the practical skills of pragmatism and compromise, into ideological debates that are hard to resolve and more likely to split the party into unelectable minorities. Second, close alignment with a particular religion may reduce a party's chance of winning elections in a pluralistic and increasingly secular nation, because in the current cultural milieu, persons tagged as religious tend also to get tagged as extremists.

Conclusion

This brief review of history and theory provides a way to evaluate the impact of religious interaction with American partisan politics. First, it seems clear that general "agenda setting" by the religious community has worked well. Groups organized against slavery, excessive drinking, economic injustice, racism, and abortion have been "winners" or potential "winners" in the sense of energizing a political party and generating policy change consonant with broader party principles. On the other hand, advocacy for or against a particular candidate, faith, or policy usually boomerangs to harm religion. Explicit advocacy of a particular candidate or issue poses the hazard of specifying God's will in a particular way, only to have events work out differently. The contradiction tarnishes the reputation of the advocates, frequently leading them and their followers to abandon either their faith or political engagement, or both.

Second, key issues or perspectives first nurtured in religious communities have affected the party system, always influencing and, arguably, often directing party realignments. Abolition, and to some extent anti-Catholicism, made Republicans the majority from the 1860s through the 1920s. In turn, the Social Gospel provided the philosophical basis for the New Deal and Democratic supremacy from the 1930s through the 1960s. And, finally, concern about overly permissive social policy from the late 1970s to the present has helped restore the Republican Party to national parity and southern dominance.

Third, religious preference and depth of religious commitment explain a great deal of partisan attachment and partisan voting throughout most of American history, suggesting that the role of religion in political partisanship and in changes to the party system is important.

Fourth, the failure to recognize the complex relationship between public and personal morality has proved a persistent difficulty in American religious engagement with politics. Often leaders have forgotten that the redeemed can still act sinfully and that even some obvious sinners can advance the public good. Too often the assertion has been made that deep religious commitment *by itself* makes one a superior policy analyst, election strategist, campaign organizer, or party candidate. But effective political analysis requires the ability to examine both public positions and personal beliefs. Unfortunately, such comprehensive analysis has often been missing.

Fifth, the argument that America's church-state separation requires the secularization of partisan activities has often been made but rarely followed. Employed sometimes by religious opponents to keep churches with threatening social agendas from engaging the parties, it has more often been resisted by political-party establishments threatened by the possibility of losing power within their own party. And although the secularized interpretation has dominated jurisprudence and most official histories of the American party system, in actual practice religion and American politics have always been mixed.

It seems certain that persons of deep religious faith will continue to influence elections and government. In the increasingly diverse American religious community, however, a separate Christian or religious political party would fail to accomplish most of the goals that viable political parties seek. A broader "religious" party would require such a watered-down religious commitment and broad set of policy objectives that it would have a difficult time distinguishing itself from today's major parties.

The most effective strategy might be to establish Christian or religious caucuses within every major political party. Much as members of the Christian Coalition often operate as part of the GOP coalition, so a liberal "religious coalition" could profitably work within the Democratic Party. Other religious groups organized for political action could be independent of the major parties, weighing in on specific races or during specific election years. A multiplicity of religious voices, working within existing parties, probably holds the best chance of successfully bringing religious views to bear on the operations and ends of politics and government, without harming either religion or political parties.

References

Conkle, Daniel O. 1993. "Different Religions, Different Politics: Evaluating the Role of Competing Religious Traditions in American Politics and Law." *Journal of Law and Religion* 10, no. 1:1–33.

Dreisbach, Daniel. 1996. "Religious Traditionalists and Church-State Controversy in the Age of Andrew Jackson." Paper presented at the annual meeting of the American Political Science Association, San Francisco, Calif., 29 August–1 September.

Dunn, Charles. 1984. *American Political Theology*. New York: Praeger.

Fowler, Robert Booth. 1985. *Religion and Politics in America*. Metuchen, N.J.: Scarecrow Press.

Fowler, Robert Booth, and Allen D. Hertzke. 1995. *Religion and Politics in America*: *Faith, Culture, and Strategic Choices*. Boulder, Colo.: Westview Press.

Hertzke, Allen D. 1988. *Representing God in Washington: The Role of Religious Lobbies in the American Polity*. Knoxville: University of Tennessee Press.

Howe, Daniel. 1979. *The Political Culture of American Whigs*. Chicago: University of Chicago Press.

Hunter, James Davison. 1991. *Culture Wars: The Struggle to Define America*. New York: Basic Books.

Jensen, Richard. 1971. *The Winning of the Midwest*: *Social and Political Conflict, 1888–1896*. Chicago: University of Chicago Press.

Kleppner, Paul. 1970. *The Cross of Culture*: *A Social Analysis of Midwestern Politics, 1850–1900*. New York: Free Press.

———. 1979. *The Third Electoral System, 1853–1892: Parties, Voters, and Political Culture*. Chapel Hill: University of North Carolina Press.

———. 1982. *Who Voted? The Dynamics of Electoral Turnout, 1840–1940*. New York: Praeger.

Marty, Martin. 1970. *Righteous Empire: The Protestant Experience in America*. New York: Dial Press.

Napolitano, Gary. 1994. "A Christian Political Party for America?" Masters thesis, Regent University, Virginia Beach, Va.

Noll, Mark. 1988. *One Nation under God? Christian Faith and Political Action in America*. San Francisco: Harper & Row.

———. 1992. *A History of Christianity in the United States and Canada*. Grand Rapids: Eerdmans.

Reichley, A. James. 1985. *Religion in American Public Life*. Washington, D.C.: Brookings Institution.

Wald, Kenneth. 1997. *Religion and Politics in the United States*. 3d ed. Washington, D.C.: Congressional Quarterly Press.

Teaching Tools

Discussion Questions

1. Is the compromise and power-brokering characteristic of political parties that different from other aspects of life, such as education or church involvement? What makes the idea of partisanship so offensive, and is it really so objectionable?

2. Are religious groups and movements still a promising source of ideas and supporters for the two major political parties, or has American society become too "secular" for open religious commitment to mix with politics?

3. Is it better for Christians to join one of the major political parties and to work within current structures, or is it a better strategy to

develop a separate Christian, Judeo-Christian, or even a more broadly religious political party?

4. The Prohibition movement was able to enact anti-drinking laws in the late 1800s and early 1900s, but these laws failed to sufficiently modify drinking behavior and were mostly repealed. Can the Prohibition movement really be termed a success? Are there other moral issues or movements that might achieve legislative success but not change citizen behavior?

Student Exercise: Party Platforms

Search the Internet for websites on the major and minor political parties in the United States and in other countries. One place to start your search is the site called Political Parties and Youth Organizations in the United States of America (http://home.luna.nl/~benne/pp/nam/us/index.htm). Read the platforms or statements of principle for some of these parties. Does any party match what you think a Christian political party should stand for? If so, which one and why? If not, is there any party that seems close to your views?

Faculty Exercise: A Platform for a "Christian" Political Party

After students have reviewed the platforms or principles of existing parties, divide the class into several groups. Try to get each group to agree to a limited number of principles for its own Christian political party, as each group might define it. Compare the results of each group, hopefully generating a discussion over the plausibility of Christian political parties.

Research Topics

Research the impact of religion on partisan politics in the immediate postindependence era, such as the 1800 election between Jefferson and Adams, and in the emergence of mass-based political parties in the 1820s.

8

Religion in American Elections and Campaigns

PETER WIELHOUWER WITH THOMAS YOUNG

American political life has always been influenced by American religious life, and religion continues to be at the center of many aspects of American politics (e.g., Ahlstrom 1972; Noll 1990; Reichley 1985). From the settlement of our nation onward, religion has shaped the goals and aspirations of our citizens—ranging from John Winthrop's 1630 admonition to a Puritan congregation to be "as a city on a hill," to Martin Luther King Jr.'s hope that his children would live in a nation where they would be judged simply by the content of their character.

Given that elections reflect decisions about what should be the direction and goals of a nation's political life, it is not surprising that religion has also affected the direction and outcome of American elections and

The data used for this paper were obtained from the American National Election Studies Cumulative Data CD (Sapiro et al. 1998) and were made available through the Inter-University Consortium for Political and Social Research at the University of Michigan. We would like to thank Stephen King for his comments on an earlier draft of this chapter. Sole responsibility for the conclusions drawn from these data lie with the authors.

campaigns. This chapter addresses the role religion plays in American elections. The first part of the chapter discusses how religion serves to structure political attitudes and behavior generally; the second part compares and contrasts the political attitudes and behavior of different religious groups with regard to attitudes and behavior relevant to political campaigns. The third part examines how the religious faith of some presidential candidates may have affected campaigns and the American political system. The chapter concludes with a discussion of the emergence and development of the so-called Christian Right as a social and political movement.

How Religion Structures Political Attitudes and Behavior

There are two basic ways to think about how religion might affect the political behavior of individuals and groups. First, it is common to think of religion as a subset of individual attitudes, or a system of *internal* cognitive beliefs or affections. A second approach to analyzing the intersection between religion and political behavior emphasizes the *external* social context within which such attitudes and behavior are shaped.

Wald and Smidt (1993, 32) suggest that there are two principal approaches to studying internal religion in social science, the first of which conceives of "religion as a mental phenomenon—*believing*," based on a "*personal-subjective*" approach to religion. This school of thought is similar to a more general cognitive-psychological approach to studying opinion and behavior. This approach emphasizes the internal, psychological role of beliefs and the effect that a particular attitude or set of attitudes may have on the adoption of other beliefs or on a person's behavior. One might ask, for example, how attitudes toward the nature of biblical authority might shape attitudes such as trust in political figures, government institutions, or other people more generally. Likewise, one might examine how the beliefs regarding a statement such as "all major religions of the world are equally good and true" is related to willingness to tolerate different kinds of social behavior, or how the belief that "the values of Christians are under attack in America today" shapes the likelihood that those who hold such beliefs turn out to vote on election day. But regardless of the attitude examined, this more "psychological" approach to the relationship between religion and politics sees religion more as an internal motivator and views the individual in isolation from the social context within which that individual is located.

162

A second approach to studying religious beliefs conceives of "religion as a social phenomenon—*belonging* . . . [based on] a *social-collective* perspective that stresses the community basis of religious identity and expression" (Wald and Smidt 1993, 32). This approach follows the social-scientific approach to studying politics from a group perspective, based on the observation that individuals within different social groups generally share certain common perspectives or attitudes. For example, members of the African American community in the United States share a specific set of collective experiences, rooted in the social, political, and economic oppression associated with slavery and white supremacy, that shapes their social and political perspectives. Likewise, members of the Jewish community share a common history and set of experiences that influences the political and social orientations of its members. From this perspective, religious beliefs and attitudes are viewed more as reflections of sociological, rather than psychological, processes.

Suppose one is constructing a questionnaire to ask individuals about their religion. An initial question might approach the nature of the respondent's religious faith in general fashion. One might ask: "Do you consider yourself to be part of some religious faith—Christianity, Judaism, Islam, or some other religious faith—or are you an agnostic or an atheist?" Some individuals might choose to call themselves Christian (a mental reflection of a religious faith) even though they do not belong to or attend a church (the more sociological reflection of a religious faith)—such people are more "cultural Christians" than "religious Christians." But if religion has a political impact, is it the mental facet of religion (identification as a Christian) or the sociological facet of religion (association with others who hold similar beliefs) which is likely to explain how religion shapes political attitudes and behavior?

More specifically, among those who consider themselves to be Christians, one could ask: "Do you identify yourself as a member of any particular religious denomination, and if so, which one?" Or, one might ask: "Are you affiliated with or a member of any particular religious denomination, and if so, which one?" While these two questions are closely related in that many respondents might give the same answer to either question, they reflect different approaches to understanding a person's religion—the first taps a more psychological approach, the second a more sociological approach. For example, Joe Smith might have been reared as a member of a small denomination located only in particular areas of the country (e.g., as a member of the Nazarene church). But, because Joe has moved to another region of the country where such churches are not found, he has become a member of a different denomination (e.g., a member of a Mennonite congregation). Now if one were to ask Joe how he identifies religiously, he might state that he identifies as a Nazarene, but if one were to ask Joe his religious affiliation, he would likely respond that he is a member of a Mennonite church.

The same kind of dilemma arises when we think about who should be labeled an evangelical. One approach would be to treat evangelicals simply as a categorical group composed only of those who profess particular religious beliefs (e.g., those who hold strong views on the nature of biblical authority, who hold that Jesus is the only way to salvation, and who believe that witnessing to one's faith is an important component of the Christian life). Thus, religion is treated as a mental phenomenon, reflecting the expression of certain beliefs. On the other hand, evangelicals might be treated more as a sociological group, composed of people who share a common heritage and who interact socially through different networks, including, but not limited to, worshiping and serving together in congregational life. If an evangelical is one who expresses particular religious beliefs, then many African Americans would be included. But if being an evangelical encompasses the sharing of a common heritage and the likelihood of exhibiting patterns of social interaction on a regular basis, then simply expressing particular religious beliefs is not sufficient to warrant classification as an evangelical. According to this latter approach, that some Roman Catholics may express particular evangelical beliefs does not warrant their being classified as evangelicals, because they have been part of a different religious heritage and tend to interact within other social and religious groups.

If we analyze the impact of religion more from a sociological, rather than a cognitive, approach, then we must consider how social roles, friendship patterns, or church activities shape the ways in which religion is interpreted and applied within the political arena. Churches, for example, provide one such external social context. Churches can be thought of as communities within which people who generally agree on certain theological principles can interact (or fellowship) with one another (Wald, Owen, and Hill 1988; see also Huckfeldt, Plutzer, and Sprague 1993). Churches can serve as an agent of socialization, not only by "conveying the institutionalized roles and attitudes of the particular faith," but by teaching the values and behaviors that they wish to see instilled within their members (Chalfant, Beckley, and Palmer 1994, 68).

For example, some religious groups, such as Jehovah's Witnesses, eschew any political activity, including voting. Other churches—for example, churches within the African American community, and other church-related organizations, such as the Sojourners or the Christian Coalition—strongly encourage political activism on the part of members and sympathizers. Thus, in the context of particular congregations, there is wide variation in *the extent to which* political messages are conveyed to church members.

There is also wide variation in *how* such political messages are conveyed to church members. In some church congregations, one might hear explicit references to the political teachings of their faith. Members of Mennonite congregations, as well as those within other churches that are historically pacifist in nature, might hear sermons specifically stating that the church is committed to nonviolence, separation of church and state, and service to others. But political messages may be transmitted differently in other churches, "through posters and wall hangings, the choice of hymns, . . . bumper stickers affixed to the minister's car, announcements during worship services and articles in the church bulletin" (Wald 1997, 28).

The source of political messages may also be important sociologically. Ministers, because of their formal positions of leadership, have a great opportunity to influence the political ideas of their congregations. Research has shown that contemporary pastors take part in a wide variety of political activities and that they vary widely in their perceived political roles and in their willingness to deliver explicitly political cues to their congregants (Guth et al. 1997). African American congregations, on the other hand, are frequently pastored by politically active ministers who provide political cues to their church members. Such ministers "may issue pastoral endorsements, help to organize church members as volunteer workers in political campaigns, organize voter registration drives, or serve on ministerial committees for campaign organizations" (Calhoun-Brown 1996, 942).

The reception of political messages may vary among congregants. Political messages delivered by clergy are most likely to be perceived by members already interested in politics (Welch et al. 1993). Evangelical Protestants are most likely to have their opinions influenced by messages from the pulpit, a likely function of the evangelical pastor's role as the perceived authority on matters of scriptural interpretation.[1]

Churches also provide a setting in which members may make political information and material available to other members. Organizations associated with the Christian Right expended substantial resources on behalf of socially conservative candidates and political agendas in both 1994 and 1996, seemingly to great effect (Rozell and Wilcox 1995 and 1997). After the 1996 election, for example, many church members recalled having been contacted by fellow church members, having had voting guides available in their church, or having had church discussions related to political issues during the campaign. People contacted through these commonly used tactics of the Christian Right were more likely both to turn out to vote and to vote Republican (Guth et al. 1998).

But politically active congregations are not limited to the Christian Right. Within politically active black churches, the "environment is such that elec-

165

toral participation is the communicated norm and political activity is facilitated by the institution itself" (Calhoun-Brown 1996, 943). Members within such "political" black churches are significantly more likely than those unaffiliated with political churches to vote in primaries and in the general election (Calhoun-Brown 1996; Tate 1991; Wielhouwer 2000).

Thus religion can influence political attitudes and behavior in a variety of ways. One approach emphasizes the manner in which individuals process political information in light of their religious beliefs. A second approach emphasizes the group nature of American politics and culture, and suggests that individuals' behavior can be meaningfully understood by examining the common groups to which they belong, including religious groupings. Social and religious institutions function as microcommunities, in which social expectations about one's attitudes and behaviors are disseminated to both children and adults. Cues on political matters can come from pastors, friends within one's church, or through informational media provided by others attending the church.

Differences in Engagement in Politics

The most straightforward approach to using religion as a framework for studying Americans' political behavior and attitudes is to compare different religious groups. We will examine the political orientations and behaviors of several major religious groups: African American Protestants, white Mainline Protestants, white Evangelical Protestants, Roman Catholics, Jews, and Americans who identify with no particular religious group, or who consider themselves atheists or agnostics.[2] Given our previous discussion, it should be noted that this classification scheme reflects more of a social, rather than a mental or belief-centered, approach to classifying people religiously, because it is based on denominational affiliation and not the expression of particular theological beliefs, and because it separates Black Protestants from other Protestants. In addition, the analysis will, at times, separate southern Protestants from nonsouthern Protestants in order to account for some of the most important changes in American politics, changes that have largely been centered in the South (e.g., Black and Black 1987; Scher 1997).

One important gauge of a religious group's political orientation is the degree to which its members are psychologically engaged in politics. Do members of a particular religious tradition pay attention to political campaigns? Are they concerned who wins the election? Do they vote in elections, and do they participate in politics beyond the mere act of voting? The data presented in tables 8.1 and 8.2 address these kinds of questions.

Table 8.1 Political Engagement of Religious-Group Members, 1960–1996

A. Percentage of Group Respondents Who Care a Great Deal Which Party Wins the Presidency

Year	Black Protestants	Mainline Protestants[a]	Evangelical Protestants[a]	Roman Catholics	Jews	Other/ None
1960	37.5	70.7	64.7	69.8	70.5	51.4
1964	78.4	64.6	58.8	67.0	71.1	62.0
1968	76.0	66.2	65.4	62.5	64.1	47.3
1972	66.7	62.4	57.6	57.5	61.7	59.4
1976	68.8	57.2	56.6	54.2	67.2	46.3
1980	73.1	57.7	51.7	52.2	58.8	51.6
1984	69.2	66.2	65.6	61.7	71.7	62.6
1988	64.6	62.7	61.8	59.5	58.1	54.0
1992	71.1	77.9	76.7	75.9	95.7	67.1
1996	83.3	79.0	78.1	77.0	92.6	71.7

B. Percentage of Group Respondents Who Are Very Much Interested in the Presidential Election

Year	Black Protestants	Mainline Protestants[a]	Evangelical Protestants[a]	Roman Catholics	Jews	Other/ None
1960	25.9	43.5	35.0	36.6	40.3	28.9
1964	49.3	38.9	31.6	37.8	46.7	39.4
1968	32.6	40.4	41.8	35.2	47.5	39.0
1972	35.6	32.1	27.8	31.6	39.3	33.3
1976	41.4	37.2	36.7	35.6	44.9	27.5
1980	31.9	29.7	30.0	26.3	43.1	28.9
1984	33.2	28.8	25.4	26.6	34.0	33.3
1988	26.5	27.6	27.9	28.9	32.3	26.0
1992	34.7	41.1	38.2	40.9	65.2	33.2
1996	31.7	25.1	25.2	23.7	51.9	16.7

Source: 1948–1997 American National Election Study CD-ROM (Sapiro et al. 1998).

[a]Mainline and Evangelical Protestants include white respondents only.

The top half of table 8.1 presents the percentage of respondents within each religious group that stated that they "cared a great deal" which party won the presidential election in that year. Two main kinds of comparisons can be made from this kind of table. First, we can compare the extent to which different religious groups cared about the outcome of the election for a particular year. In 1996, for example, a higher percentage of Jews (92.6 percent) than Roman Catholics (77.0 percent) cared about the outcome of the election, while those who had no religious affiliations expressed the lowest level of caring (with 71.7 percent indicating that they cared). Second, we can compare the same group across years to see how that group may have changed over time. When one compares Black Protestants in the 1960 election with Black Protestants in the 1964 election one observes a very large increase in the percentage who cared about the outcome. This massive shift was likely a result of the Republican presidential candidacy of Barry Goldwater and his extreme version of conservatism (particularly as reflected in his opposition to the historic Civil Rights Act of 1964).

The top portion of table 8.1 reveals that majorities (frequently quite large majorities) within each group in virtually all election years express that they care a great deal about the election outcome. There is, however, substantial variation across years. The elections of 1976 and 1980 exhibited generally low levels of concern, while the 1992 and 1996 elections revealed the highest levels of concern. Even as concern over election outcomes has waxed and waned, the level of concern exhibited in 1996 by all religious groups is consistently greater than the level evident among these same groups in 1960, a year in which there was considerable controversy over the fact that John F. Kennedy, a Catholic, was running for the presidency. Generally speaking, the percentage of Black Protestants who express concern has exceeded the percentage associated with the other religious groups; white Evangelical Protestants were among the least-concerned groups through 1980, but after that year they have maintained levels of concern comparable to the other religious groups. People with no religious affiliation generally express the lowest levels of concern about election outcomes.

The bottom portion of table 8.1 presents the percentage of each group that reports being "very much interested" in the presidential election campaign in that year. In contrast to concern over election outcomes, relatively few people express very high levels of interest in election campaigns. However, while interest in political campaigns is low, it is not declining. Overall, the portion of those who express high levels of campaign interest is about one-third of the electorate, and it is rare for more than 40 percent of any group to express high levels of campaign interest. Jews usually exhibit the highest level of interest in the campaign, while Roman Catholics tend to be the least interested. Overall, table 8.1 presents us with a paradox. While most Americans, regardless of their religious affiliation, indicate that they care a great deal about which candidate wins a presidential election, they generally indicate that they are not very interested in the campaign while it is happening.

Another way to examine the engagement of citizens in politics is to look at the extent to which they actually participate in the political process.

168

There are many ways in which citizens can participate in politics. They may write to their member of Congress, attend city council meetings, or take part in protest marches. In table 8.2 we examine two important kinds of participation in the electoral process, voting and campaign activism.

Table 8.2 Political Participation of Religious-Group Members, 1960–1996

A. Percentage of Group Respondents Who Report Voting in the Presidential Election

Year	Black Protestants	Mainline Protestants[a]	Evangelical Protestants[a]	Roman Catholics	Jews	Other/ None
1960	51.7	85.2	70.6	87.0	85.5	52.6
1964	65.5	83.7	66.2	84.0	94.7	63.1
1968	67.7	82.0	66.6	79.5	97.1	50.0
1972	65.8	77.1	61.1	79.2	90.5	70.1
1976	64.6	77.1	67.1	73.5	81.8	57.0
1980	67.9	76.5	65.0	72.6	87.8	60.8
1984	66.7	77.5	65.1	79.2	86.4	68.2
1988	62.2	77.9	59.4	75.1	82.1	62.0
1992	66.3	81.2	72.1	81.0	97.4	66.8
1996	64.5	79.1	71.1	76.2	92.0	58.5

B. Average Number of Campaign Activities (out of Five) Taken Part in by Group Respondents[b]

Year	Black Protestants	Mainline Protestants[a]	Evangelical Protestants[a]	Roman Catholics	Jews	Other/ None
1960	0.54	0.93	0.73	0.73	0.44	0.58
1964	0.65	0.79	0.62	0.77	0.58	0.58
1968	0.73	0.75	0.66	0.70	1.06	0.54
1972	0.68	0.79	0.45	0.66	1.37	0.90
1976	0.54	0.78	0.56	0.73	1.29	0.69
1980	0.43	0.67	0.58	0.62	0.66	0.61
1984	0.53	0.62	0.51	0.63	1.26	0.67
1988	0.56	0.58	0.45	0.64	0.64	0.56
1992	0.50	0.74	0.72	0.64	1.33	0.60
1996	0.40	0.63	0.57	0.47	0.62	0.42

Source: 1948–1997 American National Election Study CD-ROM (Sapiro et al. 1998).

[a]Mainline and Evangelical Protestants include white respondents only.

[b]The five possible political activities are displaying campaign materials, attending political rallies or meetings, working for a political party, attempting to influence someone else's vote, and contributing money to a candidate.

Voting is the easiest, and therefore the most common, form of political behavior. The top portion of table 8.2 presents the reported turnout rates of respondents in each of our groups.[3] Comparing these groups, we can see that turnout among Jews exceeds that of all other groups in every year since 1964. Roman Catholics and Mainline Protestants have the next-highest turnout rate, and with few exceptions are similar to each other in the extent of their voting. On the other hand, Black Protestants and white Evangelical Protestants tend to exhibit the lowest turnout rates over time, though evangelicals increased their level of turnout during the 1990s. Finally, those with no religious connections have exhibited the lowest levels of voter turnout over time.

To get a broader picture of political participation, five different campaign activities (displaying campaign materials, attending political rallies or meetings, working for a political party, attempting to influence someone else's vote, and contributing money to political campaigns) were combined into an index ranging from 0 (representing no activities) to 5 (all five activities). The bottom portion of table 8.2 presents the average number of campaign activities in which members of each group took part in each election year. Historically, Black Protestants and Evangelical Protestants have been the least active in campaign activity, though their level of such activity has been fairly stable since 1972. Mainline Protestants have been the most active Christian tradition, though since 1976 their level of campaign involvement has not matched the level prior to that time (except for 1992). Jews have generally had the highest participation rate in presidential election years since 1968.

To summarize, then, we have seen considerable variation in the extent to which different religious traditions express psychological engagement and exhibit participation in campaigns. Generally speaking, Jews tend to be more engaged and active, while Black Protestants, Evangelical Protestants, and people with no religious affiliation tend to be the least active. There likely are different reasons for the lack of activism among these groups. Evangelical thought tends to focus less on temporal concerns and more on personal relationships with God, and, since the 1920s, with the fundamentalist-modernist divide, evangelicals have generally avoided extensive political involvement. The emergence of the Christian Right as a political force has likely affected only a portion of evangelicals (primarily a portion of church-attending evangelicals), and so its effects are muted here. Those with no religious affiliation may have lower participation rates due to the fact that they are less likely to be engaged in social institutions, especially the church, wherein many civic and political skills are developed (Verba, Schlozman, and Brady 1995, chap. 9). And, finally, African Americans historically have had lower levels of political participation than whites, due to legal and socioeconomic barriers, as well as a perceived paucity of real political options in the current party system (see, e.g., Walters 1988).

Religious Groups and Partisanship

Observers of politics (not to mention politicians and their campaign managers) are frequently interested in the orientations of the electorate regarding politicians and political institutions. Changes in the president's popularity affect the policies he can pursue, as well as his relations with Congress. And substantial attention has been paid to the declining attachment (or "dealignment") of Americans to the two major political parties (Wattenberg 1996). Two aspects of the intersection of religion and party politics are of interest. First, to what extent do members of these different religious groups vary in their party identifications? And, second, what changes, if any, have occurred in these party identifications? The first question is important because it speaks to the ability of parties and candidates to count on their "base" vote in the electorate—that is, who can largely be counted on to cast their votes based on party. The second question is important because politics is dynamic, and a critical aspect of that dynamism involves changes in the issue and partisan alignments among voters. When changes occur in those alignments, important political and policy changes may follow (Sundquist 1983).

Party Identification

Table 8.3 presents the level of identification with the two major political parties, along with the percentage of political independents, within our six religious categories over the last forty years.[4] The figures presented in the table represent the average percentage in each group who identified as a Democrat, independent, or Republican in each decade. So, for example, during the 1960s, the average percentage of Roman Catholics identifying with the Democratic Party was 57.3 percent, the figure derived when one averages the percentage of Catholics who identify as Democrats in each of the three presidential elections of that decade. The figures in the line "'60s–'90s Change" represent the change in those averages between the 1960s and 1990s—for example, the percentage of Democratic Party identifiers among Catholics decreased by 15.6 percent, from 57.3 percent to 41.7 percent. The figures in the line "% Change" indicate how much of a change the "'60s–'90s Change" is for each group. Thus, the 15.6 percent decrease in Democratic identification among Catholics represents a 27.2 percent decrease from the

Table 8.3 Party Identification of Religious-Group Members,

	Black Protestants	Mainline Protestants[a]		Evangelical Protestants[a]	
		Non-South	South	Non-South	South
Democratic					
1960s	68.0	32.3	52.1	40.4	64.4
1970s	69.0	25.4	42.9	33.2	45.1
1980s	68.0	27.0	33.4	26.1	44.5
1990s	65.8	26.0	26.8	26.7	33.2
'60s–'90s Change[b]	-2.2	-6.3	-25.3	-13.7	-31.2
(% Change)[c]	-3.2	-19.5	-48.6	-33.9	-48.4
Independent					
1960s	15.3	23.5	26.1	25.4	22.6
1970s	23.1	35.4	29.5	37.7	35.1
1980s	24.6	32.1	33.3	36.5	34.7
1990s	29.0	33.9	37.7	32.4	37.0
'60s–'90s Change	+13.7	+10.2	+11.6	+7.0	+14.4
(% Change)	+89.5	+43.4	+44.4	+27.6	+63.7
Republican					
1960s	8.7	43.7	21.5	30.6	10.9
1970s	7.0	38.5	26.4	27.5	18.8
1980s	5.2	39.5	33.0	35.3	18.4
1990s	4.2	39.6	35.1	39.1	28.8
'60s–'90s Change	-4.5	-4.1	+13.6	+8.5	+17.9
(% Change)	-51.7	-9.4	+63.3	+27.8	+164.2

57.3 percent level of the 1960s. For purposes of our discussion, we consider any changes of 5 percent or less between the 1960s and the 1990s to be insignificant and attributable to sampling error.

Looking first at changes in identification with the Democratic Party, we see that neither Black Protestants nor those without religious affiliation exhibited any real change in their level of identification with the Democratic Party. There was a small decrease among nonsouthern Mainline Protestants, while there were substantial losses among southern Mainline Protestants, evangelicals, and Roman Catholics. Only among Jews did the level of identification with the Democratic Party

1960s–1990s (by percentage)

Roman Catholics	Jews	Other/None
57.3	51.3	38.9
49.8	53.4	29.6
40.9	56.4	28.7
41.7	62.6	33.6
-15.6	+11.3	-5.3
-27.2	+22.0	-13.6
26.2	42.4	37.4
34.6	37.2	55.3
36.3	35.5	47.5
35.9	29.7	46.3
+9.7	-12.7	+8.9
+37.0	-29.9	+23.8
15.9	6.3	23.2
14.6	8.6	11.4
21.6	8.2	19.6
21.0	7.7	18.4
+5.1	+1.4	-4.8
+32.1	+22.2	-20.7

Source: 1948–1997 American National Election Study CD-ROM (Sapiro et al. 1998).

[a]Mainline and Evangelical Protestants include white respondents only. Table entries are decade means and include presidential election years only.

[b]" '60s–'90s Change" represents the absolute change in identification for a group between the 1960s and 1990s (e.g., Roman Catholic identification with the Democrats changed from 57.3 percent to 41.7 percent, a decrease of 15.6 percentage points).

[c]"% Change" represents the relative change in identification for a group between the 1960s and 1990s (e.g., Roman Catholic identification with the Democrats changed from 57.3 to 41.7; that 15.6-point decrease [see note b] represents a 27.2 percent decrease).

increase over this period. On the whole, then, there is a clear movement away from the Democratic Party during this period, particularly among evangelicals, and especially among people in the South. These declines in identification with the Democratic Party have been largely matched by increases in the percentage of independents within these religious groups. Looking at the middle section of the table, we can see that, with the exception of Jews, there is a substantial increase in the percentage of independents within each of these religious groups over this period.

Significant changes in Republican identification occur in three of the religious traditions analyzed. Southern Mainline Protestants in the 1990s, unlike their nonsouthern counterparts, increased their identification with the Republican Party by 63 percent over 1960s levels. Among Evangelical Protestants outside the South, identification with the GOP increased by more than 27 percent, while within the South, identification with the GOP among Evangelical Protestants increased a whopping 164 percent. These changes are a function of the attractiveness of the Republican Party's social conservatism to southerners and evangelicals (along with the liberalism of Democratic candidates), real efforts by GOP candidates to court the southern vote, and the increasing activism of the Religious Right during the 1980s and early 1990s, when the most important changes take place.

Since southern Evangelical Protestants have exhibited considerable change in their partisan identifications over time, it may be interesting to look at this group in a little more detail. Figure 8.1 shows the changing nature of the group's party identification for each presidential election year between 1960 and 1996 (rather than simply being averaged across decades). In 1960 about 70 percent labeled themselves Democrats, but by 1996 only about 40 percent did. What were the causes and timing of these changes? Identification with the Republican Party has been steadily increasing among southern Evangelical Protestants, with the exception of 1980, while self-classification as an independent increased only in 1968. Between 1964 and 1968, the percentage of southern Evangelical Protestants who labeled themselves independents increased from about 15 percent to about 35 percent, and that level has since remained constant. One significant factor affecting the deterioration of Democratic strength in the South was the 1968 American Independent Party candidacy of George Wallace, who gained a substantial share of the vote—and a large number of electoral college votes—from southern states. Another source of change was the aligning of the Democratic Party with liberal and African American interests during the early 1960s, which alienated conservative whites from the party. In sum, a large chunk of southern Evangelical Protestants left the Democratic Party in the mid-1960s and never returned.

Today, Black Protestants and Jews are predominantly Democrats but also include large numbers of independents. Mainline Protestants and nonsouthern Evangelical Protestants are more evenly divided, but tend to be more Republican or independent in their partisan identifications. Southern Evangelical Protestants, despite their massive shift toward the Republican Party, are still slightly more Democratic than Republican in their partisan self-classifications. Roman Catholics continue to label themselves primarily as Democrats, but at significantly lower levels than forty years ago, while those who claim no religious affiliation are clearly the most likely to label themselves independents.

To summarize these changes in party identifications, there has been a substantial movement away from the Democratic Party between the

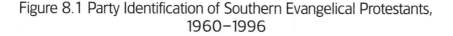

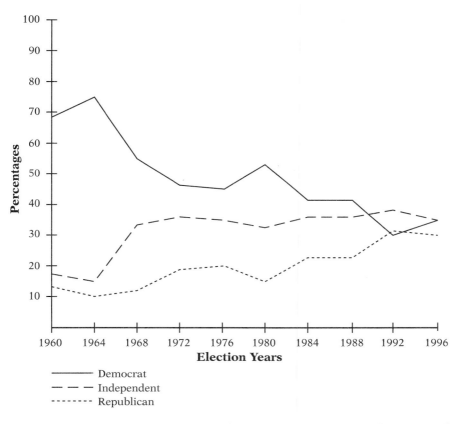

Figure 8.1 Party Identification of Southern Evangelical Protestants, 1960–1996

1960s and 1990s, coupled with a large increase in the willingness of members of all religious groups to label themselves as independents. Additionally, important increases in Republican identification occurred among southern white Protestants and among Evangelical Protestants. These changes reflect shifts in the U.S. electorate that have been documented elsewhere (e.g., Miller 1991; Nie, Verba, and Petrocik 1979; Stanley and Niemi 1999). But as important as these changes have been for American politics, elections are not won or lost solely on party loyalties. Not all voters cast their ballots on the basis of their partisan identifications. Nor do partisan identifications fully reveal which voters choose to cast their ballots in an election. Therefore, it is also important to examine the extent to which members of these religious groups report casting their votes for the candidates of the two parties.

Table 8.4 Presidential Vote Choices of Religious–Group Members,

		Mainline Protestants[a]		Evangelical Protestants[a]	
	Black Protestants	Non-South	South	Non-South	South
Democratic Vote Share					
1960s	88.8	37.1	39.7	39.0	47.1
1970s	89.7	32.6	28.6	32.5	34.2
1980s	91.8	30.7	36.5	27.9	33.6
1990s	94.6	42.0	35.2	33.1	37.5
'60s–'90s Change[b]	+5.8	+4.8	-4.4	-5.9	-9.6
(% Change)[c]	+6.6	+13.0	-11.1	-15.2	-20.4
Republican Vote Share					
1960s	11.2	60.6	54.9	56.5	39.0
1970s	10.3	67.4	71.4	67.5	65.8
1980s	7.8	66.6	61.4	67.6	66.0
1990s	3.4	42.7	54.9	53.7	50.4
'60s–'90s Change	-7.8	-17.9	0.0	-2.8	+11.4
(% Change)	-69.7	-29.5	0.0	-5.0	+29.2

Presidential Voting

Table 8.4 presents how the members of these different religious groups voted in the presidential elections since the 1960s. Not only have Black Protestants voted consistently for Democratic candidates, but their voting for Republican candidates has steadily declined. Historically, Mainline Protestants have voted largely Republican, though this decreased among nonsoutherners in the 1990s, in part because Mainline Protestants were among Ross Perot's biggest supporters. Mainline Protestants in the South voted increasingly Republican through the 1980s. Prior to the 1970s, Evangelical Protestants in the South tended to vote Democratic, while their nonsouthern counterparts tended to vote Republican. However, southern evangelicals have increased their support of GOP candidates over time. While Roman Catholics have consistently voted Democratic, their level of support for Democratic candidates has declined since John F. Kennedy's 1960 candidacy, so that today they tend to divide their votes more evenly. In contrast, Jews vote strongly Democratic, despite

176

1960s–1990s (by percentage)

Roman Catholics	Jews	Other/None
72.3	89.2	59.8
48.8	70.0	62.6
46.7	64.0	48.4
53.0	83.3	60.8
-19.3	-5.9	+1.0
-26.7	-6.6	+4.7
25.3	9.7	33.5
51.2	30.0	37.4
50.2	31.5	45.1
32.9	6.3	21.9
+7.6	-3.4	-11.6
+30.0	-35.1	-34.6

Source: 1948–1997 American National Election Study CD-ROM (Sapiro et al. 1998).

[a]Mainline and Evangelical Protestants include white respondents only. Table entries are decade means and include presidential election years only.

[b]"'60s–'90s Change" represents the absolute change in party vote share for a group between the 1960s and 1990s (see note in table 8.3).

[c]"% Change" represents the relative change in party vote share for a group between the 1960s and 1990s (see note in table 8.3).

casting significant portions of their votes for the GOP candidates of the 1970s and 1980s. People with no religious affiliation tend to vote Democrat, so that the substantial decline in Republican voting during the 1990s benefited the Perot candidacies of 1992 and 1996.

Congressional Voting

While partisanship and reasonably well-informed evaluations influence voting for president, the factors that affect voting for members of Congress are more varied, and include name recognition, incumbency, and campaign spending (e.g., Fiorina 1989; Herrnson 1995; Jacobson 1990, 1997). Table 8.5 reveals the average percentage of each religious group voting for the Republican House candidate in each decade. (The Democratic vote shares are not presented because they are virtually the opposite of GOP votes, unlike the presidential vote figures in which third-party candidates have diverted significant numbers of votes in certain years.) Once again, a 5 percent change will be used as a rough thresh-

Table 8.5 Congressional Vote Choices of Religious-Group Members,

		Mainline Protestants[a]		Evangelical Protestants[a]	
	Black Protestants	Non-South	South	Non-South	South
U.S. House Republican Vote Share					
1960s	10.6	61.4	37.4	56.1	20.0
1970s	4.9	47.7	29.5	36.9	24.4
1980s	8.0	45.3	30.8	46.4	31.0
1990s	11.4	51.4	58.2	56.7	57.6
'60s–'90s Change[b]	+0.9	-10.0	+20.8	+0.6	+37.7
(% Change)[c]	+8.3	-16.3	+55.7	+1.0	+188.7
U.S. Senate Republican Vote Share					
1970s	8.5	56.9	48.0	48.9	38.4
1990s	15.0	54.8	46.5	60.0	58.2
(% Change)	-16.5	-9.9	+37.0	+8.7	+93.0

old for ascertaining whether any significant changes have occurred in voting for members of Congress.

It is clear from table 8.5 that Black Protestants have exhibited considerable stability in their voting patterns, rarely voting for Republican candidates for Congress (though such support is higher than their support for GOP presidential candidates). Those with no religious affiliation have also tended to vote Democratic.

Evangelical Protestants outside the South have varied over time in their support for Republican congressional candidates, but in the 1990s they continue to vote in a Republican direction, as they had in the 1960s. Since at least the Civil War, Evangelical Protestants in the South had voted for Democratic congressional candidates, and they continued to do so through the 1980s. The voting patterns of Mainline Protestants also vary by region. However, differences between the two regional groups are narrowing, becoming more consistently Republican. Historically, Mainline Protestants in the South generally voted Democratic,

Corrected Table 8.5, page 178

	Black Protestants	Mainline Protestants[a]		Evangelical Protestants[a]	
		Non-South	South	Non-South	South
U.S. House Republican Vote Share					
1960s	10.6	61.4	37.4	56.1	20.0
1970s	4.9	47.7	29.5	36.9	24.4
1980s	8.0	45.3	30.8	46.4	31.0
1990s	11.4	51.4	58.2	56.7	57.6
'60s-'90s Change[b]	+0.9	-10.0	+20.8	+0.6	+37.7
(% Change)[c]	+8.3	-16.3	+55.7	+1.0	+188.7
U.S. Senate Republican Vote Share					
1960s	17.9	63.0	34.0	55.2	30.1
1970s	8.5	56.9	48.0	48.9	38.4
1980s	11.5	58.5	43.3	61.4	42.9
1990s	15.0	54.8	46.5	60.0	58.2
'60s-'90s Change	-2.9	-6.2	+12.6	+4.8	+28.0
(% Change)	-16.5	-9.9	+37.0	+8.7	+93.0

1960s–1990s (by percentage)

Roman Catholics	Jews	Other/None
29.4	19.4	35.8
27.6	13.8	28.2
27.9	21.9	28.3
43.3	25.4	36.7
+13.9	+5.9	+0.9
+47.4	+30.5	+2.4
32.6	36.1	46.1
37.9	34.4	41.2
43.0	21.6	41.9
43.6	24.0	40.9
+11.0	-12.1	-5.2
+33.9	-33.5	-11.2

Source: 1948–1997 American National Election Study CD-ROM (Sapiro et al. 1998).

[a]Mainline and Evangelical Protestants include white respondents only. Entries are decade means and include all election years.

[b]"'60s–'90s Change" represents the absolute change in Republican vote share for a group between the 1960s and 1990s (see note in table 8.3).

[c]"% Change" represents the relative change in Republican vote share for a group between the 1960s and 1990s (see note in table 8.3).

but, by the 1990s, they voted primarily for Republican candidates for the House (though their support for GOP candidates for the Senate was less). Mainline Protestants outside the South have tended to vote Republican, but this support has weakened somewhat over time. Thus, by the 1990s, southern and nonsouthern evangelicals have come to mirror each other in their congressional voting patterns, while some regional disparities remain between southern and nonsouthern Mainline Protestants.

On the other hand, Roman Catholics cast approximately 70 percent of their votes for Democratic candidates for the House and Senate in the 1960s, but Catholic support for Democratic House and Senate candidates had diminished to less than 60 percent by the 1990s. Such change clearly reflects the deterioration of the New Deal Democratic coalition in the post–civil rights era. Jews have also increased their support of Republican House candidates, but they have decreased their support of GOP senatorial hopefuls. This pattern may well reflect the more important foreign policy role played by Senate, particularly as it may relate to U.S. policy toward Israel.

What can we conclude about the candidate preferences of group members? Clearly Black Protestants and Jews are the most consistent partisans of any group, as it is common for 75 percent or more of their ranks to vote Democratic for federal offices. Historically, Mainline Protestants, at least those located outside the South, constituted the core of the Republican Party in their substantial support for GOP candidates. Since the 1980s, however, Evangelical Protestants have voted more Republican than Mainline Protestants, both within and outside the South. Southern evangelicals turned toward GOP presidential candidates in the 1970s and to GOP congressional candidates in the 1990s. Roman Catholics have varied their partisan support in presidential elections, trending toward Republican candidates, while they continue to vote Democratic in congressional races (though not at the levels evident only ten to twenty years ago). Finally, those who express no religious affiliation tend to vote Democratic.

On the whole, table 8.5 provides additional evidence that political orientations and voting behavior vary among members of different religious groups, and, in the case of Protestants, by region as well. While religious differences continue to be evident, however, regional differences have diminished over time. Of course, the way in which religion may affect campaigns and elections is not limited to the religious affiliations of members of the electorate. The religion of the candidate at the top of the ticket can also have an impact on the dynamics of the election campaign.

The Impact of Candidates' Religion

This section briefly examines three cases in which a candidate's religion played an important role in elections during the last half of the twentieth century. The 1960 campaign, when John F. Kennedy's Catholicism was an important issue, will be addressed first, followed by the 1984 and 1988 campaigns of Jesse Jackson and Pat Robertson.

John F. Kennedy (1960)

Al(fred) E. Smith, the Democratic presidential nominee in 1928, was the first Roman Catholic candidate for president in American history. His candidacy ignited wild and fantastic attacks. His critics charged, among other things, that if Smith were elected he would make Catholicism the national religion, that Vatican forces would tunnel under the Atlantic

180

Ocean and set up a new Vatican City in the Mississippi Valley, and that a new dollar bill would be inscribed with the rosary (Burner 1988, 47).

With the 1960 candidacy of John F. Kennedy, the prospects of having a Roman Catholic president again became an issue in the election campaign. Early in the 1960 nomination campaign, JFK won the West Virginia presidential primary; this was important because he ran well outside his native region, the Northeast, and because he won within a highly Protestant, largely fundamentalist, state. The victory helped clear the way for his nomination. Suddenly it became conceivable that a Catholic could be elected president. Kennedy worked to turn the issue of religious diversity to his advantage by raising the issue of bigotry— suggesting that a vote against him for any reason would lead to the label of bigot (Burner 1988, 52).

Kennedy also addressed the religion issue directly in a critical speech before a group of Protestant ministers in Houston. In the speech, he stated his belief in the separation of church and state and declared that his actions as president would not be influenced by anything other than his perception of the national interest. His speech seemed to defuse much of the anti-Catholicism that fueled many of his critics, but in so doing he also asserted the complete segregation of a president's religious views (including the direct teachings of his religion) from the actions that he would take "in the national interest."

> I believe in a President whose views on religion are his own private affair, neither imposed upon him by the nation or imposed by the nation upon him as a condition to holding that office. . . .

> I am not the Catholic candidate for President. I am the Democratic Party's candidate for President, who happens also to be a Catholic.

> I do not speak for my church on public matters—and the church does not speak for me. Whatever issue may come before me as President, if I should be elected—on birth control, divorce, censorship, gambling, or on any other subject—I will make my decision in accordance with . . . what my conscience tells me to be in the national interest, and without regard to outside religious pressure or dictate. (Quoted in White 1961, 392–93)

In the campaign, Kennedy mobilized Catholics firmly behind him. More than 80 percent of Catholic voters cast their ballots for JFK. But, as discussed in the previous section, Catholics have not since supported the Democratic Party to such an extent. It is not surprising that such a level has not been attained subsequently. Catholics, as an "out-group" in American politics, rallied to support one of their own to a much greater extent than they would have supported a candidate outside their faith.

Kennedy's candidacy was historically important for two reasons. First, he successfully challenged the anti-Catholic bigotry of much of the American electorate and almost completely undermined that bigotry as a basis for political attack. However, second, and perhaps more important, Kennedy's strategy for defusing the "Catholic" issue was to compartmentalize his religion, separating it from his public service. By promising that he would not allow his religion to impinge on his interpretation of the national interest, he helped set the stage for the contemporary political debates about the role of religion in public life—namely that the religious beliefs of public officials should be completely separated from their political beliefs and actions.

Jesse Jackson (1984 and 1988) and Pat Robertson (1988)

In the mid-1980s two grassroots religious figures arose to challenge mainstream candidates. Both candidates were well-known preachers with established social and political networks. Jesse Jackson, a black pastor, political activist, and associate of Martin Luther King Jr., competed for the 1984 and 1988 Democratic presidential nominations. His message emphasized a "moral economy," a "moral community," and social and economic justice (Hertzke 1993b, 66–79), and he would frequently speak in places of economic or social suffering. Political life in black communities radiates from the church, and Jesse Jackson made full use of this fact to aid his campaign. The preexisting network of black churches became Jackson's vote bloc, his means of fund-raising, and his means of mobilizing and spreading his message (Hertzke 1993b, xi). One of Jackson's first goals was to register black voters. He did this with remarkable success, and through his efforts the number of registered black voters mushroomed. African American turnout in primary and general elections peaked during the decade (Tate 1994).

Likewise, the 1988 campaign of Marion (Pat) Robertson, a white, Pentecostal, television evangelist, was aimed largely at mobilizing Christian conservatives. Robertson made use of his Christian Broadcasting Network and emphasized a socially conservative response to America's troubles. Specifically, Robertson focused on three main issues: the moral decline of America, the breakup of the family, and the secularization of public schools (Hertzke 1993b). By making a strong showing in a number of early state contests, Robertson was able to be a "player" in shaping the Republican Party platform in 1988. Moreover, following his failed candidacy to secure the nomination, Robertson and his team established the Christian Coalition to help organize and mobilize Christian Right voters. The Christian Coalition has played an important role in subsequent presidential and congressional elections.

The candidacies of Jesse Jackson and Pat Robertson would leave a lasting impact on American politics. Their campaigns successfully mobilized important voting blocs that would have to be courted in future elections—the black vote and the Christian Right vote. Their campaigns created coalitions to ensure the future political representation of each constituency in its respective party. Finally, their campaigns revolutionized the use of grassroots campaigning outside the architecture of the major party organizations (Hertzke 1993b, chap. 5). Thus, the lasting legacy of the 1984 and 1988 campaigns of Jackson and Robertson was an improved ability of populist candidates to use churches as venues for organizing people at the grassroots level, and for channeling them into various aspects of political activism and fund-raising (Hertzke 1993a).

Religious Activists and Political Campaigns

Religion in political campaigns is not limited to the way it may shape one's political attitudes and voting behavior. Nor is it limited to the impact that the religious faith of a candidate may have in the election process. Religion also can play a role by mobilizing activists to work on behalf of issues, candidates, and parties in the election.

In contemporary American politics, the Christian Right has helped shape the course of political campaigns. The term "Christian Right" (alternatively labeled the Religious Right, Christian conservatives, the new Christian Right, etc.) usually refers to a rather broad, though somewhat amorphous, segment of the electorate who are theologically conservative Christians and who are also characterized by social and political conservatism. Typically, issues such as sexual immorality, pornography, abortion, and education are central political concerns to these "orthodox" Christians (Guth et al. 1997).

Social movements by their very nature are rather amorphous, though facets of social movements are linked to particular organizations. In the Christian Right, the movement includes adherents and contributors to a variety of parachurch religious ministries, such as Focus on the Family, and a variety of politically active groups with socially and theologically conservative roots, such as the Christian Coalition, Concerned Women for America, the Family Research Council, Eagle Forum, and the American Center for Law and Justice (see, e.g., Guth et al. 1995). Less clearly associated with the group might be individuals whose beliefs coincide with many of the goals and ideals of the movement, but who do not consciously associate with it. The point is, the Christian Right is a heterogeneous group that lacks a single leader[5] and is subject to the high levels of factionalism that have historically characterized religiously conservative Protestantism (Fowler, Hertzke, and Olson 1999, 138–40).

The catalysts for the rise of the Christian Right into politics can be traced to three sets of events in the 1960s and 1970s (Fowler, Hertzke, and Olson 1999, 141–45; Wald 1997, 218–25). The first was a series of Supreme Court decisions interpreted as threatening to Christian beliefs and, more generally, as harmful to the society. These included the removal of the Ten Commandments, prayer, and Bible reading from public schools, and the establishment of the constitutionality of abortion. The second was the widespread dissatisfaction with the presidency of born-again evangelical Jimmy Carter, who was more liberal in his policies than many evangelicals would have liked. The third set of events was a series of political and cultural conflicts at the local level during the mid-1970s, which galvanized conservative Christians at the grassroots level. The result was an effort to build a political and social coalition of single-issue groups that would have as its basis "a frontal attack on 'big government' as a threat to traditional religious and economic values. With that theme [the coalition's organizers] hoped to harness evangelicals to a comprehensive conservative program" (Wald 1997, 226).

The groups initially coalesced in 1979 under the leadership of Reverend Jerry Falwell and his organization, the Moral Majority, which was a force in the nomination and election campaigns of Ronald Reagan in 1980 and 1984. The Moral Majority was, in reality, however, not much of a grassroots organization. For the most part, its membership consisted of Baptist pastors tied to the cooperative fellowship of Baptist churches with which Falwell was associated. By 1988, however, the Moral Majority had run out of money and was disbanded.

In its wake, following the failed presidential campaign of Pat Robertson in 1988, the Christian Coalition was formed, and it created a much more extensive set of grassroots organizations. The coalition's goal was to strengthen its local activists. Its national spokesman, Ralph Reed, built a wide-ranging operation, designed to coordinate local chapters through modern communication tools such as faxes, computers, local workshops, and the annual "Road to Victory" conference (Fowler, Hertzke, and Olson 1999, 145). The organizational capacity of the coalition was utilized in the 1992 Bush reelection campaign, and the group was given a position of importance on the platform committee of the 1992 Republican National Convention.[6]

The midterm elections of 1994 marked a high-water mark for the Christian Right. Their grassroots efforts helped the Republican Party capture control of Congress for the first time in forty years and helped it make important gains in state legislatures and governor's mansions, particularly in the South (e.g., Rozell and Wilcox 1995). The coalition also played a major lobbying role in efforts to pass the new Republican majority's "Contract with America" (Oldfield 1996).

In 1996, its influence continued in presidential, congressional, and state electoral politics (Rozell and Wilcox 1997). Organizations associated with the Christian Right expended substantial resources on behalf of socially conservative candidates, and the organizations' members worked hard on the candidates' behalf, seemingly to great effect (Rozell and Wilcox 1995 and 1997; Guth et al. 1998). Fellow church members contacted other church members to encourage them to vote for particular candidates; voter guides were placed in church lobbies; and discussion of political issues occurred among church members. Following the election, those who indicated that they had been contacted by one of these commonly used tactics of the Christian Right were more likely not only to vote, but to vote Republican (Guth et al. 1998).

Though having the support of the Christian Right does not guarantee victory for Republican candidates, these candidates appear obligated to court this constituency. At the Christian Coalition's 1999 "Road to Victory" conference, for example, every candidate for the 2000 Republican presidential nomination (Gary Bauer, George W. Bush, Elizabeth Dole, Steve Forbes, Alan Keyes, John McCain) made appearances. GOP candidates who antagonize Christian conservatives do so at their own risk: During the 2000 nomination campaign, John McCain, during the final days of the Virginia primary contest, lashed out at icons of the Religious Right such as Falwell and Robertson in their home state, and was soundly defeated. On the other hand, recorded telephone messages by Robertson attacked McCain in the subsequent Michigan primary, and negative publicity about this strategy probably contributed to McCain's victory in that state over the favorite, George W. Bush.

Still, it appears that those with ties to the Christian Right have begun to reassess what it can and cannot accomplish. In particular, the movement has come under criticism recently by prominent evangelical figures who earlier had been leaders within the Moral Majority (Thomas and Dobson 1999). In addition, the Christian Coalition has suffered from internal difficulties, particularly the tension between standing firm on principled positions of public policy and seeking compromises in order to get some of the organization's goals passed into legislation (half a loaf of bread being better than no loaf at all). Recent unfavorable IRS rulings against the Christian Coalition appear to bode ill for its nonprofit status and its formal organizational structures. Finally, the Christian Coalition's efforts to reach out to Catholics and to the black community, with which there are many shared moral values, have to this point largely failed. The future influence of the Christian Right will likely be tied to its ability to cope successfully with both its strengths and weaknesses (Green 1997), to coordinate the disparate elements within its fold, and to overcome tensions that have emerged in the Republican Party as a result of its influence.

Conclusion

Religion can operate in at least two ways to influence people. First, it can influence people as an internal belief system, shaping the adoption of other beliefs or affecting behavior. Religion can also operate as an external set of influences, in which one's church, pastor, or social group convey messages and expectations about one's political beliefs and actions along with the associated social pressures to conform. These two types of influences can also work in concert, so that one's prior beliefs *and* social-religious context both influence one's attitudes and behaviors.

As evidence of these processes, this chapter revealed that there is, at times, considerable variation in the political engagement and participation rates of members of different religious traditions. For example, Black Protestants and white evangelicals have generally been less active in voting and campaign politics since the 1960s, though those patterns changed during the 1980s. Moreover, there is considerable variation in the political preferences of members of different religious traditions. Black Protestants are strongly Democratic in their party identification and voting choices, while white Protestants are more divided; all white Protestants became less Democratic during the last half of the twentieth century, but southern white Protestants (especially evangelicals) became much more Republican than nonsoutherners.

There are also other ways in which religion can affect American campaigns and elections. At times, the religious affiliation and beliefs of presidential candidates (such as Al Smith and John F. Kennedy) can become issues in election campaigns. In fact, two aspects of the 2000 presidential election campaign suggest that the religious affiliation and beliefs of candidates remain important features in contemporary politics: (1) the reaction to George Bush Jr.'s statement in the GOP nomination debate that Jesus Christ was his favorite political philosopher and (2) the reaction to Al Gore's nomination of Joseph Lieberman, an orthodox Jew, as his vice-presidential running mate. Moreover, the candidacies of Jesse Jackson and Pat Robertson show that the religious beliefs of candidates can drive the prominent issues and themes (and legislative remedies) they emphasize, while church networks can become core logistical elements in campaigns. Finally, religion can affect political campaigns and elections through the activities of religio-political movements, as noted in the discussion of the development and influence of the Christian Right beginning in the late 1970s.

American democracy was founded on a widely shared set of religious presuppositions. Moreover, religious beliefs and religious associations have always influenced American culture and politics, and arguments that religion has been only a minor factor are specious at best. Contemporary politics continues to reflect that influence, as evident in the campaign for the Republican nomination for president in 2000. Religious beliefs are frequently held with considerable intensity, and religious associations frequently serve as bases of group loyalty and commitment. As a result, it is likely that religion will continue to affect the political behavior and preferences of American citizens for a long time to come, and that it will influence the law- and policy-making processes at local, state, and national levels well into the future.

References

Ahlstrom, Sydney E. 1972. *A Religious History of the American People*. New Haven: Yale University Press.

Black, Earl, and Merle Black. 1987. *Politics and Society in the South*. Cambridge: Harvard University Press.

Burner, David. 1988. *John F. Kennedy and a New Generation*. Glenview, Ill.: Scott Foresman.

Calhoun-Brown, Allison. 1996. "African American Churches and Political Mobilization: The Psychological Impact of Organizational Resources." *Journal of Politics* 58 (November): 935–53.

Chalfant, H. Paul, Robert E. Beckley, and C. Eddie Palmer. 1994. *Religion in Contemporary Society*. 3d ed. Itasca, Ill.: F. E. Peacock.

Fiorina, Morris P. 1989. *Congress: Keystone of the Washington Establishment*. 2d ed. New Haven: Yale University Press.

Fowler, Robert Booth, Allen D. Hertzke, and Laura R. Olson. 1999. *Religion and Politics in America: Faith, Culture, and Strategic Choices*. 2d ed. Boulder, Colo.: Westview Press.

Green, John C. 1997. "The Christian Right and the 1996 Elections: An Overview." In Rozell and Wilcox 1997.

Guth, James L., et al. 1995. "Onward Christian Soldiers: Religious Activist Groups in American Politics." In *Interest Group Politics*, edited by Allan Cigler and Burdett Loomis. 4th ed. Washington, D.C.: Congressional Quarterly Press.

———. 1997. *The Bully Pulpit: The Politics of the Protestant Clergy*. Lawrence: University Press of Kansas.

———. 1998. "Thunder on the Right? Religious Interest Group Mobilization in the 1996 Election." In *Interest Group Politics*, edited by Allan Cigler and Burdett Loomis. 5th ed. Washington, D.C.: Congressional Quarterly Press.

Herrnson, Paul S. 1995. *Congressional Elections: Campaigning at Home and in Washington*. Washington, D.C.: Congressional Quarterly Press.

Hertzke, Allen D. 1993a. "Churches as Precincts in Party Politics: The Legacy of Pat Robertson and Jesse Jackson." *Vox Pop Newsletter of Political Organizations and Parties* 11, no. 3.

———. 1993b. *Echoes of Discontent: Jesse Jackson, Pat Robertson, and the Resurgence of Populism*. Washington, D.C.: Congressional Quarterly Press.

Huckfeldt, Robert, Eric Plutzer, and John Sprague. 1993. "Alternative Contexts of Political Behavior: Churches, Neighborhoods, and Individuals." *Journal of Politics* 55 (May): 365–81.

Jacobson, Gary C. 1990. *The Electoral Origins of Divided Government: Competition in U.S. House Elections, 1946–1988*. Boulder, Colo.: Westview Press.

———. 1997. *The Politics of Congressional Elections*. 4th ed. New York: Longman.

Kellstedt, Lyman A. 1993. "Religion, the Neglected Variable: An Agenda for Future Research on Religion and Political Behavior." In *Rediscovering the Religious Factor in American Politics*, edited by David C. Leege and Lyman A. Kellstedt. Armonk, N.Y.: M. E. Sharpe.

Kellstedt, Lyman A., et al. 1997. "Is There a Culture War? Religion and the 1996 Election." Paper presented at the annual meeting of the American Political Science Association, Washington, D.C.

Miller, Warren E. 1991. "Party Identification, Realignment, and Party Voting: Back to Basics." *American Political Science Review* 85 (June): 557–68.

Nie, Norman H., Sidney Verba, and John R. Petrocik. 1979. *The Changing American Voter*. Enlarged ed. Cambridge: Harvard University Press.

Noll, Mark A. 1990. *Religion and American Politics: From the Colonial Period to the 1980s*. New York: Oxford University Press.

Oldfield, Duane M. 1996. *The Right and the Righteous: The Christian Right Confronts the Republican Party*. New York: Rowman and Littlefield.

Reichley, A. James. 1985. *Religion in American Public Life*. Washington, D.C.: Brookings Institution.

Rozell, Mark J., and Clyde Wilcox, eds. 1995. *God at the Grassroots: The Christian Right in the 1994 Elections*. New York: Rowman and Littlefield.

———. 1997. *God at the Grassroots: The Christian Right in the 1996 Elections*. New York: Rowman and Littlefield.

Sapiro, Virginia, et al. 1998. *American National Election Studies, 1948–1997*. ICPSR edition. Ann Arbor, Mich.: ICPSR.

Scher, Richard K. 1997. *Politics in the New South: Republicanism, Race, and Leadership in the Twentieth Century*. Armonk, N.Y.: M. E. Sharpe.

Stanley, Harold W., and Richard G. Niemi. 1999. "Party Coalitions in Transition: Partisanship and Group Support, 1952–1996." In *Reelection 1996: How Americans Voted*, edited by Herbert F. Weisberg and Jane M. Box-Steffensmeier. New York: Chatham House.

———. 2000. *Vital Statistics on American Politics, 1999–2000*. Washington, D.C.: Congressional Quarterly Press.

Sundquist, James L. 1983. *Dynamics of the Party System: Alignment and Realignment of Political Parties in the United States*. Rev. ed. Washington, D.C.: Brookings Institution.

Tate, Katherine. 1991. "Black Political Participation in the 1984 and 1988 Presidential Elections." *American Political Science Review* 85:1133–58.

———. 1994. *From Protest to Politics: The New Black Voters in American Elections.* Enlarged ed. Cambridge: Harvard University Press.

Thomas, Cal, and Ed Dobson. 1999. *Blinded by Might: Can the "Religious Right" Save America?* Grand Rapids: Zondervan.

Verba, Sidney, Kay L. Schlozman, and Henry E. Brady. 1995. *Voice and Equality: Civic Volunteerism in American Politics.* Cambridge: Harvard University Press.

Wald, Kenneth. 1997. *Religion and Politics in the United States.* 3d ed. Washington, D.C.: Congressional Quarterly Press.

Wald, Kenneth D., Dennis E. Owen, and Samuel S. Hill. 1988. "Churches as Political Communities." *American Political Science Review* 82 (June): 531–48.

Wald, Kenneth D., and Corwin E. Smidt. 1993. "Measurement Strategies in the Study of Religion and Politics." In *Rediscovering the Religious Factor in American Politics,* edited by David C. Leege and Lyman A. Kellstedt. Armonk, N.Y.: M. E. Sharpe.

Walters, Ronald. 1988. *Black Presidential Politics: A Strategic Approach.* Albany: State University of New York Press.

Wattenberg, Martin P. 1996. *The Decline of American Political Parties, 1952–1994.* Cambridge: Harvard University Press.

Welch, Michael R., et al. 1993. "Are the Sheep Hearing the Shepherds? Cue Perceptions, Congregational Responses, and Political Communication Processes." In *Rediscovering the Religious Factor in American Politics,* edited by David C. Leege and Lyman A. Kellstedt. Armonk, N.Y.: M. E. Sharpe.

White, Theodore H. 1961. *The Making of the President 1960.* New York: Atheneum.

Wielhouwer, Peter W. 2000. "Releasing the Fetters: Parties and the Mobilization of the African-American Electorate." *Journal of Politics* 62 (February): 1.

Teaching Tools

Discussion Questions

1. Discuss the differences in your religious identification compared with your religious affiliation. What are the specific teachings of your church or religious tradition with regard to politics and your political behavior? How does each affect your attitudes toward politics?
2. Why do you think some religious traditions cause people to affiliate with certain political parties and to vote for the candidates of those parties? Specifically, why do members of some religious groups tend to be Democrats while members of others tend to be Republicans?
3. Looking at table 8.3, we can see that people unaffiliated with a religious tradition are also the most likely to identify as political

independents, as opposed to affiliating with one of the major parties. Why do you think that is true?

4. What evidence can you find of the role religion plays in the current (or most recent) elections?

5. Do you think that the religious affiliation of political candidates will ever be as polarizing as Kennedy's was in 1960? What would be the reaction of the American electorate if a Buddhist ran for president? Or a Hindu? Or a declared atheist?

6. A core element of Kennedy's effort to defuse the issue of his Catholicism was his commitment to separate the teachings of his religion from the decisions he would make as president. Is this something that can really be done? Is this something that presidents must do? If you were to become president (or the governor of your state, or a member of Congress), would you be able to separate your most closely held values from the decisions you would make in those positions?

9

Religion and the American Presidency

JEFF WALZ

If the 2000 presidential election is any indication, religion will continue to be an integral part of the White House for years to come. Both the Republican presidential nominee, George W. Bush, and the Democratic nominee, Al Gore, "wore God on their campaign sleeves." Bush described his decision to "recommit my life to Jesus Christ," and Gore declared himself "a child of the Kingdom and a person of strong faith" (Goldstein 1999). While presidential religious language may not be new, the link Bush and Gore forged between faith and public policy is nevertheless significant. By advocating a role for faith-based organizations in federal initiatives, Bush and Gore followed in the footsteps of other "godly" policies, such as the environmentalism of Theodore Roosevelt (1901–9), Prohibition, and the abolition of slavery. The lesson from the campaign and the early days of the new Bush administration that includes Christian conservatives is clear: religion is here to stay at 1600 Pennsylvania Avenue.

This chapter analyzes the relationship between religion and the American presidency by focusing on the four most recent presidents—Jimmy Carter (1977–81), Ronald Reagan (1981–89), George Bush (1989–93), and Bill Clinton (1993–2001). The first section, "The President's Religious Background," examines the religious faith that each brought to office. In what religious faith were these presidents reared and to what extent did they take that faith into political life? The second section, "Religion, the Electoral Connection, and White House Access," focuses on the use of religion in presidential elections. How important is religion to the nomination and general-election campaigns? The third section, "The President as Religious National Leader," explores the role of faith in leading the public. To what degree do presidents demonstrate personal, private piety in the White House? How frequently do presidents use civil religion in speeches, inauguration addresses, and other public pronouncements? How may presidents use this public religion toward persuasive ends? The fourth, and final, section, "Religion and Executive Action," probes the connection between presidential faith and policy decisions and appointments.

Religion plays an important, yet limited, role in the presidency. The religion that presidents bring to office does affect their use of religious language, the policies they pursue, and the manner in which they pursue them. Though Americans want a president who practices a religion, they may not necessarily desire one who is too outwardly religious, as Carter found out in 1976. When making public pronouncements of a religious nature, presidents are generally acting more to unite the country than to enhance its religious convictions. Religious beliefs do influence how presidents govern and the policy goals they pursue. But religious faith is only one factor in White House management and policy pursuits; the partisan makeup of Congress, the country's economic condition, and a host of other variables interact with presidential faith, as the Carter, Reagan, Bush, and Clinton administrations illustrate.

The President's Religious Background

Before considering the influence of religion on a presidency, it is important to understand the faith that presidents bring to office. Religious faith may serve to guide not only the president's conduct in office but also the types of policies he pursues.[1] Later we examine how the religious faith of our four most recent presidents may have shaped their conduct and policies while in office, but here we simply begin to understand the distinctive faith each brought to his presidency.

Perhaps no contemporary president personifies a strong religious background as well as Jimmy Carter. Carter was born in Plains, Georgia, in 1924, to a "matter-of-fact" Baptist father and a "free-thinking and free-speaking" Methodist mother (see Ribuffo 1989, 146–47). Much later in life, Carter had a spiritual rebirth. The turning point may have been a question posed in a sermon by his pastor, the Reverend Robert Harris of the Plains Baptist Church. In the sermon, Harris asked: "If you were arrested for being a Christian, would there be enough evidence to convict you?" In response, Carter felt that there would not, and he compared himself to the self-righteous Pharisee in Luke 18:10–13. Later, in 1966 or early 1967, Carter went for a walk with his sister Ruth, and he asked her, "What is it that you have that I haven't got?" When she replied that "everything I am" belonged to Jesus, Carter opened his heart more fully to the Lord.

If Carter's religion was transparent and life-altering, Ronald Reagan's faith prior to his presidency was less public and more constant. Above all, Reagan's early values were derived from two people: Ben Hill Cleaver, the minister of the First Christian Church (Disciples of Christ) in Dixon, Illinois, during the 1920s; and his mother Nelle, whose religiosity served to shape her son (Vaughn 1995). Foreshadowing his later career as a Hollywood movie star, Reagan combined acting and speaking with church activities. He was part of a Sunday school pageant that Nelle wrote, and he helped lead an Easter sunrise prayer service. In Christian Endeavor, a group of young people that met on Sunday nights, Reagan led discussions on topics like "What Would Happen If All Church Members Were Really Christians?" and "What Difference Does It Make What We Do on Sundays?"

George Bush, an Episcopalian, also had strong religious training in his youth. In his own words (Bush 1988), "My upbringing was conventional Christianity. We had prayer at home, we attended church regularly. There was never any doubt that Jesus Christ was my Savior and Lord." Bush's parents were active in Christ Episcopal Church in Greenwich, Connecticut, where George was raised. Bush's mother, Dorothy, was raised a devout Presbyterian, and she led family devotions after breakfast each morning. Bush maintained his strong Episcopalian religion, solidified primarily by mother Dorothy, throughout his political and personal life (Hutcheson 1989).

Rather than fitting neatly into one particular denominational heritage like Carter (Baptist), Reagan (Disciples of Christ), or Bush (Episcopalian), Clinton had several different religious ties: Baptist, Catholic, and Methodist. Like Reagan, Clinton used to socialize with Christian young people during adolescence. In fact, Clinton's nanny even mused that one day he might become a minister like Billy Graham (Maraniss

1995). The second part of Clinton's religious heritage was the Catholicism to which he was exposed during his undergraduate years at Georgetown University in Washington, D.C., while Clinton's Methodist ties came from his marriage to Hillary.

Religion, the Electoral Connection, and White House Access

Faith like that expressed by Carter, Reagan, Bush, and Clinton has been an issue in many presidential campaigns, particularly those following corrupt administrations or times. In 1896, during a time of farm and labor unrest, fundamentalist Democratic candidate William Jennings Bryan injected heavy religious overtones into his unsuccessful bid. Prior to Byran and during the "gilded era," a period of American history noted for its corruption, Rutherford B. Hayes (1877–81) and James A. Garfield (1881) "made the point that they were church members and spoke very staunchly about their faith, their church affiliations and the union of God and country" (Goldstein 1999, citing historian Thomas C. Reeves).

More recently, in the wake of the Watergate scandal,[2] voters in the 1976 presidential election chose Democrat Carter over Republican Ford. Voters selected the deeply religious Carter, in part, to restore a sense of dignity and ethics to the presidency. As Carter emerged in early 1976 as a viable presidential candidate, much of the American media and public did not know what to make of Carter's strong Christian convictions. Though the press was confused by Carter's "born-again" Christian status,[3] a Gallup poll conducted later in 1976 found that 48 percent of American Protestants and 18 percent of American Catholics had been "born again" in Christ (Ribuffo 1989, 142). While some perceived Carter's Southern Baptist religion negatively, it appears his faith actually helped him win the election by enabling him to capture key segments of Christian voters.

In fact, in putting together their electoral coalitions, presidential candidates and their strategists try to woo particular religious groups. From the middle of the nineteenth century until the 1960s, Democratic presidential candidates could count on the Roman Catholic vote. Reagan in 1980 brought many Evangelical Protestants—those "born again" in Christ whose mission is to spread the good news of Jesus Christ—into the Republican column, a trend that continued in the 1990s. And Democratic presidential candidates generally anticipate receiving the Jewish vote (Fowler, Hertzke, and Olson 1999, 109). At times, however, candidates will target religious groups normally outside of their coalition. For example, in 1984, Reagan went after both the Catholic and Jewish vote, but only after he had first secured his electoral "base" in the South and the West. Reagan's first-term policies assisted this strategy, as he had renewed a call for tuition tax credits to assist, in part, those who sent their children to Catholic schools and had appointed the first ambassador to the Vatican ("Going after the Democrats' Turf" 1984).

Reagan demonstrated another truism about religion on the campaign trail—articulation of favorable policy positions may count for more than personal piety. Evangelicals were smitten with Reagan in the 1980 and 1984 elections, despite the fact that he was not in church every Sunday, was divorced, came out of Hollywood, and had a wife (Nancy) who had some belief in astrology. But Reagan had two things going for him. First, he could "speak the language" of evangelicals, even if he did not necessarily live that life fully. Second, he addressed issues—values, families, patriotism, for example—that resonated with the evangelical constituency (Fowler, Hertzke, and Olson 1999, 119).

Once the campaign is over, the difficult job of governing begins. A key to effective leadership is serving electoral constituencies, including religious ones, that put you into office. As a rule, certain religious groups with liberal leanings, such as Jews, Catholics, and Mainline Protestants, have better access to Democratic presidents, whereas conservative groups like Evangelical Protestants have better access to Republican presidents.

A case study of the Reagan White House bears this out. Allen Hertzke (1989) suggests that a formal relationship between the White House and domestic groups is a fairly new development. Carter was the first to appoint a director of public liaisons to work with blacks, Hispanics, women, and other constituencies. Reagan later extended this practice by assigning a Protestant, a Catholic, and a Jew the task of "establishing and maintaining contacts with religious constituencies" (Hertzke 1989, 264). The Protestant liaison, a Baptist, served as an effective liaison for religiously conservative Protestants, but liberal Mainline Protestant groups had almost no access to Reagan. On the other hand, the Jewish constituency had more access to the Republican White House than one might have expected given the more Democratic inclinations of most Jews. When groups, including religious groups, do not enjoy access to the president, they frequently work to have someone else occupy the White House.

The President as Religious National Leader

To be an effective national leader, presidents need to "go public" by making direct presidential appeals to the people (Kernell 1986). Religion can play a part in such leadership. Presidents may publicly express their religious faith in different ways and seek to unify the nation through some form of civil religion. Such Oval Office faith and religious rhetoric can facilitate progress on a variety of constituency and issue fronts. Recent presidents have exhibited different ways of bringing religious expression to the White House, with such expressions resulting in different outcomes.

Though Carter took his strong, born-again faith with him to the White House, he did not always "wear his religion on his sleeve." In Washington, he attended services and taught Sunday school at First Baptist Church. Overall, however, he displayed much less personal piety than other presidents with seemingly weaker religious convictions. Perhaps this was due to the fact that "because he was so pious, Carter felt little need for official declarations of piety" (Ribuffo 1989, 151).

Reagan's White House faith was much more opaque and ambiguous than that of his early religious endeavors. Still, many evangelicals viewed Reagan as a brother in Christ. Pat Robertson viewed Reagan as "probably the most evangelical president we have had since the founding fathers" (Pierard and Linder 1988, 266). But others, such as Lutheran historian Martin Marty, viewed Reagan's faith as "sincere but unauthentic" (1984). Still, it can be difficult to distinguish genuine public professions of faith from mere religious rhetoric, though some would contend that the latter was a much more prominent part of Reagan's White House years than the former.

Unlike Reagan, Bush and wife Barbara attended church regularly during his presidency. Bush stated: "I don't want to act like I'm holier than thou . . . and yet I want to do what many who have gone before me have done, and that is to try to amplify as best one can that we are one nation under God" ("Bush Affirms Role of Religion" 1991). The Bushes generally rotated attending several different Episcopal churches in the Washington area, but they also visited other churches, such as a black Baptist church. Unconstrained by security concerns, Barbara Bush said that one of her responsibilities as First Lady was to "get my husband to church" (Lawton 1989).

Clinton's diverse religious experiences were reflected in his church attendance as chief executive during the early days of his administration. Initially, he generally attended First Baptist Church near the White House, a theologically liberal church, though about as often he attended the Foundry United Methodist Church, where Hillary and daughter Chelsea attended. He also worshiped at St. John's Episcopal Church and St. Matthew's Catholic Church. While away from Washington, Clinton attended a variety of worship services. During such services, Clinton has been observed taking notes on sermons, underlining Bible passages, and singing hymns from memory. Prior to the Lewinsky scandal, First Baptist pastor Everett C. Goodwin stated that he saw Clinton as "a man obviously at prayer, searching for God's presence" (Solomon 1993).

Beyond what religion presidents bring to the White House—and how they practice their faith while in office—presidents speak the language of religion. From inaugural addresses to prayer breakfasts, from Memorial Day speeches to policy addresses, presidents since Washington have engaged in "civil religion." While the religious faith of presidents has policy implications (to be addressed in the next section), civil religion is largely symbolic and rhetorical in nature, though it may be used as a means to policy ends.

Perhaps no term has linked the American presidency and religion more than the term *civil religion*. Just what is civil religion? Robert Bellah (1967) first applied the term to American politics in his essay "Civil Religion in America," but the roots of the discussion of civil religion can be traced to the eighteenth-century political philosopher Jean-Jacques Rousseau. Rousseau, who moved from Calvinism to Roman Catholicism and from Roman Catholicism to Deism, suggested that many citizens embraced a "public faith" that enhanced civic spirit. Borrowing from political philosopher John Locke, Rousseau viewed civil religion as a creed based on "the existence of God, the messiahship of Jesus, and adherence to biblical ethics" (Pierard and Linder 1988, 33). Societies used religion to enhance social harmony. Since Christians' greatest allegiance was to God, civil religion could help develop a secondary allegiance to the state. Civil religion, then, "would be the general will of the people expressed religiously in the life of the state with a benign but watchful Supreme Being to preside over the keeping of the public faith" (Pierard and Linder 1988, 34).

According to Bellah, the roots of American civil religion are found in the Declaration of Independence, the words and actions of the founders, and other important early national events. Simply put, religion was important to early Americans. Moreover, religion continues to play a stabilizing role in America's social and political system. Even the separation of church of state, as articulated in the First Amendment, has failed to dilute religion's impact. Civil religion includes "the widely but informally held set of fundamental political and social principles concerning the history and destiny of a state or nation that help to bind that state or nation together." Thus, civil religion serves to unify Americans much like other ideas, such as the notions of democracy, freedom, justice, and concern for others (Linder 1996, 734).

The extensive literature on civil religion generally focuses on how religion and politics come together in presidential inaugural addresses. Cynthia Toolin's study (1983) of inaugural addresses from Washington to Reagan found that almost every address contained a specific reference to a divine being. Allusions might be made indirectly to "Almighty Providence" or more directly to a personal God. For example, Franklin D. Roosevelt (1933–45), in his first inaugural address during the Great Depression, referred to "almighty God" and later said, "We humbly ask the blessings of God. . . . May He protect each and every one of us" (quoted in Toolin 1983, 41). This use of religious language at the inauguration of a new administration is designed, in part, to unify the American people in the aftermath of a political campaign that divides them into partisan camps. In addition, the use of such language can enable a president to rally the public behind his leadership, and, at times, even behind his policy proposals.

Like their predecessors, Carter, Reagan, Bush, and Clinton have used civil religion to unite the country, to draw attention to specific issues and events, and to serve as a "prophet," "priest," or "pastor" to the nation. Before assessing the civil religion of recent presidents, it is first important to understand the different ways in which civil religion may be expressed by presidents. A president who uses civil religion in a prophetic role acts like an Old Testament prophet in pronouncing judgment on the American people and in calling them to repentance for their failure to keep their "sacred" commitments. A president who serves in the role of a priest speaks as an advocate for the people and "pronounces words of comfort, praise, and celebration" (Pierard and Linder 1988, 24). A president who serves in the role of a pastor provides spiritual inspiration and comforts the afflictions of American citizens (Linder 1996, 734). Obviously, presidents can assume all three roles at different times during their administration. But during their tenure, presidents tend to adopt one role more than the other two. Within this framework, it appears that Clinton was more a pastor, Reagan a priest, and Carter a prophet, while Bush does not fit neatly into this categorization. In each role, presidents don the garb of civil religion to move the nation in a certain philosophical or policy direction.

Despite his strong religious convictions, Carter did not engage in civil religion to the same extent that some of his predecessors had. Like other presidents, Carter took his oath of office in 1977 on two Bibles, one used by President Washington and the second a gift from his mother, Lillian Carter. Both Bibles were open to Micah 6:8 (KJV): "He hath showed thee, O man, what is good; and what doth the Lord require of thee, but to do justly, and to love mercy, and to walk humbly with thy God" (White 1996, 153). Carter noted the uniqueness of the United States, "the first society to openly define itself in terms of both spirituality and of human liberty." After completing his brief inaugural address, the president and his family walked from the Capitol to the White House.

During Carter's tumultuous four-year term, the country endured an energy crisis, inflationary pressures, and the hostage-taking at the American Embassy in Iran. As a result, Carter fluctuated between a prophet and priest of American civil religion, though most remember him as the former. At the 1977 National Prayer Breakfast, for example, Carter stressed "the need for national humility." As a "city on a hill," America has a mission to uphold, one that should not be jeopardized by national arrogance. It was only during a 1980 address, given during the Iran hostage crisis, that Carter turned from prophetic concerns to more pastoral ones, when he emphasized the need for Americans to pull together during this difficult time (Pierard and Linder 1988, 249).

No speech signified Carter's prophetic civil religion more than his "crisis of confidence" speech in 1979. Though Carter's accomplishments were noteworthy—civil service reform, industrial deregulation, and the Panama Canal treaties, for example—the administration's problems overwhelmed these achievements. Aside from the energy crisis and unemployment, America's power seemed to be waning. To address these issues, Carter invited 130 national leaders, including ten religious figures, to Maryland for consultation on these crises. The July 15 "crisis-of-confidence speech" that resulted from these meetings showcased a prophetic president. The government and the people were to blame for the country's ills. Carter suggested that "too many of us now tend to worship self-indulgence and consumption. Human identity is no longer defined by what one does but by what one owns." The press described the speech as a sermon around which to unite the American public (Pierard and Linder 1988, 253).

Unfortunately for Carter, the people seemed to desire a benevolent high priest more than a condemning prophet. While Jimmy Carter may never be rated by historians as a great president, "It will be difficult in the long run to sustain censure of a president motivated to do what is right" (Jones 1988, 217). Carter lacked some of the pragmatic political skills for which many Southern Baptists are known, skills some thought would characterize Carter's presidency (Baker 1977). But, as the 1980 election neared, Carter's honesty and forthrightness were popular with neither the public nor the press, and many evangelicals wanted someone to confirm and promote the significant status of the nation, rather than to criticize it as Carter had done.

Reagan appeared to be the ideal antidote, as he was a charismatic leader who epitomized the priestly chief executive. Pierard and Linder (1988) argue that civil religion reached its apex under Reagan and actually competed with the sectarian religion practiced in churches, synagogues, and temples. Just as there are weekly religious services, it was "The Great Communicator" who in 1981 began the weekly radio address (Barilleaux and Yenerall 1999). But while Reagan's use of civil religion may have been unprecedented, the religious language he used in his two inaugural addresses was typical. Moreover, during both his inaugurals, Reagan took the oath of office with his left hand on his mother's Bible, open to 2 Chronicles 7:14 (KJV): "If my people, which are called by my name, shall humble themselves, and pray, and seek my face, and turn from their wicked ways; then will I hear from heaven, and will forgive their sin, and will heal their land." Dwight Eisenhower, the last president to serve two full terms (1953–60), had used the same passage (White 1996, 157).

Four themes were inherent in Reagan's civil religion and presidential outlook (Pierard and Linder 1988). One theme was that of American exceptionalism, a sense that the United States has a special role to play in history. According to this theme, America is a nation chosen by God, and the American people need to act as an example to other nations and peoples. The president stated: "I believe in the goodness of the American people," who are "blessed in so many ways [because] we're a nation under God, a living and loving God." Moreover, as Reagan suggested at a celebration of the Constitution in 1987, he believed that God had designed specific tasks for the American people: "The guiding hand of providence" created America "for a higher cause: the preservation and extension of the sacred fire of human liberty. This is America's solemn duty" (quoted in Pierard and Linder 1988, 275–76).

Second, Reagan's civil religion emphasized America as a spiritual nation. Our nation, Reagan contended, takes its spiritual strength from God, and "standing up for America means standing up for the God who has so blessed our land." Echoing Theodore Roosevelt's belief that the presidency is a "bully pulpit" from which to lead the country, Reagan believed that the country was "hungry for a spiritual renewal." With this renewal underway, America would be better equipped to tackle its myriad social and economic problems (Pierard and Linder 1988, 277).

Third, Reagan's civil religion posited that a vibrant religious life within society is a prerequisite for a healthy nation. He believed that the Bible provided answers to our nation's problems and even proclaimed 1983 as the year of the Bible. At an "ecumenical prayer breakfast" during the Republican Convention in Dallas in 1984, Reagan emphasized the key role that faith, religion, and churches play in American society and contended that God is the foundation of civic virtue (Pierard and Linder 1988, 278–79).

Finally, Reagan's civil religion foresaw a strong military and spiritual country resisting the power of communism. One of Reagan's most memorably anticommunism speeches was to the National Association of Evangelicals in 1983, when he asserted that the United States must do everything in its power to fend off the evils of communism, an ideology that would force Americans to "abandon our faith in God." As a type of pastoral benediction, Reagan urged: "Let us pray for the salvation of all those who live in that totalitarian darkness—pray they will discover the joy of knowing God." A strong military, Reagan argued, would help bring such a godless system to its knees (Pierard and Linder 1988, 279–80). Reagan, more so than Carter, used civil religion as a means to accomplish specific policy ends.

Bush, who served as Reagan's vice president for eight years, used civil religion in a more typical fashion. At his swearing-in, Bush also had his hand on two Bibles, the Washington Bible and the Bush family Bible. Both were opened to Matthew 5, the Sermon on the Mount. Consistent with the Beatitudes, Bush's opening prayer and the tone of his inauguration suggested a kinder and gentler administration. Bush hoped this would distinguish him from Reagan. What defined Bush's inauguration were two actions: he was the first to hold a public reception at the White House since Taft in 1909, and he declared a National Day of Prayer and Thanksgiving for January 22, 1989 (White 1996, 162–63).

During his four-year term, Bush did not invoke civil religion nearly to the same extent that Reagan had. At the National Prayer Breakfast early in his term, Bush's speech was devoid of much of the religious rhetoric of his predecessor. Still, echoing his first act as president, in which he offered a prayer, Bush called on Americans to join together: "There is no greater peace than that which comes from prayer and no greater fellowship than to join in prayer with others" (quoted in McCarthy 1989, 22).

Generally speaking, Bush probably did not use civil religion either to the extent or in the fashion that many evangelicals might have preferred. But Bush could use civil religion effectively—even if he did so sparingly—during his term, as seen in Bush's use of civil religion during Desert Storm, the American-led effort to extract Iraq from Kuwait in 1991. When Bush took office, war seemed unlikely as America's greatest military rival, the Soviet Union, began to break apart in 1989 and eventually dissolved in 1991. But when Iraqi troops invaded adjacent Kuwait on August 1, 1990, Bush called Iraq's action "naked aggression" and promised to make Iraq an example to other aggressors. On the eve of the military campaign with Iraq, Bush, in his January 16, 1991, address to the American public, emphasized the importance of prayer to a successful campaign. Citing economic sanctions and other nonmilitaristic actions to encourage Saddam Hussein to pull Iraqi troops out of Kuwait, Bush contended that "while the world prayed for peace, Saddam prepared for war" (Nelson 1999, 238). At the close of his speech, Bush concluded with a benediction: "Tonight, as our forces fight, they and their families are in our prayers. May God bless each and every one of them, and the coalition forces at our side in the Gulf, and may He continue to bless our nation, the United States of America" (Nelson 1999, 240).

Much like the outspoken Reagan, and diverging from the religiously reticent Carter and Bush, Clinton resurrected a more vigorous civil religion. Whereas Carter practiced prophetic civil religion, calling on the people to make sacrifices for the good of the nation, and Reagan practiced priestly civil religion, leading the citizens in a celebration of the country, Clinton acted more as a national pastor. In this role, the president "provides spiritual inspiration to people by affirming American core values and urging them to appropriate those values, and by comforting them in their afflictions" (Linder 1996, 734).

The scope and depth of Clinton's pastoral civil religion may be seen in various contexts, beginning with his first inaugural address in 1993. In that address, Clinton invoked more of the language of civil religion than had his hero, John Kennedy (1961–63), in his inaugural address and more than Reagan had in either of his two inaugural addresses. In fact, Clinton drew upon the very language of Scripture. He also made reference to the Almighty, reinforcing America's reliance on God, and he employed the religious language of covenant as well as notions of renewal and rebirth. Clinton closed his address by quoting Scripture, "And let us not be weary in well-doing: for in due season we shall reap, if we faint not" (Gal. 6:9 KJV), and by recognizing God's role in this process (Linder 1996, 738). There was also a "universalist emphasis" within the inaugural address, almost as if Clinton was hinting that he desired to be "political pastor of the world," perhaps foreshadowing his administration's internationalist flavor (Linder 1996, 739).

This pastoral quality of Clinton's civil religion was particularly evident in the aftermath of the bombing of the federal building in Oklahoma City in 1995. The work of anti-government extremists, the bombing claimed the lives of 168 innocent people. In seeking to address the hurts and fears of the families of the victims as well as the American people, Clinton was able to salve the wounds, calm the fears, and "minister" to the families and citizens alike. "Wounds take a long time to heal, but we must begin." This event may well have been a major turning point in the Clinton presidency. Prior to the Oklahoma City memorial service, the GOP had recaptured control of Congress and Clinton's job-approval rating, as opposed to his personal-approval rating, had reached its lowest point (Mead, Sward, and Wilson 1995).

Religion and Executive Action

Two generalizations about the American presidency and religion have thus far emerged. First, American presidents have been religious men who have taken their faith with them to the White House. And, second, once in office presidents have drawn upon a civil religion within their inaugural addresses and other speeches to rally the public behind general administration goals. What is less understood, and what is now considered, is how a president's religious faith may affect his (or someday her) approach to the role of government and the specific public policies that he chooses to pursue. An analysis of the four most recent presidencies suggests that presidential faith does influence these factors, although the strength of this relationship is unclear.

Carter's deep, vibrant faith had a significant impact on the policies he pursued in office, particularly with regard to human rights issues. In his autobiography, *Living Faith*, Carter discusses at some length the impact of his church membership on the policies he pursued in government. All Americans, Carter said, want to do what is right and just. Unfortunately, churches too often fail to move their members toward upholding basic human rights, both at home and abroad. In Carter's estimation, "The majority of church members are more self-satisfied, more committed to the status quo, and more exclusive of nonsimilar people than are most political officeholders I have known" (1996, 108). Since many congregations are unwilling to address difficult questions and issues, it is up to government to fill that void. The role of government, therefore, should be an activist one. In promoting this perspective, Carter would often cite theologian Reinhold Niebuhr: "The sad duty of politics is to establish justice in a sinful world" (Ariail and Heckler-Feltz 1996, 72), with establishing justice encompassing more than the administration of law.

This pursuit of justice motivated Carter's concern for one of his major policy objectives—namely, human rights at home and abroad. In his autobiography, Carter cites the human rights model to which Jesus spoke: "The Spirit of the Lord is on me, because he has anointed me to preach good news to the poor. He has sent me to proclaim freedom for the prisoners and recovery of sight for the blind, to release the oppressed" (Luke 4:18). This faith was tied closely to Carter's southern upbringing. How, Carter wondered, could far too many white southerners for far too long have reconciled racial segregation and discrimination with the teachings of Christ?

Carter matched his human rights optimism with policy achievements (Ribuffo 1989). Carter's efforts saved civilian lives, particularly in Argentina, Brazil, and Chile. Carter expanded the conventional notion of human rights by viewing religious liberty as a central human right. He encouraged the Soviet Union to lift restrictions on Jewish emigration to Israel and (secretly) asked the People's Republic of China to allow Bibles to circulate and to allow the return of Christian missionaries. In the Middle East, Carter brokered the Camp David accords, an agreement between Israel and Egypt that sought to make the region more peaceful and stable.

If Carter's faith-based human rights actions pleased many Christians, his position on church-state issues evoked a very different response. Though a self-proclaimed Christian who prayed daily, Carter interpreted the establishment clause of the First Amendment ("Congress shall make no law respecting an establishment of religion . . .") in a "strict separationist" or "no aid" manner. In other words, government should not aid or support religion at all, a position that Baptists have traditionally supported.

> Separation is specified in the law, but for a religious person, there is nothing wrong with bringing these two together, because you can't divorce religious beliefs from public service. And at the same time, of course, in public office you cannot impose your own religious beliefs on others. (Flowers 1983, 117)

This position had implications on several church-and-state policy issues. Unlike his 1976 opponent, Gerald Ford, and many Christians, Carter did not support government financial assistance to parochial schools. He did support certain forms of indirect state aid—such as the loaning of secular textbooks and school lunches—that contributed to an educated citizenry. However, he drew the line on government support when it helped advance the mission of religious schools. He opposed tax credits to support parochial schools and prayer in public schools. Further, Carter favored taxing church properties other than the church building itself (Flowers 1983). Carter's Baptist faith, then, led him to strongly support a role for government in human rights but not in public assistance to religious education. More than specific policy initiatives, Carter's faith—and the desire to recapture a sense of ethics in the wake of Watergate—led him to what Pierard and Linder (1988, 245) call a "moral presidency."

Reagan's Disciples of Christ faith, along with other personal, political, and economic factors, led him down a different path. Whereas Carter's Baptist faith emphasized a corporate responsibility, leading to his focus on human rights, Reagan's religion focused more on individual responsibility and a reduced role for government, themes that would be prominent during his two terms. Growing up in Dixon, Illinois, Reagan observed that the wealthy were admired and the poor viewed as especially sinful. Some Disciples members believed that the poor needed moral improvement more than material assistance to improve their situation. Charity was not central to the Disciples' mission during the first part of the century, and the church was suspicious of communism and skeptical of unions. Thus, some of the seeds for Reagan's later policies were likely sown in the faith in which he had been reared (Vaughn 1995).

Reagan's laissez-faire philosophy, that government should play only a small part in citizens' lives, may also be traced to what J. Mark Thomas (1984) calls Reagan's social ethic. Thomas contrasts the ethical goals that Reagan pursued in his first term—such as equal rights for women, racial equality, quality public education, and peace—with Reagan's lack of emphasis on institutional means to implement them. This individualistic, as opposed to institutional, approach stemmed from Reagan's belief in the American people. In the "state of nature," to use political philosopher John Locke's term, there was no need for government. Each person was his or her own authority. Government was needed only to protect property and keep the peace. Reagan's priestly belief in the goodness of American society decreased the need for government solutions to the vexing problems of equal rights, public education, and so on. Unlike Carter, Reagan had much more confidence in the ability of citizens and communities to achieve ethical goals without government involvement. Reagan's faith and civil religion, then, were connected to his policy goals.

Compared with Reagan and Carter, Bush used his faith less openly or consistently to form policy objectives. Bush, as an Episcopalian, was a member of a denomination known for its moderation, for its penchant to be inclusive and conciliatory. At the same time, Bush, like Reagan, aligned himself with conservative Christians. Both pursued policies to weld the Republican Party's religious and free-market constituencies.

Accordingly, the Republican Party's 1988 platform, crafted by the Bush team, was consistent with the policy goals of the so-called Christian Right (Hutcheson 1989). Bush also supported prayer at high school commencements and voluntary prayer in public schools. He called for stronger families and urged parental involvement in issues such as condom distribution at schools. And, like many of his Republican colleagues today, Bush supported school choice and the provision of public assistance to enable parents to send their children to parochial schools if they desired (Lawton 1991). On these issues, it may be difficult to discern what, if any, impact Bush's Episcopalian faith may have had on the positions he adopted. Still, in the end, it is likely that whether or not his Episcopalian faith had any moderating influence, Bush's political commitment to these positions associated with the program of the Religious Right probably reflected well his own personal convictions (Hutcheson 1989, 38).

Clinton's Baptist and Catholic roots likely led him, at least in part, toward an activist role for government in many policy areas. Clinton was known to employ a very inclusive model in decision making, listening to all opinions and then hoping to arrive at a consensus decision. Similarly, the ecclesiastical structure of Baptist churches, in which there is no church hierarchy to control the decisions and doctrine in local churches, emphasizes the priesthood of all believers and puts a premium on consensual decision making. And, consistent with Catholic social tradition, Clinton sought to find a middle ground between opposing positions. While some may consider this effort to find middle ground simply a form of political expediency or politics as usual, it may also reflect the Catholic church's emphasis on the common good and its associated criticism of individual rights (Casey 1993).[4]

Using this consensual style, Clinton addressed certain policy issues consistent with the Baptist and Catholic traditions—for example, his emphasis on service toward fellow citizens. Clinton cited the Catholic social mission in a speech he delivered at the University of Notre Dame in September 1992, saying that we must follow President Kennedy's aspiration: "Here on earth God's work must truly be our own" (Casey 1993, 33). He went on to emphasize that the focus should be on the working class, as these folks must sweat and sacrifice in their daily struggle. Thus, rather than simply offering handouts to the underprivileged, Clinton followed Catholic theology by urging a balance between rights and responsibilities.

Consistent with Carter and the Democratic Party position, Clinton was a strong supporter of church-state separation. During the colonial period, as well as during the early years of the republic, Baptists struggled against established churches. This history of the church helps shed light on its traditional suspicion of government support of religion. Clinton opposed government subsidies for private or religious schools, suggesting that the nation's founders "knew that there needed to be a space of freedom between government and people of faith that otherwise government might usurp" (Solomon 1993, 3015).

These sketches of the political impact of Carter's, Reagan's, Bush's, and Clinton's religious lives should be viewed cautiously. Since the president is beholden to multiple interest groups with varying agendas, the influence of a president's religion on his agenda will likely be constrained by other factors as well. Moreover, presidents may pursue certain policy goals more to win over constituents than to follow their hearts. Did Carter and Clinton pursue human rights and working-class policies, respectively, because of their religious traditions, because it was the right thing to do, or because of political pressure? In examining the relationship between a president's religion and his policy goals, it must always be recognized that many forces are at work. Nevertheless, religious forces should not be undervalued, just as they should not be overemphasized.

A good example of this cautionary note is when one considers other ways in which executive action and religion may be linked. A primary way for presidents to put their religious stamp on their presidency, and to please religious groups, is through executive appointments. But little is known about the religious values of either career civil servants or the political appointees in the executive branch.

Higher-profile appointments, to the president's cabinet or the U.S. Supreme Court, present a somewhat muddied picture. Even in these instances, religion is likely to be one of a variety of factors that a president considers in making choices. For example, in his effort to put together a cabinet that looked more like America, Clinton focused on selecting more women and minorities, not on their religious qualifications. Presidents may well consider the religious affiliation of their appointees, but they generally seek to reward their political loyalists first, while using lower-level appointments to bring greater diversity to the executive branch. Like Reagan, Bush appointed few evangelicals to prominent positions within his administration, increasing tension with a constituency that believed that "people are policy" (Martin 1996, 312).

Religion has played a more prominent role in federal court appointments. Prior to World War II, as Catholics and Jews sought political recognition, presidents customarily set aside a seat on the Supreme Court for each group (Perry 1991). During Truman's administration, for example, 30 percent of all federal court appointments were given to Catholics and 10 percent to Jews (Lubell 1955). More recently, Reagan and Bush responded to conservative groups by developing plans to appoint more conservative judges to the Supreme Court and other federal judiciary posts (Fowler, Hertzke, and Olson 1999). In fact, anti-abortion groups since 1980 have encouraged the Republican National Convention to adopt a policy limiting federal judicial nominations to those who "respected the sanctity of human life." One study suggests that Reagan and Bush did keep this promise (Goldman 1993). But, as in other policy areas, organized religion does not speak with one voice on federal judiciary appointments. While this division in political perspective among religious groups provides presidents with greater latitude in making presidential appointments, it also complicates the president's appointment process. For example, while Reagan's unsuccessful appointment of Robert Bork to the Supreme Court in 1987 was supported by the National Association of Evangelicals, it was opposed by the National Council of Churches ("Religious Groups Are Not Taking Sides" 1988).

Finally, the president's role as chief executive does allow him on occasion to "make laws" without congressional approval, or to weigh in on crucial issues, as several recent examples illustrate. Citing the denial of religious freedom in Sudan, Clinton signed an executive order in 1997 prohibiting transactions with that African country. Later, in responding to an appeal from Pope John Paul II, Clinton issued an executive order in 1998 permitting religious and charitable groups to send humanitarian aid to Cuba with fewer strings attached (Hendon, Dwight, and Greco 1998). Short of making their own "law," administrations may also weigh in and be heard on contentious bills with religious implications. For example, though religious groups lobbied on both sides of the Civil Rights Restoration Act of 1988, the Reagan administration voiced strong opposition; the act became law anyway ("New Rights Act May Affect Church Groups" 1988). Presidents can also seek to establish better relations with religious groups through the use of their executive powers. Clinton, for example, permitted a Minnesota church in 1994 to keep a $13,450 tithe from a couple that later went bankrupt, by instructing the Justice Department to remove its argument ordering the money be returned to the couple's creditors (Fowler, Hertzke, and Olson 1999).

Conclusion

There is a clear, though somewhat perplexing, nexus between religion and the American presidency. As candidates, presidents bring their faith to the campaign. Once in office, presidents owe allegiance and access to religious groups that helped make them the chief executive. The public, however, sees a different side of the presidency. Using civil religion, presidents speak the language of religion to build a reservoir of goodwill for a broad philosophy of government and specific policy outcomes. A variety of factors, including the president's religious faith, his political philosophy, and a host of competing political demands, motivate these governing directives. But any attempt to sort "religious motivation from political calculation" is a "difficult business" (Fowler, Hertzke, and Olson 1999, 122). Likewise, there are considerable difficulties in seeking to determine whether the importance of religion to the presidency is likely to grow, as recent developments suggest.

A good example of the challenge and mystery of religion and the American presidency is Harry S. Truman. A compromise vice-presidential candidate for Franklin D. Roosevelt (1933–45) in the 1944 elections, Truman became president when Roosevelt died only a year later. The former Missouri farmer and haberdasher (men's clothes dealer) grew up in a strict Baptist home, where, by the age of twelve, he had read the Bible through for the second time and could cite specific chapters and verses. He was especially taken with Exodus 20 (the Ten Commandments), the Beatitudes in Matthew, and how people shaped history (Barber 1992, 307). Though Truman felt unprepared for the presidency, he took solace that, in his role as a shaper of history, he was under the guidance of God. Truman's management style stressed individual accountability, even for the president ("the buck stops here"), and it may be attributed to principles he derived from his religious upbringing. At the same time, however, many other variables affected Truman's approach to government and his policy agenda, from public opinion to party directives to political realities. Thus, in the end, it is clear that much more work needs to be done before we can more fully understand the dynamic relationship that exists between a president's religious faith and the public policies he pursues and the political actions he takes. This is true whether we are examining the past, as in Truman's case, or the present, as we seek to understand the role religion may play in the administration of our newly elected president, George W. Bush.

References

Ariail, Dan, and Cheryl Heckler-Feltz. 1996. *The Carpenter's Apprentice: The Spiritual Biography of Jimmy Carter*. Grand Rapids: Zondervan.

Baker, James T. 1977. *A Southern Baptist in the White House*. Philadelphia: Westminster Press.

Barber, James David. 1992. *The Presidential Character: Predicting Performance in the White House*. 4th ed. Englewood Cliffs, N.J.: Prentice Hall.

Barilleaux, Ryan, and Kevin Yenerall. 1999. "Bill Clinton and American Civil Religion." Paper presented at the annual meeting of the American Political Science Association, Atlanta, Ga., September.

Bellah, Robert. 1967. "Civil Religion in America." Daedalus 96 (winter): 1–21.

"Bush Affirms Role of Religion in Public Life." 1991. *Christianity Today* 35 (29 April): 38–39.

Bush, George (interview). 1988. "Bush on Faith: A Personal Issue." *Christianity Today* 32 (16 September): 40.

Carter, Jimmy. 1996. *Living Faith*. New York: Time Books.

Casey, Shaun. 1993. "The President's Religion." *Nieman Reports* (summer): 32–35, 54.

Flowers, Ronald. 1983. "President Jimmy Carter, Evangelicalism, Church-State Relations, and Civil Religion." *Journal of Church & State* 25 (winter): 113–32.

Fowler, Robert Booth, Allen Hertzke, and Laura Olson. 1999. *Religion and Politics in America: Faith, Culture, and Strategic Choices*. 2d ed. Boulder, Colo.: Westview Press.

"Going after the Democrats' Turf." 1984. *Business Week* 2858 (3 September): 22–23.

Goldman, Sheldon. 1993. "Bush's Judicial Legacy: The Final Imprint." *Judicature* 76:287–97.

Goldstein, Laurie. 1999. "White House Seekers Wear Faith on Sleeve and Stump." *New York Times*, 31 August, A1, A16.

Hendon, David, Dwight Allman, and Donald Greco. 1998. "Notes on Church-State Affairs: Cuba." *Journal of Church & State* 40 (autumn): 921.

Hertzke, Allen D. 1989. "Religious Constituencies and Washington Elites." In *Religion and Political Behavior in the United States*, edited by Ted G. Jelen. New York: Praeger.

Hutcheson, Richard G., Jr. 1989. "Religion in the Bush White House." *The Christian Century* 106 (18 January): 37–38.

Jones, Charles O. 1988. *The Trusteeship Presidency: Jimmy Carter and the United States Congress*. Baton Rouge: Louisiana State University Press.

Kernell, Samuel. 1986. *Going Public: New Strategies of Presidential Leadership*. Washington, D.C.: Congressional Quarterly Press.

Lawton, Kim. 1989. "White House Religion." *Christianity Today* 33 (17 February): 36–37.

Linder, Robert. 1996. "Universal Pastor: President Bill Clinton's Civil Religion." *Journal of Church & State* 38 (autumn): 733–49.

Lubell, Samuel. 1955. *The Future of American Politics*. Rev. ed. Garden City, N.Y.: Doubleday, Anchor Books.

Maraniss, David. 1992. "Roots of Clinton's Faith Deep, Varied." *Washington Post*, 29 June.

———. 1995. *First in His Class: The Biography of Bill Clinton*. New York: Simon & Schuster.

Martin, William C. 1996. *With God on Our Side: The Rise of the Religious Right in America*. New York: Broadway Books.

Marty, Martin. 1984. "Presidential Piety: Must It Be Private?" *Christian Century* 101 (22 February): 187–88.

McCarthy, Colman. 1989. "Bush Doesn't Beat around the Bible: God with Ham and Eggs." *National Catholic Reporter* (3 March): 22.

Mead, Tyra, Susan Sward, and Yumi Wilson. 1995. "New Arrest as Clinton Comforts Blast Survivors." *San Francisco Chronicle*, 24 April, A1.

Nelson, Michael. 1999. "George Bush's Persian Gulf War Address (1991)." In *The Evolving Presidency*, edited by Michael Nelson, 235–40. Washington, D.C.: Congressional Quarterly Press.

"New Rights Act May Affect Church Groups." 1988. *Christianity Today* 32 (22 April): 38–39.

Painton, Priscilla. 1993. "Clinton's Spiritual Journey." *Time* 41 (5 April): 49–51.

Perry, Barbara. 1991. *A Representative Supreme Court? The Impact of Race, Religion, and Gender on Appointments*. Westport, Conn.: Greenwood Press.

Pierard, Richard, and Robert Linder. 1988. *Civil Religion and the Presidency*. Grand Rapids: Zondervan, Academie Books.

"Religious Groups Are Not Taking Sides on High Court Nominee." 1988. *Christianity Today* 32 (15 January): 38, 40.

Ribuffo, Leo. 1989. "God and Jimmy Carter." In *Transforming Faith: The Sacred and Secular in Modern American History*, edited by M. L. Bradbury and James B. Gilbert, 141–59. New York: Greenwood Press.

Sharman, J. Michael, ed. 1995. *Faith of the Fathers*. Culpepper, Va.: Victory.

Solomon, Burt. 1993. "White House Notebook: Inside the Yuppie from Yale . . . Is a Southern Baptist's Soul." *National Journal* 25 (18 December): 3014–15.

Thomas, J. Mark. 1984. "Reagan and the State of Nature." *Christianity and Crisis* 17 (September): 321–25.

Toolin, Cynthia. 1983. "American Civil Religion from 1789–1981: A Content Analysis of Presidential Inaugural Addresses." *Review of Religious Research* 25 (September): 39–48.

Vaughn, Stephen. 1995. "The Moral Inheritance of a President: Reagan and the Dixon Disciples of Christ." *Presidential Studies Quarterly* 25 (winter): 109–28.

Wald, Kenneth. 1997. *Religion and Politics in the United States.* 3d ed. Washington, D.C.: Congressional Quarterly Press.

White, Daniel E. 1996. *"So Help Me God": The U.S. Presidents in Perspective.* New York: Nova Science Publishers.

Teaching Tools

Discussion Questions

1. How would you characterize the religious denominations from which presidents have come?
2. How important are religious constituencies to a candidate's presidential campaign?
3. What religious groups may have the best White House access under a Republican administration? Under a Democratic administration? Why?
4. Would you consider Carter, Bush, Reagan, and Clinton to be religious? Why or why not?
5. Why do presidents engage in so much civil religion, and what do they hope to accomplish through the use of such religious rhetoric?
6. How did religion affect how our last four presidents viewed the role of government and their specific policy agendas?
7. Will the importance of religion in presidential campaigns and administrations increase or decrease in the future?
8. How should a Christian assess the fitness of presidential candidates and the performance of presidential administrations?

Topics for Further Student Research

1. As chief executive, the president may make laws without congressional approval, using executive agreements and other methods. Trace such presidential lawmaking, directed toward religion, in a recent administration.
2. Religious groups have been clamoring for a place at the policymaking table. To what extent have presidents brought religious

representatives, including those from their own denomination, into their administrations?

3. Using your denomination or a selected one, identify the presidents from that tradition. What is this denomination's theology and its attitudes toward politics? How consistently have presidents upheld their tradition's theological and political beliefs?

4. Using public-opinion survey data, determine what people want today in a president. How prominently does religion play in that profile?

5. Describe how religion has moved into the White House during the last thirty years or so. Include such aspects as church services, prayer breakfasts, religious advisers, and so forth.

Exercises

1. View the video series *With God on Our Side: The Rise of the Religious Right in America* (Alexandria, Va.: PBS Home Video, 1996), which not only chronicles the rise of the Religious Right but focuses on the role of presidents in fostering this movement. This documentary series has a companion volume that may be of interest: William Martin, *With God on Our Side* (New York: Broadway Books, 1996). How does this series help us better understand the role of religion in the 2000 presidential election? How might the four major candidates in the 2000 election (Buchanan, Bush, Gore, Nader) view the role of the Religious Right and its impact on politics today?

2. During or shortly before election years, assign groups of students to assess the "presidential Christian fitness" of the major candidates. Parts of the project may include the candidates' religious backgrounds, religion in the campaign, the role of faith in platforms, and how religious groups and individuals view the candidates. Presentations will educate the class on the religious dimensions of the candidates.

3. Debate the usefulness and desirability of using Christian Coalition voting guides to educate parishioners on the major presidential candidates. Have students self-select themselves into groups of those who support the guides, those who oppose them, and those "on the fence." This is an interesting way to discuss the candidates, their positions, and how best to educate religious voters.

10

Religion and Congress

JAMES L. GUTH AND LYMAN A. KELLSTEDT

Religion has a very spurious relationship with political ideology and voting. It's one of those variables that just explains nothing independently.

Political scientist Thomas E. Mann, in *The Arizona Republic*, August 25, 1990,
on the role of religion in Congressional voting

All politicians, Democrats and Republicans alike, love God. Or, more accu-
rately, they love to use God to baptize their political agendas. In the *Congressional Directory* . . . no one is an atheist. Even those who have not been
to church or synagogue in years (or have never gone) and probably claim
nothing more than a generic Protestant, Catholic, or Jewish "faith" list
themselves as something under the category "Religion." You never know
when it might help you to be religious.

Columnist Cal Thomas, *Blinded by Might:
Can the "Religious Right" Save America?* (1999), 83

The authors gratefully recognize the contributions of several institutions and individuals
to this project. Furman University and Wheaton College provided financial support. We
also acknowledge the generous financial assistance of the Dirksen Congressional Center.
Finally, we thank student colleagues who have worked on this project: Krista Brinkley of
Wheaton College, Tom Rudolph of the University of Minnesota, Tobin Grant and Tim Hill
of Ohio State University, and Michael Cassabon and Mark Horner of Furman University.

While political scientists have painted an increasingly rich picture of the complex role that religion plays in electoral politics, the study of religious influences in Congress is moribund. Indeed, a quick search of the literature reveals only one book and a handful of articles. The book, Peter Benson and Dorothy Williams's *Religion on Capitol Hill* (1982), was based on interviews with eighty members of the Ninety-sixth Congress and is now quite dated. The few journal articles available are usually confined to reporting members' religious "preferences" and comparing these to the mass public, or to analyzing the influence of religion on a single issue, such as abortion (Duke and Johnson 1992; Tatalovich and Schier 1993).

This scholarly neglect has several causes. For many years, social scientists have assumed that economic, rather than cultural, issues create the most important divisions in American politics. In addition, scholars have often assumed that modern societies are inevitably secular or, at least, that political elites are immune to religious influences. Other impediments to understanding are more ideological in nature. For example, many academics favor strict separation of church and state and assume that the historic American commitment to that ideal means that religion does not influence legislative decisions, or that if it does, it shouldn't. There are also more practical barriers: most political scientists are unwilling to invest the time and energy required to understand the complex structures of American religion (Leege and Kellstedt 1993, 4–8). Indeed, the few extant analyses of religious influence in Congress use crude measures long abandoned in the study of electoral behavior. Simplistic religious classifications such as "Catholic/Non-Catholic," "Protestant, Catholic, Jew," or "Baptist, Methodist, Catholic" are now avoided in electoral analysis but are still used in legislative studies (see, e.g., Tatalovich and Schier 1993; Page et al. 1984; Rae 1998). Finally, gathering data on members' religion is a difficult, sensitive task that scholars would rather avoid (Benson and Williams 1982, 17–18).

This chapter will demonstrate the value of religious variables in analyzing congressional behavior through an intensive study of the House of Representatives in the 105th Congress (1997–98). In the first section, we examine the religious transformation of the House over the past forty years, along with a more detailed analysis of the 105th Congress. Unlike earlier studies, we aggregate members into meaningful religious traditions, permitting a more accurate assessment of religion's impact on congressional behavior. We also introduce a new "unobtrusive" measure of religious commitment, demonstrating its utility—in combination with religious tradition—as an indicator of religious influence. Next, we look at the political location of different religious groups within the party leadership and committee structures of the House. Finally, we use our measures of religious tradition and commitment in a study of voting behavior, showing how these factors influence legislators' decision making.

The Religious Composition of the U.S. House of Representatives

What changes have taken place in the religious affiliations of House members? Have some traditions gained representation, while others have lost? Have religious groups changed their political alignment or remained in their historic political homes?

In table 10.1 we trace the broad contours of developments in the past half-century.[1] Such historical work has obvious limitations, especially with respect to members in the distant past. Although most representatives have claimed some religious affiliation, it is often difficult to determine that affiliation with specificity. Thus, it is sometimes impossible to discover whether a "Lutheran" in the 1950s belonged to the old mainline Lutheran Church in America, or to the more conservative Lutheran Church–Missouri Synod, or perhaps to some other Lutheran group. Many "Baptists," "Presbyterians," and other religious adherents present similar problems.

Our analysis is based on a careful historical classification of members using categories from our earlier work on electoral and interest-group alignments (Green et al. 1996).[2] The results differ considerably from the typical summaries based purely on entries in the *Congressional Directory, Congressional Quarterly*, or *Almanac of American Politics*, usually drawn from members' responses to questionnaires. Those responses often leave a lot to be desired, both in ambiguous responses such as "Baptist," and also in the large number of vague answers such as "Christian." We have gone beyond these more general labels to employ more precise denominational affiliations that, in turn, permit us to locate members in their proper religious tradition. Table 10.1 presents snapshots of the religious composition of the House of Representatives at twenty-year periods beginning in 1953, collapsing specific denominational affiliations into America's historic religious traditions (see Green et al. 1996). Though these estimates still contain a good amount of "measurement error," given the lack of denominational precision found in these historical sources, we can still learn much about religion in Congress.

Several dramatic trends appear in table 10.1. First, we see significant changes in the overall religious affiliations of House members. Most striking is the declining proportion of Mainline Protestants, who have long dominated America's political elite. Constituting over half the

215

House's membership in 1953–54, Mainline Protestants accounted for only two-fifths forty years later. As mainliners make up only about one-fifth of the electorate, this is still a case of massive overrepresentation. Nevertheless, the much-discussed decline in mainline church membership is reflected here by smaller losses in the House. Evangelical Protestants, about a quarter of the electorate, appear to have lost slightly in House representation, despite their massive political mobilization in the 1980s and 1990s. On the other hand, Catholics have become more numerous in the House, especially if one counts African American and Hispanic Catholics, almost precisely matching their numbers in the electorate (about 25 percent). Jewish numbers also increased over the period, going from slightly more than 2 percent to more than 7 percent of the House. Other smaller traditions, such as Black Protestants, Mormons, and Orthodox, have a greater presence in the contemporary House, but one older minority, Unitarians, has lost numbers. The proportion of members with no religious affiliation seems to have declined, but part of that "drop" is an artifact of data limitations for the Eighty-third Congress (1953–54).

The shifts in partisan religious composition are no less striking. First, note the decline of the Mainline Protestant contingent among Republicans. At midcentury *more than two-thirds* of all House Republicans were mainliners, but this dropped to less than half in 1993. This shift has two sources: the striking movement of evangelical members from the Democratic to the Republican side, and the rapid numerical growth of Republican Catholics. Evangelicals dropped from 21.4 to only 8.7 percent of the Democratic caucus, but rose from 6.9 to 15.3 percent of the GOP by 1993; Catholic Republicans increased from 10.6 to 22.7 percent of the party, if all Catholics are included. In the Democratic caucus, mainliners declined from 42.3 to 36.5 percent over the same period. White Catholics remained steady at about a quarter of the party, but the number of black and Hispanic Catholics added to Catholic ranks. By the 1990s, Catholics of European extraction were equally large elements in each party, although the Democrats almost had a monopoly on minority Catholics. Growing numbers of Jews and Black Protestants, with a scattering of other faiths, filled the remaining Democratic ranks.

The implications for the religious coalition-building in the two parties are evident. By the 1990s, the Republican Party was no longer the "mainline Protestant Church at prayer" but included large contingents of evangelical, mainline, and Catholic Christians, plus a small but solid bloc of Mormons. The Democratic Party, always the electoral home of religious, ethnic, and racial minorities, now exhibited that identity in its congressional corps. Mainline Protestants were still the largest sin-

Table 10.1 Religious Traditions in Congress, 1953–1994 (percentage by Congress)

	All Members			Republican			Democrat		
	1953–54	1973–74	1993–94	1953–54	1973–74	1993–94	1953–54	1973–74	1993–94
Major Traditions									
Evangelical	14.2	13.3	11.4	6.9	11.4	15.3	21.4	14.9	8.7
Mainline	55.5	52.3	41.7	68.8	66.8	49.4	42.3	41.0	36.5
Catholic (white)	18.5	21.9	23.0	10.6	16.1	21.6	26.5	26.5	24.0
Catholic (other)	0.0	2.6	4.1	0.0	0.5	1.1	0.0	2.4	6.1
Jewish	2.3	2.7	7.3	.5	1.0	2.8	4.1	4.0	10.3
Black Protestant	0.5	2.5	6.4	0.0	0.0	0.6	0.9	4.4	10.3
Others									
Unitarian	2.3	1.1	1.1	3.7	0.5	0.6	0.9	2.0	1.5
Mormon	0.7	1.6	2.1	1.4	1.6	4.0	0.0	1.6	0.8
Christian Science	0.7	0.9	0.9	0.5	1.6	2.3	0.9	0.4	0.0
Orthodox	0.0	0.7	0.9	0.0	0.0	2.3	0.0	1.2	0.0
None	5.7	1.1	1.1	7.8	0.5	0.0	3.6	1.6	1.9
Totals[a]	100%	100%	100%	100%	100%	100%	100%	100%	100%

[a]Due to rounding errors, columns do not add up to exactly 100%.

gle Democratic group in 1993, but they constituted just a little more than a third of its membership, with the combined Catholic forces close behind at about 30 percent. Clearly, the old Protestant domination of both parties that persisted well into the 1960s has given way to more religious diversity among both Republicans and Democrats, with mainliners suffering especially severe representational losses.

A Closer Look at Religious Affiliation

Although the religious data in our historical overview are good approximations, we can do a good bit better when it comes to the contemporary Congress. Fortunately, modern computer technologies permit extensive investigation into members' religious activities as chronicled in the *Congressional Record*, the national press, religious publications, local newspapers, and a myriad of other sources, often providing much more detailed information. For example, a local newspaper's report on a legislator's membership in a specific Lutheran church permits us to identify him as an affiliate of the conservative Lutheran Church–Missouri Synod rather than the mainline Evangelical Lutheran Church in America. Or a report on a member's affiliation with the First Christian Church of a specific town prompts a quick trip to denominational websites to confirm that she is an adherent of the mainline Christian Church (Disciples of Christ), rather than the evangelical Christian Churches and Churches of Christ. And sometimes a member who is listed only as "Protestant" can be placed in the proper religious tradition by virtue of his or her local church affiliation, assuming there is one.

These more precise findings for the 105th Congress are reported in table 10.2. Generally, the House's religious composition in 1997 reveals the same patterns and trends that we saw in the historical data. The mainline numbers show evidence of further erosion in the late 1990s. Just over 30 percent of House members fell into this category—though it rises to 36 percent if we include those who called themselves "Protestant," but for whom we could find no evidence of specific religious affiliation or behavior. Evangelicals achieved an all-time high proportion of 16.7 percent of the membership, finally reflecting their grassroots political mobilization of the 1980s and 1990s. (It should be noted that many mainline members are distinctly "evangelical" in conviction and behavior, and in some cases identify with that movement; Frank Wolf of Virginia, Sue Myrick of North Carolina, and Tony Hall of Ohio are just three prominent examples.) All Roman Catholics together make up almost 30 percent of the House, with minority Catholics (primarily Hispanics) a small proportion of that total. A wide variety of smaller religious groups fills out the picture: Jews and Black Protestants are the largest, each with about 6 percent, while Mormons, Christian Science, Eastern Orthodox, and Unitarians have even smaller representation. Six members (1.4%) list "none" as their affiliation.

Members of the various religious traditions are not distributed randomly by party. Evangelicals are mostly Republican and now constitute more than a quarter of the GOP conference, but amount to only a minuscule part of the Democratic caucus. Mainline Protestants are also predominantly Republican, making up more than one-third of the GOP (40 percent if "Protestants" are counted); their Democratic counterparts constitute a quarter of that party. Both House parties have substantial white Catholic groups: more than one in five Republicans and almost

Table 10.2 Religious Tradition by Party Affiliation, 105th Congress

Religious Tradition	Total (%)	GOP (%)	Dem. (%)
Evangelical	16.7 (74)	27.3 (63)	5.2 (11)
Mainline	31.0 (137)	35.5 (82)	26.1 (55)
"Protestant"	4.5 (20)	5.2 (12)	3.8 (8)
Catholic	25.1 (111)	22.1 (51)	28.4 (60)
Minority Catholic	4.1 (18)	0.9 (2)	7.6 (16)
Jewish	5.7 (25)	1.3 (3)	10.4 (22)
Black Protestant	6.8 (30)		14.2 (30)
Mormon	2.5 (11)	4.3 (10)	0.5 (1)
Christian Science	1.1 (5)	2.2 (5)	
Orthodox	0.7 (3)	0.9 (2)	0.5 (1)
Unitarian	0.5 (2)	0.4 (1)	0.5 (1)
Secular	1.4 (6)		2.8 (6)
Totals[a]	100% (442)	100% (231)	100% (211)

[a]Due to rounding errors, columns do not add up to exactly 100%.

three in ten Democrats. The Hispanic Catholics bolster the Democratic Catholic forces, while the GOP contains only two Hispanic Catholics, both Cuban Americans. Black Protestant representatives are all Democratic (Republican J. C. Watts of Oklahoma is a *Southern* Baptist and therefore is included within the Evangelical Protestant ranks).[3] Members of the Church of Jesus Christ of Latter-day Saints (Mormons) are all Republican, but one Reorganized Latter Day Saint (Leonard Boswell of Iowa) is a Democrat. The religious "nones" are all Democrats. Clearly, each religious tradition has a partisan bent, revealed in the location of its "representatives" in the U.S. House.

The Religious Commitment of Congressmen

In addition to locating members in the correct religious tradition, we also wanted to provide some gauge of their religious commitment, although that is no simple task. Indeed, only one previous study has attempted such a project. Benson and Williams (1982) argued on the basis of interviews that our national legislators were quite religious, even more than the American public, one of the most observant in any developed nation. There is some room for skepticism on this count. In the twenty years since their study, legislators may have succumbed to secularizing influences in the general culture. Even so, Cal Thomas's statement at the beginning of the chapter suggests there are still electoral incentives for members to emphasize publicly whatever religious attachments they may have, given a continuing "positivity bias" toward religion among most Americans. In any case, informal interviews with current or recent House members suggest that religious commitment on the Hill is still fairly high.

Our preliminary reconnaissance of religious commitment involves intensive use of "unobtrusive" measures. Rather than attempting to interview all members or to persuade them to fill out questionnaires about their religious practice, we have relied on the new resources afforded by the Internet to do a thorough inventory of members' religious affiliations and behavior.[4] While we eventually hope to make finer distinctions in the level and type of members' religious commitment, here we limit ourselves to a crude dichotomous judgment about religious involvement. We have adopted a rather generous standard: any substantial religious activity—regular church attendance, private devotional activity, or leadership role in religious institutions—qualifies a member as "active." Conversely, the absence of such evidence puts the member in the "not active" category.

According to the data we collected, about 60 percent of House members have an active religious commitment. As Benson and Williams (1982) suggested, this seems somewhat higher than one finds in the American public. For example, about 40 to 45 percent of Americans report to Gallup that they attend religious services every week, but that figure is probably inflated (Hadaway, Marler, and Chaves 1993). As our measure generally incorporates visible and substantial types of involvement beyond even regular attendance, we are confident in our conclusion that these political elites are more active religiously than the public. This should not be surprising; after all, legislators are by definition organizational animals and likely to be involved in all sorts of community activities, including churches. Indeed, among Black Protestants and, increasingly, evangelicals, one reads repeated stories of candidate recruitment through church channels.

Although we cannot present all the data here, they reveal that the entire Mormon contingent is religiously active, and that evangelicals are the most active of the large religious groups, with 86 percent exhibiting strong religious involvement. Black Protestants follow at 73 percent. Almost two-thirds of the Mainline Protestants are religiously active, followed closely by white Catholics at 60 percent. Minority Catholics and Jewish members exhibit fairly low levels of religious commitment, as do Christian Scientists. "Protestants" and, naturally, "secular" members almost universally fall in the "not active" category (for these data, see Guth and Kellstedt 1999).

At this point we should note the limitations of religious activity as a measure of commitment. As many scholars have observed, involvement may tap the *degree* of religious commitment, but not the *kind*. While doing this research, we have been reminded once again of the differing content of commitment, especially among Mainline Protestants and Catholics. For most evangelicals and many Mainline Protestants, high activity is associated with a traditional theological perspective, drawing on what we have referred to elsewhere as an *individualistic social theology*, emphasizing an individual's relationship with God and personal responsibility for proper moral behavior. Indeed, this perspective may be defined as the historic Protestant social theology. For some Protestants, however, activism is coupled with a *communitarian social theology*, in which the fundamental religious problem is the alienation of human beings from their fellows and the ultimate solution is reconciliation, often fostered by governmental activism. While such interpretations are more common among mainline religious leaders than among the laity, they are not hard to find among mainline legislators, especially on the Democratic side of the aisle (Guth et al. 1997; cf. Benson and Williams 1982).

This conflict of social theologies is especially evident among Catholics. Most of the active Catholics on the GOP side identify with an orthodox Catholic faith, linked to a strong traditional moral code. Among Democrats, in contrast, the active Catholics are often part of the "peace and justice" wing of the church, with roots in the labor movement of the 1930s and branches in the liberation theology of the 1970s. In any event, in the future we hope to assign Catholics and Protestants to a more sophisticated set of commitment categories, based on both the extent and kind of involvement. Nevertheless, here we will use the simple religious-commitment measure as an explanatory variable in our analysis of congressional voting.

Religion and the Distribution of Power in the House

Of course, neither the size of religious contingents nor the extent of members' religious commitment tells the full story of the changing role of religion in the House. For example, the distribution of religious traditions in the House may be becoming more representative of the American public, but the distribution of power within the institution may still not reflect that diversity. Or, most members may be active religionists, but the less religious may dominate leadership roles. How is power distributed within the formal structure of the House? As a preliminary assessment, we first look at party leadership positions and then consider the location of different religious groups within the congressional committee structure, two important sources of formal power.

Although evangelicals have long been underrepresented in the House, in the 105th (and 106th) Congress they certainly dominated the House majority leadership. Republican Speaker Newt Gingrich (Southern Baptist), Majority Leader Dick Armey (a born-again Presbyterian who attends a nondenominational evangelical church), and Majority Whip Tom DeLay (Southern Baptist) were all from the evangelical tradition, as was Chief Deputy Whip Dennis Hastert, a graduate of Wheaton College. The Republican Conference chair and vice chair, John Boehner of Ohio and Susan Molinari of New York, were both Catholics, but only the conference secretary, Jennifer Dunn of Washington, was a Mainline Protestant. Indeed, the historically dominant mainliners had "proportional" representation only among the sixteen deputy whips. On the House Republican Steering Committee, which assigns GOP members to House committees, the situation was slightly different: evangelicals, mainliners, and Catholics were all slightly overrepresented, with Republican Mormons, Jews, and seculars shut out. The larger Republican Policy Committee exhibited yet a different pattern, dominated by evangelical, mainline, and Catholic members—but primarily those with high levels of religious commitment. Less-active members from all traditions and most religious "minorities" were underrepresented. On the whole, party leadership posts among Republicans went disproportionately to evangelicals and to those with strong religious commitments.

Among the Democrats, party leadership positions were more widely distributed. Minority Leader Dick Gephardt (Baptist) came from the evangelical tradition, while Minority Whip David Bonior was a Catholic who once considered entering the priesthood. Vic Fazio, the caucus chair and a mainliner (Episcopalian), made national headlines in 1994 for his vigorous attacks on the Christian Right. Finally, the caucus vice chair, Barbara Kennelly of Connecticut, was also a Catholic. The Democrats' four chief deputy whips included an evangelical, a Catholic, a Black Protestant, and a Hispanic Catholic. Of the twelve regional whips, however, seven were Catholics. If one combines all these positions into a collective "party leadership," the distribution of religious groups is almost exactly that of their contribution to the House Democratic membership. On the other hand, the important Democratic Steering Committee, which makes committee assignments, has proportionately more Catholics than the House Democratic delegation, and proportionately fewer Black Protestants and secular members. Nevertheless, committee posts in the Democratic Party tend to reflect the same "proportionality" that Democrats require of their National Convention delegates on other grounds.

A glance at the distribution of religious groups in House committees provides some different insights into the "power locations" of each religious tradition. Here we follow Deering and Smith's (1997) classification of House committees as "prestige," "policy," and "constituency." On "prestige" committees such as Appropriations, Ways and Means, and Budget and Rules, religious groups are proportionately represented, with only a slight advantage to mainliners. But some groups do better than others on particular panels: evangelicals are overrepresented on Appropriations, mainliners dominate Budget and Rules, while Catholics are slightly overrepresented on Ways and Means. On policy committees, the situation is somewhat different, with evangelicals, mainliners, and Catholics all slightly underrepresented, while Jews and Black Protestants are slightly overrepresented. Jews tend to concentrate on International Relations and Judiciary, and Black Protestants are numerous on Education and Judiciary. Catholics are heavily represented on the Banking and Commerce committees. Finally, evangelicals are slightly more numerous on "constituency committees," especially Small Business and Agriculture, while mainliners are overrepresented on Agriculture, and Catholics are proportionately more numerous on the National Security and Resources panels.

There are some interesting differences, however, in committee assignments by party. On policy committees, the GOP tends to assign evangelicals, mainliners, and Catholics with strong religious commitments, while the Democrats follow the opposite pattern, appointing *less*-active members from these same traditions, plus a disproportionate number of religious minorities. This pattern no doubt contributes to the oft-noted ideological polarization within committees such as Judiciary and

Education. On constituency committees the result is different: the Republicans still give proportionately more assignments to the religiously active members, but so do the Democrats. These committee patterns no doubt reflect many factors—members' interests and constituency concerns, leadership preferences, and available slots—but these religious differences across committees may nevertheless have important implications for the way such committees work.

Religion and Voting in the House of Representatives

Many political scientists are likely to play along with us this far, agreeing that our religious portrait of the contemporary House has some intrinsic value. But at this point they are likely to echo Tom Mann's assertion at the beginning, "Yes, but religion just doesn't make any difference where it counts: when members put their voting card in the machine!" Here we demonstrate that this conclusion is incorrect. Not only is there a strong bivariate relationship between religious variables and voting on a wide range of issues, but these relationships often survive the most stringent multivariate tests, incorporating the most powerful factors normally used in congressional voting studies.

Table 10.3 reports the relationship between religious traits and five summary voting scales. We have calculated the percentage of "liberal" votes cast by members in each religious category, using *National Journal* scales for social, economic, and foreign policy issues. In addition, we report *Congressional Quarterly* "Clinton support" scores (how often the member supported the administration's announced position) and the quarterly's "party unity" scores (how often members voted with a majority of their party when opposed by a majority of the other party). The top of the table shows that religiously active members as a whole are considerably less liberal than their inactive counterparts on the first four scores, with the "gap" being approximately fifteen percentage points for each of the four scores. Note also that religious commitment makes a difference not only on social issues, where it "should," but on economic and foreign policy as well. The religiously committed, however, are not uniformly more loyal to their party—or more prone to defect—than the uncommitted. As we shall see later, however, these global scores hide considerable divergence between parties.

As table 10.3 also shows, Mormons are clearly the leaders in religiously based conservatism in Congress, usually voting on the liberal side less than one-fifth of the time. Evangelicals are not far behind, however, voting with the liberals on only about one vote in four on policy issues, and

Table 10.3 Voting Behavior of House Members by Religious Tradition and Activism, 105th Congress

Religious Tradition and Activism	Social Issues (%)	Economic Issues (%)	Foreign Policy (%)	Clinton Support (%)	Party Unity (%)
All Members	47	47	48	51	88
Not active	57	56	57	59	86
Active	41	41	42	45	87
Mormons	19	19	11	28	92
Evangelical	23	25	24	31	90
Not active	39	41	45	45	81
Active	19	22	21	28	91
Christian Science	33	23	34	34	85
Orthodox	40	44	32	42	91
Mainline	45	42	45	47	86
Not active	52	49	52	52	84
Active	40	38	41	44	88
"Protestants"	48	47	46	48	85
Catholic	49	53	53	53	85
Not active	53	55	55	56	85
Active	47	52	52	52	85
Minority Catholic	74	72	74	75	91
Jewish	77	75	72	76	89
Unitarians	79	69	68	70	81
Black Protestant	82	77	84	80	93
Secular	87	82	84	82	95

Note: The first three columns show the percentage of times members of the category voted in a "liberal" fashion, based on the *National Journal's* selection of floor votes cast on social, economic, and foreign policy issues in the 105th Congress. The fourth and fifth columns (based on issues selected by the *Congressional Quarterly*) show the percentage of times members of the category supported President Clinton's position and their party's majority position.

supporting Bill Clinton less than one-third of the time. Among evangelicals there is also a considerable gap between the inactive and the active, the latter being much more conservative across the board—and more loyal to their party. Mainline Protestants as a group are markedly more liberal than evangelicals, falling just short of the mean scores for the whole

House, but once again the religiously committed are more conservative than their inactive counterparts. The nominal "Protestants" look much like the inactive mainliners, with whom they might easily be combined. Catholics of European descent are more liberal than Mainline Protestants across the board, but once again active Catholics are consistently more conservative than their inactive counterparts, if only by small margins. Among Black Protestant and Jewish members of Congress, uniformly liberal religious involvement has little impact on voting (data not shown).

This preliminary assessment certainly makes a strong case for the influence of both religious affiliation and religious commitment on voting behavior. Nevertheless, these patterns might result from spurious correlations among religion, voting, and other factors. To submit our conjectures to a more rigorous test, we incorporated our religious variables in a series of multivariate analyses, using each of the voting scores in turn as the dependent variable. In addition to including the religious variables as independent predictors, we added other variables typically used in congressional voting analysis. First, we incorporated the member's party affiliation and used the proportion of the vote received by Bill Clinton in 1996 in his or her district to measure *district* partisanship and ideology. We also entered other personal traits of the member, including gender, age, and minority ethnic status (black and Hispanic).

To control for the effects of the district's cultural and religious characteristics, we also included estimates for the evangelical, mainline, Catholic, and Mormon population derived from the Glenmary Research Center data (Bradley et al. 1992). Not surprisingly, House members naturally tend to come from constituencies with large numbers of co-religionists, with the correlations between member affiliation and corresponding district religious membership being quite substantial for Mormons ($r = .54$), Catholics ($r = .35$), evangelicals ($r = .33$), and Jews ($r = .30$). Ironically, the correlation between mainline representation and district population is stronger for evangelical ($r = .20$) than for mainline church membership ($r = .10$), suggesting that the large mainline presence in the House has benefited from the tendency of evangelical voters to support mainline candidates.

In any case, these data hint that the voting habits of members may derive not from their personal religious attributes but from their "embodiment" or "transmission" of the religious traits of their constituency. Although many so-called regional voting tendencies are likely to result from different geographical distributions of various religious and ethnic groups, we also incorporated regional variables to control for any remaining geographical traits. Finally, we included the black and Hispanic population of each district, as these variables have often been shown to be important sources of voting behavior in the House. In addition, these census estimates are probably better proxies for Black Protestant and Hispanic Catholic populations than figures produced by the Glenmary studies—as the latter figures are based primarily on official denominational estimates, which are notoriously inadequate for minority churches.

What do we find? Not surprisingly, party affiliation is the most powerful influence on voting on all four substantive scales, with Democratic identity predicting liberal votes (for full tabular presentation of these data, see Guth and Kellstedt 1999). Not surprisingly, members from constituencies showing strong Clinton support in 1996 were more likely to cast liberal votes and to support the president's program. Democratic Party unity is strongly influenced by the strength of the Clinton vote, but a stronger Clinton vote in 1996 in Republican-held districts is associated with partisan defections among GOP members. Other constituency characteristics also help explain members' votes: legislators with large evangelical constituencies are consistently more conservative, are more loyal to their party (if Republican) or less loyal (if Democrats). Large mainline and Catholic populations, however, do not seem to produce distinctive member behavior, although large mainline constituencies seem to push Republicans toward higher levels of party voting, and large Catholic populations make for somewhat more liberal stances on economic issues. Thus, with the critical exception of evangelical population, the religious composition of the constituency adds relatively little to our ability to explain members' votes, once the member's own religious traits and other variables are in the equation. In addition, legislators' demographic traits are seldom much help: women tend to be slightly more liberal and loyal Democratic voters (and less loyal if Republican). Age, on the other hand, occasionally produces slight conservative tendencies.

Even after all these constituency and personal traits are incorporated into the regression, we find that religion continues to matter. Evangelical legislators are consistently more conservative than their political, demographic, regional, and district characteristics would predict. They are also more loyal in the GOP. Catholic commitment shows the same tendency, especially on social issues, but at lower levels than for evangelicals. Finally, mainline commitment is associated with slightly more conservative voting, but none of the coefficients approaches statistical significance, although active mainliners (like their evangelical and Catholic counterparts) are more loyal to the GOP. In the final analysis, we explain 80 percent or more of the variance in congressional liberalism on the four policy scores, and between two-fifths and almost half the variance in party unity.

We should stress that this operation clearly *understates* the total impact of religion on voting. A district's religious composition and the member's own religious traits are powerful factors determining whether members are Republican or Democratic to begin with. Indeed, using only the member's religious profile and that of the district, a discriminant analysis puts 76 percent of members in the correct party, including 81 percent of the Republicans and 70 percent of the Democrats. The point of the present exercise is merely to demonstrate that religious influences meet the strongest test, retaining *direct* influence even when their indirect impact is accounted for by other variables also directly influenced by religion. Thus the total direct and indirect effects of religion are substantial.

Religion and Factional Alignments in the 105th House

A final way to look at the impact of religion on Congress comes from considering the factional location of various religious groups. We produced an estimate of factional alignments in each party by using the SPSS (Statistical Package for the Social Sciences) Quick Cluster routine on the *National Journal* and *Congressional Quarterly* scores used above, specifying a tri-factional composition for each party, based on journalistic accounts of within-party struggles. We designate the three House GOP factions as *Moderates* (16.0 percent of the party), *Traditional Conservatives* (38.3 percent), and *Christian Right* (45.5 percent). Similarly, three factions constitute the House Democratic caucus: *Moderates* (17.5 percent), *Traditional Liberals* (37.4 percent), and *New Politics Liberals* (45.0 percent). That the two largest factions sit at the extremes of the ideological continuum is perhaps statistical confirmation of the celebrated polarization of the contemporary House of Representatives.

To illustrate the factional distribution of religious groups, we have combined the two party distributions into a single continuum, running from the New Politics Liberals (appropriately on the left) to the Christian Right (on the right). As table 10.4 demonstrates, religious groups have dramatically different partisan locations. Mormons are solidly in the Christian Right faction, with only one Traditional Conservative and one Democratic Moderate, Reorganized Latter Day Saint Leonard Boswell (D, Iowa). Active evangelicals are concentrated in the Christian Right faction, but more than half the inactive evangelicals have found their way into other groups, such as the Traditional Conservatives and Democratic Moderates. A very solid majority of active mainliners resides in the Christian Right and Traditional Conservative factions, but the remainder is spread across the continuum, including even a few in the New Politics contingent. Among inactive mainliners, the entire distribution shifts "left" a cell or two, with the largest bloc voting as Tradi-

228

Table 10.4 Religious Variables and Factional Alignments

Religious Tradition and Activity	Democratic Factions			Republican Factions		
	New Politics Liberals	Traditional Liberals	Democratic Moderates	Republican Moderates	Traditional Conservatives	Christian Right
Percent of House	21.5	17.9	8.4	8.4	20.1	23.8
Mormons			9.1		9.1	81.8
Evangelical Actives		6.5	4.8	1.6	21.0	66.1
Evangelical Inactives		16.7	25.0		16.7	41.7
Mainline Actives	9.2	14.9	14.9	4.5	26.9	31.3
Mainline Inactives	16.0	16.4	10.4	13.4	31.3	11.9
Christian Science				40.0	20.0	40.0
Orthodox		33.3			33.3	33.3
Catholic Actives	19.4	23.9	10.4	10.4	19.4	16.4
Catholic Inactives	25.0	22.7	6.8	11.4	22.7	11.4
Minority Catholics	50.0	38.9		5.6	5.6	
Unitarian	50.0			50.0		
Seculars/Nominal	42.3	7.7	3.8	15.4	23.1	7.7
Jewish	52.0	32.0	4.0	12.0		
Black Protestants	70.0	26.7	3.3			

Note: Percentages are based on row totals. Due to rounding errors, percentages do not always add up to exactly 100%.

tional Conservatives, but with more legislators in each of the two most liberal Democratic factions than in the Christian Right. The five Christian Science adherents distribute themselves across the GOP factional alignment, while two of the three Orthodox members also locate themselves in the two most conservative Republican factions.

Active Catholics are close to a microcosm of the entire House in factional distribution, with similar numbers in New Politics and Christian

Right factions, a close balance among the Traditional Liberals and Traditional Conservatives, and identical numbers of Democratic and Republican Moderates. Among inactive Catholics, once again the distribution shifts to the left, with half in the two most liberal Democratic factions. The overwhelming majority of minority Catholics are either in the New Politics or Traditional Liberal factions, a location also favored by secular/nominal, Jewish, and Black Protestant legislators. Looking at the situation from the other direction (data not shown), each faction has a distinctive religious composition. The Christian Right's membership comes primarily from active evangelicals (41 percent), active mainliners (20 percent), and active Catholics (15 percent), with support from almost all the Mormons. The New Liberal faction, on the other side, consists primarily of Black Protestants (22 percent), Jews (14 percent), active Catholics (14 percent), inactive Catholics (12 percent), secular members (12 percent), and minority Catholics (10 percent). The Traditional Liberals and Conservatives draw somewhat more broadly from their own party's religious constituencies, while Moderates from both parties tend to be drawn from religious constituencies more numerous in the *other* party. Thus, it is clear that both religious tradition—as measured by religious affiliation—and religious commitment are fundamental forces structuring the factional alignments within each party, and hence, within Congress.

Conclusion

Despite its exploratory nature, this research has demonstrated the potential value of studying the religious composition of Congress. Our data on the House of Representatives present a *prima facie* case for the explanatory power of religious variables. We have shown that the House has undergone a dramatic religious restructuring over the past two decades, in which its religious composition has approached more closely the religious distribution of the nation, as Catholics, Black Protestants, Mormons, and perhaps evangelicals have approached something like proportional representation. Mainline Protestants still retain a disproportionate number of seats, but that "overrepresentation" has faded rapidly in recent years. Jewish voters are also overrepresented, but Jewish legislators remain a relatively small contingent in the House (unlike the Senate, where they constitute 10 percent of the membership).

We find that both old and new alignments structure the congressional party system. Evangelical Protestants have made a dramatic move from the Democratic to the Republican side of the aisle, while Catholics have infiltrated the GOP in large numbers. At the same time, the most religiously committed members in the evangelical, mainline, and Catholic traditions have shifted toward the Republican side, both reflecting and shaping trends in electoral choice by their "parent" groups in the mass public. During a time when voters, religious activists, and political party elites have been realigned by new religious divisions, it would indeed be surprising if the same forces failed to influence the "people's House," even if that impact has been somewhat delayed by the effects of incumbency and other forces of institutional inertia.

Much of the influence of religion on the contemporary House is obviously channeled indirectly through changes in the religious composition of the two parties. Nevertheless, we have demonstrated that even when party membership, a district's religious characteristics, and a wide variety of other variables are controlled, members' religious affiliation and commitment still have a direct impact on their voting behavior. Religiously active evangelicals, mainliners, and Catholics are, on balance, more conservative on a wide range of issues than their inactive co-religionists and other religious groups. Mormons also provide the example of a distinct minority religious group strongly committed to the GOP and conservative issues, while most religious minorities and secular legislators are firmly attached to the Democrats. Thus, partisan divisions in contemporary American politics are firmly rooted in religious soil.

References

Benson, Peter L., and Dorothy L. Williams. 1982. *Religion on Capitol Hill: Myths and Realities*. San Francisco: Harper & Row.

Bradley, Martin B., et al. 1992. *Churches and Church Membership in the United States, 1990*. Atlanta: Glenmary Research Center.

Deering, Christopher J., and Steven S. Smith. 1997. *Committees in Congress*. Washington, D.C.: Congressional Quarterly Press.

Duke, James T., and Barry L. Johnson. 1992. "Religious Affiliation and Congressional Representation." *Journal for the Scientific Study of Religion* 31:324–29.

Grant, J. Tobin, Lyman A. Kellstedt, and Thomas J. Rudolph. 1995. "The Changing Religious Composition of the U.S. Congress." Paper presented at the annual meeting of the Society for the Scientific Study of Religion, St. Louis, Mo.

Green, John C., et al. 1996. *Religion and the Culture Wars: Dispatches from the Front*. Lanham, Md.: Rowman and Littlefield.

Guth, James L., and Lyman Kellstedt. 1999. "Religion on Capital Hill: The Case of the House of Representative in the 105th Congress." Paper presented at the annual meeting of the Society for the Scientific Study of Religion, Boston, Mass.

Guth, James L., et al. 1997. *The Bully Pulpit: The Politics of Protestant Clergy*. Lawrence: University Press of Kansas.

Hadaway, C. Kirk, Penny Long Marler, and Mark Chaves. 1993. "What the Polls Don't Show: A Closer Look at U.S. Church Attendance." *American Sociological Review* 58:741–52.

Leege, David, and Lyman A. Kellstedt. 1993. *Rediscovering the Religious Factor in American Politics*. Armonk, N.Y.: M. E. Sharpe.

Page, Benjamin I., et al. 1984. "Constituency, Party, and Representation in Congress. *Public Opinion Quarterly* 48:741–56.

Rae, Nicol C. 1998. *Conservative Reformers: The Republican Freshmen and the Lessons of the 104th Congress*. Armonk, N.Y.: M. E. Sharpe.

Tatalovich, Raymond, and David Schier. 1993. "The Persistence of Ideological Cleavage in Voting on Abortion Legislation in the House of Representatives, 1973–1988." *American Politics Quarterly* 21:125–39.

Teaching Tools

Discussion Questions

1. The religious composition of the Republican and Democratic parties in the House of Representatives is obviously quite different. Using the materials in chapters 5, 7, and 8, explain these differences. In other words, how do the distinctive political attitudes, electoral behavior, and partisan alignments of American religious traditions affect the House?

2. Do the voting patterns of various religious groups in Congress reflect the historic positions of their faith traditions as described in chapter 1? Or do they follow the stances of the major religious lobbying organizations described in chapter 6? Why or why not?

3. Although there is a clear empirical relationship between religious identity and voting, not all scholars and citizens think there *should* be such a relationship. What do you think? Is it appropriate for legislators to allow their religious beliefs to influence their decision making? Why or why not?

4. As the data in this chapter show, a member's religion seems to have somewhat greater impact on voting on social and moral issues, such as abortion, gay rights, or school prayer, as opposed to economic or foreign policy issues. Why? Is religious faith more closely tied to certain political values than to others?

5. As we have seen, the religious identity of a legislator also seems to influence other aspects of the legislative process. For example, different religious groups seem to gravitate toward different congressional committees. Why? Do those choices reflect religious values or other traits of the legislators? Why do Jewish members

of the House, for instance, seem more interested in the Judiciary and International Relations committees than other House panels? Why do evangelicals seek membership on Agriculture and Small Business?

6. Chapters 9 and 11 argue that religious values influence federal executive and judicial officials as well as members of Congress. In which branch of the federal government are the religious values of officeholders most likely to be reflected in their official decisions? Least likely? Why?

Topics for Further Research

1. As every student of politics knows, the Senate and the House are very different institutions. Using standard sources such as the *Almanac of American Politics* and Congressional Quarterly's *Congress and Its Members*, find the religious affiliations of senators and calculate the proportion who fall into each of the major religious traditions. How does the Senate differ from the House? Why do you think they differ?

2. Using the Internet resources described in this chapter, do a thorough search for information on your representative and senators. On the basis of your findings, write a "religious profile" of each, describing their religious affiliations, activities, and beliefs. Also speculate on how those religious traits have influenced their behavior as legislators (or not influenced that behavior). How much are you able to discover by means of such "nonobtrusive" measures? What questions would you like to ask them if you had the opportunity for an interview on these issues?

11

Religion and the Judiciary

FRANK GULIUZZA

It has been said that in America nearly every political issue becomes at some time or another a judicial question. Therefore, as students of American politics, it is essential that we study the complex array of federal, state, and local courts that make up America's multifaceted, multitiered judicial system.

Most introductory textbooks in American government include a chapter on the American judiciary. Such chapters usually cover a wide range of topics. For instance, there is likely to be discussion of the constitutional origin and subsequent development of federal courts, as well as explanation of the structure of America's federal courts and, perhaps, how national courts differ from state courts. In addition, there is certain to be some introduction to the U.S. Supreme Court and the power of the Supreme Court—most particularly its authority to evaluate the constitutionality of statutes, administrative edicts, executive proclamations, and state laws.

The purpose of this chapter, however, is not to provide a standard overview of the American judiciary. Rather, it is to address a few of the ways that religion affects the American legal system and, alternatively, how the legal system might affect people of faith. Three different topics

234

will be addressed. First, the chapter examines how religion helped shape the pillars on which our legal system rests. Specifically, it examines briefly the linkages between religion and code or statutory law, as well as the linkage between religion and common law or judge-made law.

Second, the chapter discusses the relationship between religion and the judicial process. Increasingly, religious actors *outside* the judiciary have had an impact on the judicial process. Just as these religious individuals and interest groups are active in electoral and legislative politics, they have also become increasingly active in the judicial process (e.g., the selection of judges, submitting *amicus curiae* briefs, filing lawsuits). In addition to the influence of religious actors from outside the process, religion plays an important role *within* the process. For instance, several of the past justices on the Supreme Court have been very open about their faith. Religion also intersects with judicial politics when a particular seat on the court becomes known as the "Catholic" seat or the "Jewish" seat. Furthermore, there is evidence, both historical and contemporary, that the religious perspectives of judges affect their voting behavior while on the bench.

Third, this chapter examines the impact of judicial politics on religion. How has public policy, initiated by the Supreme Court, affected religion? I suggest that judicial decisions—for example, the court's holdings on abortion, welfare, education, gay rights, pornography and obscenity—have had a rather dramatic and *direct* effect on religion as well as an indirect effect on the religious actors.

Code or Common Law? The Impact of Religion on the American Experience

I recently read John Grisham's book *The Testament*, in which he describes the efforts of an American attorney to find a Christian missionary working with a tribe of Indians deep in the rivers and forests of Brazil. When the attorney finds the tribe, he marvels at a people whose existence in the late 1990s is much as it might have been more than a thousand years ago. Even though the tribe is very small and unsophisticated, the attorney discovers that a primitive legal structure is in place. Moreover, the structure is built on the tribe's dominant religion—expressed chiefly through its witch doctor. The attorney later learns that, when the missionary arrived in the forest and began to spread the Christian gospel, she not only made a substantial impact on the spiritual climate of the tribe, but her work also initiated a ripple effect throughout the tribe's political and legal structure. I share this Grisham story to illustrate the oft-advanced contention that religious influences not only gen-erally predate the emergence of secular law, but that such religious influ-ences continue to have an impact on legal systems today, whether in small tribal communities or in very complex societies (Van Dervort 1994, 8).

Historically, the influence of religion in society was often so perva-sive that many governments were, in fact, theocracies. In a theocracy, the claim is that all power and authority emanates from a supernatural being. While contemporary Western societies are no longer theocratic states, this does not mean that religion has lost its influence on con-temporary legal systems. It simply means that religious influences are mixed with secular principles. For instance, while there is a formal dis-establishment of religion in U.S. government, the Judeo-Christian ethic still remains evident (Way 1981; Wald 1997; Berman 1986).

Throughout the Western world, nations generally have one of two types of legal systems: one built on "civil," or "code," law or one resting on "common" law. Most of the nations in Europe operate under a civil law system. A civil law nation relies almost exclusively on an exhaustive code prepared by its legislature. On the other hand, Great Britain and many of the former British colonies are predominately common law societies. Law in such societies is often called "judge-made law." Com-mon law countries may have codes crafted by their respective legisla-tures. But common law systems assume that, when people bring cases to court, their problems may not directly reflect the language of the code. In such ambiguous instances, judges are expected to find, and articu-late, a solution. The judge can look to the statutes of law for help, but ultimately the judge has to make a decision. This decision is not only binding on the parties in that particular case, but, even more important, when a judge renders a decision in a common law system, the ruling is published and serves as an important precedent (Tarr 1994, 6).

Although the United States is very much a common law country, reflecting our British roots, the extent to which we are governed by statu-tory and administrative law suggests that we are not unfamiliar with code law systems (Abadinsky 1991, 4). In fact, at the time of the Amer-ican Revolution, it looked as though the new nation might abandon its common law history in favor of the kind of codes that predominated in continental Europe. Why? For one reason, common law is based in no small part on tradition and custom, and America had not had the time to develop the customs necessary to give impetus to a sweeping com-mon law system like that which had matured in England. Furthermore, many Americans reacted against the common law system from their desire at the time to distance themselves from anything British. Had William Blackstone not published his extensive commentary on the British common law, thereby making the common law much more immediately accessible to the fledgling nation, America might have become a civil law society (Post 1963, 64–68).

Nevertheless, although America has a common law system, it has embraced elements of civil or code law. Code law was heavily influenced by religion; the earliest codes in the Western world were all administered by the religious leaders of their respective nations. For example, the Babylonian code of King Hammurabi, the earliest known code, was enforced by priests. So too was the Egyptian code (Abadinsky 1991, 4; Calvi and Coleman 1989, 19–20).[1] And Hebrew law was predicated on the premise that all law was divine in origin.

The most important of the historical legal codes was constructed within the Roman Empire. Over time, Roman law became sophisticated and extensive. And because of the Roman Empire's military success and longevity, Roman law came to dominate in the Western world. After the fall of its western empire, the emperor Justinian was determined to reestablish the grandeur of the Roman law. He put together a team of legal scholars to collect all the laws within the empire and to systematize them into code. In 533, Justinian's code, or *Corpus Juris Civilis*, was published. While Justinian's code lay dormant throughout much of the Middle Ages, it later became the skeleton for contemporary civil law systems (Calvi and Coleman 1989, 21–22). Moreover, even though the Roman codes were decidedly secular, much of the *canon law* of the Catholic church reflects Justinian's codes. Thus, Roman law influenced the Catholic church, which, in turn, had a substantial impact on both civil and common law systems (Abadinsky 1991, 15).

The legal system that developed in Great Britain was quite different from that of nations that had been under the more direct, physical control of the Roman Empire. The British did not build their law on some version of Justinian's code. Historically, the system of justice on the British Isles was administered locally by sheriffs and courts enforcing local customs. After the Norman Conquest in 1066, kings began to bring these local customs into a single body of general laws, and king's courts emerged to enforce the general laws. Judges in these courts gradually grew to rely on previous judgments, giving rise to the doctrine of *stare decisis* (Van Dervort 1994, 14–16; Calvi and Coleman 1989, 22–25).

How was common law influenced by religion? First, it was directly inspired by the Catholic church. While the king's courts were in force to administer justice in Great Britain, ecclesiastical courts existed as a separate, but substantial—and far from mutually exclusive—source of law. The king's courts heard civil disputes, enforced the king's ever burgeoning criminal law, and helped collect taxes. However, ecclesiastical courts had authority over many important aspects of day-to-day life, including marriage and property. These ecclesiastical courts relied on and enforced canon law, again highlighting the importance of code law—at least indirectly—within common law England. Even after King Henry VIII pulled England from the Catholic church, ecclesiastical courts continued to establish public law until well into the nineteenth century (Post 1963, 35–38).

Second, and more important, common law is based in no small part on the customs and general principles of the nation. Whether Catholic or Protestant, England was a Christian nation. Its customs and practices were often based on the teachings of the Bible or the directives of the church. Hence, its laws reflected the nation's commitment to Christianity (Abadinsky 1991, 40).[2]

When America established its independence, it borrowed heavily from the British legal system. While there was some concern about the adoption of common law, it became the cornerstone of American law. And, even though America formally shunned establishment of a national religion (therefore the absence of ecclesiastical courts), its common law reflects the customs and practices of a people who had generally embraced Protestant Christianity (Levy 1986, 38). Moreover, from the outset, America recognized the importance of equity—the opportunity for a person to receive preventative justice. Thus, in the Constitution, federal courts are authorized to hear all cases in law (common law) and equity.[3]

Religion and Judicial Process

When the framers crafted the Constitution, they introduced some remarkable features that distinguished it from the Articles of Confederation. First, they dramatically enhanced the power of the legislative branch. They located all authority over money and commerce with Congress. Likewise, they gave to Congress the authority to declare war and to approve peace treaties. Second, they created a national chief executive—an entity that did not exist under the earlier Articles of Confederation. As with Congress, the framers located several powers specifically within the presidency. They gave the president power to serve as the chief executive overseeing the entire executive branch. The president was also made the chief law-enforcement officer as well as the chief foreign policy maker, with the authority in the latter instance to negotiate treaties and to send and receive ambassadors. And the president was designated the commander-in-chief over the United States military.

The framers also created a third branch of the United States government—the federal judiciary. However, very little detail is included in the article outlining the judiciary. Article III of the Constitution simply created a national Supreme Court and distinguished between its original and appellate jurisdiction. The framers also specified that federal judges shall have lifetime tenure. But, beyond those basic details, the framers left it to Congress to flesh out the remainder of the federal judiciary (Walker and Epstein 1993, 2–3).

Precisely because the judicial branch, as established within the original Constitution, is without substantial structure and authority, it occupies a unique role in American political life. In the 1803 case of *Marbury v. Madison*,[4] the court formally asserted its own power of judicial review, and, in so doing, it put the judiciary on the political map. In *Marbury v. Madison*, the court armed itself with the authority to strike down national or state legislation, as well as actions by the legislative and executive branch, that it deems unconstitutional.

Federal judges are, to a certain extent, *outside* the government—most notably the government associated with the politically elected branches. Once appointed by the president, and confirmed by the Senate, federal judges enjoy lifetime tenure. As a result, they are not subject, at least theoretically, to the political pressures that can be so important to members of Congress and the president. Moreover, by its very nature, the branch with the authority to evaluate the constitutionality of government policy can claim some distance from the originators of governmental policy. Hence, federal judges are often thought to be outside critics of government.

Yet it is important to note that federal judges are also very much *within* the structure of the federal government articulated by the Constitution. That means that, as agents of the federal government, judges are often in opposition to state governments, local governments, and those in the private sector. As agents of the federal government, judges also make public policy. They have the power to hold parties in contempt. They can issue writs, or written court orders, that bind particular parties. Some of the most compelling and controversial public policy in recent American history has been crafted, not by elected officials, but by federal judges.

Actors outside the Process

Not surprisingly, actors outside the political process have come to the realization that they can affect judicial policy much as they affect legislative or regulatory policy. The methods used within the judicial arena, of course, are very different. Interest groups do not hire lobbyists to wine and dine jurists. Groups do not offer a federal judge money for his or her next campaign. Interest groups do, however, help shape the judiciary. First, they participate in the nomination and confirmation process by providing information and putting pressure on the president to nominate or not to nominate, or on senators to confirm or not to confirm, particular judges. Second, groups can shape the judicial landscape by filing suit. Third, even those who do not file suit can influence judicial decision making by filing *amicus curiae* (friend of the court) briefs (O'Brien 1996, 248–53).

Increasingly, religious actors have entered into the political process by forming interest groups and making a serious effort to affect public policy. It should not be surprising, therefore, that religious people are active in their efforts to affect the judicial process. Serving as outsiders to the process, religious people are involved in the nomination and confirmation process. They file lawsuits. They submit *amicus curiae* briefs in important cases (Ivers 1998, 289–94; den Dulk 1997 and 1999).

One example illustrating the impact that religious people can have on public policy, through the judiciary, is protecting religious exercise under the guise of free speech. As students of the Constitution are aware, two clauses within the First Amendment relate to religious liberty—the (no-) establishment clause and the free exercise clause. The establishment clause is the most familiar and is often paraphrased as requiring "separation of church and state." The clause that keeps government from "prohibiting the free exercise (of religion)" is most definitely a second-class citizen in the Constitution's hierarchy, in that when the establishment clause and the free exercise clause come into conflict, the court almost always prefers the establishment clause. And, when the free exercise clause bumps up against national or state criminal laws of general applicability, the court generally rules against the free exercise claim. The court's current position is that the free exercise clause simply protects one's right to believe as one might choose and does not necessarily protect action emanating from that belief.[5]

Recently, however, Christian groups have embraced another strategy for securing religious freedom. Whenever possible, they fold the free exercise claim under the free-speech clause (Brown 1998; Guliuzza 2000, 138–45). When the free-speech clause is pitted against either the establishment clause or the general criminal law, it fares much better. In several cases throughout the 1980s and 1990s, Christians, often with the support of various Christian legal organizations, have been involved in lawsuits predicated not on the free exercise clause but, rather, on the free-speech clause.

In 1981, the Supreme Court held in *Widmar v. Vincent*[6] that college and university students who formed prayer and Bible study organizations were entitled to use facilities on their campus—even though the university's policy might prohibit such activity as violating the establishment clause. After the *Widmar* decision, Congress passed, and President Reagan signed, the Equal Access Act, basically extending the protections secured in *Widmar* to high school students. The statute was challenged in the 1990 case of *Westside Community Schools v. Mergens*.[7] Again, attorneys for the students did not defend their clients' actions, or even the Equal Access Act, based on the free exercise clause. They argued that the high school created a limited public forum when it sanctioned after-school clubs not related to the curriculum. To allow these clubs and organizations to meet on campus and then, simultaneously, to deny a Bible club access to the facilities violated the students' free-speech rights. The Supreme Court agreed, and upheld the Equal Access Act. In 1993, a Christian church challenged the policy of the local school board that prohibited religious organizations from access to school facilities (e.g., an auditorium or gymnasium). The church wanted to use an auditorium to show James Dobson's film series, *Turn Your Heart toward Home*. The church challenged the policy, arguing that the school board was engaging in viewpoint discrimination. Although other groups, including Planned Parenthood, were welcome to do presentations on the family, the church claimed that it was not permitted to show a film discussing the same material from a Christian perspective. Again, the court held that the school board's policy violated the church's freedom of speech.[8] Two years later, the court ruled that the student-fee committee at the University of Virginia could not deny funding to a student newspaper that addressed campus issues from a Christian perspective.[9]

The success rate of Christian organizations in the courts vindicates the "free-speech strategy" for securing freedom of religion. It also illustrates the power that religious groups have and can wield in affecting public policy through the judiciary.

Actors inside the Process

Religious people certainly have had an impact on the judiciary working from outside the process. It is important, however, not to underestimate the impact of religion from within the judicial process. In other words, shifting the analysis from the macro level to the micro level, one will find that a number of the justices on the Supreme Court are, and have been, unashamedly religious. Moreover, beginning in the early twentieth century, some openings on the Supreme Court have actually, albeit quite informally, been designated as the "Catholic" seat or the "Jewish" seat (Walker and Epstein 1993, 38–39; Wasby 1988, 117).[10] Finally, there is some evidence that one's religion does affect one's voting behavior on the court.

241

One way to determine the force of religion on the American legal system is to examine its impact on important judicial actors. If one studies the biographies of the justices on the high court, one discovers that the influence of religion in the lives of the justices is as significant as for any other collection of public servants. The justices are drawn from a wide spectrum of religious faiths. Some were influenced by the religion in which they were reared, while other justices were converted to a religious faith as young adults. For some justices, religion seems to be a small, or nonexistent, component of their lives, while for other justices it is the most important aspect of their lives. In fact, some justices have reported that they felt a calling to religious service either before or after their tenure on the court (Guliuzza 1999, 15–21).

Has the importance of religion for the various justices changed over time? To answer this question, I have examined the way religion is presented in the biographies of the Supreme Court justices. To maintain some consistency, I reviewed the book *Supreme Court Justices*, edited by Clare Cushman and commissioned by the Supreme Court Historical Society, for mention of religion (either of the justice or of the justice's family). Although the biographical entries are authored by several scholars, the biographies are roughly the same length and seem to emphasize the same sort of information. My objective was to see if the importance of religion has increased, decreased, or remained fairly steady across time.[11] This review of the brief biographies was designed to reveal whether changes appeared in the beliefs of the justices—or, perhaps just as significant, if there was a change in how important the several biographers regarded religion when they presented their biographies.

Of the 108 biographies presented, 73 (or 67.6 percent) discussed either the religion of the justice or the religion of his or her family, whereas, in about one-third of the biographies, no mention was given to the religious faith of the justice.

Next, I examined the discussion of religion in the biographies across different historical "eras" of the court. To differentiate between eras, I used the standard divisions of 1789–1865 (when American jurisprudence was dominated by the federalism question), 1865–1937 (when American jurisprudence was dominated by economic issues and economic rights), and 1937 to the present (when American jurisprudence was dominated by individual rights and liberties).[12]

Table 11.1 reveals that the biographies written about the justices during the first period look very much like the total across time. The biographies written about justices appointed during the middle era contain many more references to religion. Keep in mind, however, that such discussions need not be positive. For instance, the identification of Brandeis and Frankfurter as being nonreligious or Holmes's antipathy toward

242

organized religion were coded as a "mention of religion." The biographies written about justices in the modern era discuss religion far less frequently, although the total is still close to 60 percent.

Table 11.1 The Justices of the Supreme Court and Religion, Divided by "Era"

	Total	Mention of Religion	No Mention of Religion
Period 1 (1789–1865)	39	26 (66.7%)	13 (33.3%)
Period 2 (1865–1937)	36	28 (77.8%)	8 (22.2%)
Period 3 (1937–)	33	19 (57.6%)	14 (42.4%)

Because the modern era (period 3) did have a higher percentage of biographies with no mention of religion, and because of the impact of the court's treatment of the First Amendment's establishment clause over the past fifty years, I wanted to look at biographies written before and after the seminal decision *Everson v. Board* (1947).[13] Table 11.2 reveals a substantial difference between the pre-*Everson* and post-*Everson* biographies.

Table 11.2 The Justices of the Supreme Court and Religion, Pre-*Everson* and Post-*Everson*

	Total	Mention of Religion	No Mention of Religion
Pre-*Everson* (1789–1947)	85	61 (71.8%)	24 (28.2%)
Post-*Everson* (1947–94)	23	12 (52.2%)	11 (47.8%)

Finally, I wanted to examine one other distinction in the biographies. Over the past fifteen years, scholars from a wide variety of disciplines have engaged in a healthy debate about the legitimacy of religious expression in dialogic politics (Ackerman 1980; Neuhaus 1984; Perry 1991; Rawls 1993; Carter 1993; Gedicks 1995; Greenawalt 1995; Thiemann 1996; Pasewark and Paul 1999; Guliuzza 2000). This scholarly discussion seems to coincide with a season in America when it is acceptable to talk about the religious influences on our public leaders in ways that might not have been acceptable during the rest of the post-*Everson* period. If I am correct, then we should see a difference in the biographies written about justices appointed between 1947 and 1984 and those appointed after 1984. This analysis is presented in table 11.3. The number of judges analyzed is relatively small, particularly after 1984, due to the relatively short period of time. Nevertheless, table 11.3 does seem to indicate a change in the biographers' treatment of the justices appointed since 1984.

Table 11.3 The Justices of the Supreme Court and Religion, 1947–84 and 1984–94

	Total	Mention of Religion	No Mention of Religion
1947–84	17	6 (35.3%)	11 (64.7%)
1984–94	6	6 (100%)	0 (0%)

Perhaps more important, some of the justices have talked openly about their faith in their judicial decisions. Such was, or is, the case for Justice Brennan and Justice Scalia, who have discussed the influence of Catholicism on their respective constitutional philosophies. On the other hand, for a handful of the justices, the connection between religion and their decision making on the court was much more concrete.[14] For example, William Cushing (1790–1810) was appointed to the Supreme Court even though his opinions on the Massachusetts Supreme Court were "notable for their use of biblical doctrine and Scripture to embellish the written law." And David Brewer's (1890–1910) early decisions contained references to Christian and biblical virtues, and his religious faith was the backbone of his judicial philosophy.

Sometimes the connection between faith and judicial service was not positive. James McReynolds (1914–41), raised within the then-fundamentalist Campbellite sect of the Disciples of Christ, did not enjoy a positive relationship with either of the two Jewish justices on the court (Brandeis and Cardozo). His disdain for Brandeis was so acute that for years he would walk out of the room when Brandeis spoke in conference. In 1924, no official photograph was taken of the court because McReynolds refused to sit next to Brandeis.

The influence of religion on judicial voting behavior is not limited to the Supreme Court. In a recent study that examined the impact of religion on the decision making of state supreme court justices, it was revealed that, from 1970 to 1993, justices from the Evangelical Protestant tradition were significantly more conservative than justices from the Mainline Protestant, Catholic, or Jewish traditions in cases related to the death penalty, gender discrimination, and obscenity (Songer and Tabrizi 1999). As a result, it appears that religious affiliation is a source of judicial values that is independent of other, more widely noted sources (Songer and Tabrizi 1999).

The Impact of Judicial Politics on Religion

As suggested earlier, judges make public policy. As a result, judicial rulings do not simply affect the parties involved in the case. Because we are a common law country, we respect the principle of *stare decisis*. Yet, over the past half-century, there have been several justices on the Supreme Court who have welcomed the opportunity to create policy from the bench. They are far more willing to interpret the Constitution actively, and some justices have even authored decisions that read like legislation.

In *Roe v. Wade* (1973),[15] the court did not simply decide whether or not a woman has a right to reproductive choice. They fashioned an elaborate approach to pregnancy and reproductive choice that included a trimester-by-trimester balancing of the rights of the woman and those of the state.

In *Miranda v. Arizona* (1966),[16] the Supreme Court did not simply uphold or reject the conviction of Ernesto Miranda. Instead, it put together a meticulous set of rights available to those in custody and required that police officers make suspects aware of their rights before they proceed with an interrogation. Chief Justice Earl Warren castigated police tactics that included hanging, whipping, and beating. Further, he indicated that, while modern police interrogation techniques that include coercion and psychological pressure may be less violent than more physical tactics, they are no less repugnant constitutionally. In the case of Ernesto Miranda, however, Warren provided no evidence of either physical torture or overt psychological pressure by the police. The problem, Warren surmised, was that anytime a suspect is taken into custody by the police, he or she may become "disoriented." As a result, "human dignity" requires substantial limits on the power of the police and that each suspect must be made aware of his or her rights.

Miranda is an excellent example of how an activist court can formulate public policy much as a legislative body might. Justice White's opinion in the case indicates as much:

> That the Court's holding today is neither compelled or even strongly suggested by the language of the Fifth Amendment, is at odds with American and English legal history, and involves departure from a long line of precedent does not prove either that the Court has exceeded its powers or that the Court is wrong or unwise in its present reinterpretation of the Fifth Amendment. It does, however, underscore the obvious—that the Court has not discovered or found the law in making today's decision, nor has it derived it from some irrefutable sources; what it has done is to make new law and new public policy in much the same way that it has in the

course of interpreting other great clauses of the Constitution. This is what the Court historically has done. Indeed, it is what it must do and will continue to do until and unless there is some fundamental change in the constitutional distribution of governmental powers.[17]

White's opinion in *Miranda* indicates that he was fully aware that the court was crafting public policy. In fact, he argued that the decision of the court was neither required by the Fifth Amendment nor rooted in history or the common law. White's concern was not that the court was making public policy without specific constitutional moorings. Rather, and much like a member of a legislative body, he was troubled by the public policy itself:

> But if the Court is here and now to announce new and fundamental policy to govern certain aspects of our affairs, it is wholly legitimate to examine the mode of this or any other constitutional decision in the Court and to inquire into the advisability of its end product in terms of the long-range interest of the country.[18]

The distinction between an activist approach to the Constitution and one that is more restrained is exemplified in the seminal death-penalty decision, *Furman v. Georgia* (1972).[19] Furman is a strange decision. In its 5–4 ruling, the Supreme Court struck down as unconstitutional the death-penalty statutes in more than thirty states. However, all nine justices wrote opinions in the case. It turns out that it is really a two-to-three-to-four decision. Two justices, Justices Marshall and Brennan, wanted to ban the death penalty itself as "cruel and unusual punishment" that thereby served as an unconstitutional form of punishment. Three other justices indicated that their concern was not with the death penalty per se, but with the way it was applied. The remaining four justices all found reasons to uphold the death-penalty statutes in the various states.

It is striking to compare the opinions proffered by Justice Brennan and Justice Blackman. Brennan wanted to abolish the death penalty. Akin to Warren in *Miranda*, Brennan argued that capital punishment violates "human dignity." It is unacceptable, Brennan noted, in a society that boasts an evolving standard of decency. To no small degree, Justice Blackman agreed with his colleague. He argued that the death penalty was indeed repugnant. Further, he maintained that, if he were a state legislator rather than a judge, he would vote to abolish capital punishment. But, he maintained, it was not within his authority to substitute his will for that of the various state legislatures.

Brennan's opinion is clearly an activist opinion. Although there is no textual or historical basis to read the Constitution as requiring the abolition of the death penalty, Brennan insisted it was within his authority to rule accordingly, since the Supreme Court existed, from his perception, to protect decency and human dignity. Blackman's opinion, on the other hand, represents a conservative judicial decision. Absent clear constitutional direction, Blackman argued that a judge should not substitute his or her will for that of the popularly elected officials.

These two judicial philosophies of activism and restraint are evident in the court's treatment of cases that have a direct impact on religion—namely, the cases dealing with the establishment clause and the free exercise clause.

With regard to the free exercise clause, the court has moved full circle since its early opinions in the late nineteenth century. In a decision in 1878 (*Reynolds v. United States*) that upheld a federal law banning polygamy, the court fashioned a belief-action dichotomy. Simply put, the majority held that the free exercise clause must protect one's beliefs, without equivocation, but does not protect the actions that emanate from those beliefs.[20]

More than fifty years later, the court seemed to suggest that the limited protection given to free exercise was not enough. In the early 1940s, the justices defined the clause as protecting one's right to refuse to participate in a state-sponsored activity that violated one's beliefs.[21] For example, one could not be forced to pray; one could not be forced to salute the flag or to pledge allegiance; ultimately, one could not be forced to participate in the armed forces.[22]

The court's treatment of the free exercise clause reached its zenith in the 1960s and early 1970s. In *Sherbert v. Verner* (1963)[23] and *Wisconsin v. Yoder* (1972),[24] the court pushed the free exercise clause even further. It held that laws which threaten one's religious freedom must be subject to strict scrutiny by the courts. Thus, for the laws and regulations to pass constitutional muster, one must demonstrate a "compelling" interest. Furthermore, if government is to encroach on one's religious liberty, the government must show that no less drastic means could have been used to accomplish its desired objectives.

Throughout the 1980s and 1990s, the court began to step back from the protections articulated in *Sherbert* and *Yoder*. Eventually, in *Employment Division v. Smith* (1990),[25] the so-called peyote decision, it reestablished the belief-action dichotomy ordered by *Reynolds*. As long as a state law is neutral toward religion and of general applicability, it will survive judicial scrutiny despite its impact on religion.

How might the court's approach to the free exercise clause affect religious freedom? On one hand, it streamlines the system substantially. The court's holding does not require special or unique protection for religion. For instance, employees, prisoners, students, and the like will not likely receive exemptions from regulations simply because they assert a religious-liberty claim. On the other hand, religious people have very little protection against such laws as long as the laws do not specifically target religion or religious activity. If the state of Texas decided to enforce existing laws against underage drinking—laws of general applicability—against churches that routinely offer wine for communion to minors, then the churches would have little protection. A church that is large and able to muster significant political clout, like the Roman Catholic church, might be able to fashion exemptions to the existing laws. Churches that are quite small, or those that lack political power, are subject to the decisions made by legislative and regulatory bodies.

Recognizing the problems that might emanate from *Smith*, Congress passed, and President Clinton signed, the Religious Freedom Restoration Act (RFRA) in 1993. In RFRA, Congress attempted to restore much of muscle granted the free exercise clause in *Sherbert*. Congress put the compelling-interest test back into place through statutory legislation.

The Religious Freedom Restoration Act was a short-lived remedy, however. In the 1997 decision in *City of Boerne v. Flores*,[26] the court delivered a sharp rebuke to the legislative branch. First, the court held that Congress did not have the authority to do an end run around the court's interpretation of the Constitution. While Congress might have the authority to pass legislation that bolsters the Constitution's mandates, it does not have the power to create statutory language that attempts to trump the court. Second, the majority reaffirmed *Smith*, thereby setting aside the revised compelling-interest test.

For lovers of religious liberty, the court's record on the establishment clause over the past fifty years might contain even more important decisions. It is hard to imagine a list of American constitutional liberties, like the Bill of Rights, without the establishment clause. Because many people came to the New World to escape religious persecution, the framers placed the establishment clause in the amended Constitution to protect religious minorities. At the very least, the establishment clause was intended to prevent a national religion and the collection of governmental revenues in support of religion.

Over the past half-century, however, the establishment clause has taken on a different meaning. In the seminal *Everson* decision, the court decided that the establishment clause erected a high wall of separation between church and state. The clause meant more than a constitutional prohibition against governmental establishment of *a* religion. In *Everson*, the court suggested that the clause barred any action by government that established, or touched on, *religion*.

The court has backed away from the interpretation of the establishment clause it pronounced in *Everson*. In fact, from the outset, the court has fashioned two different meanings for the term *separation*. First, there is "strict separation"—that no law should touch religion. The court has embraced strict separation in several cases (e.g, on-campus released time programs, prayer in public schools, after-school enrichment programs).[27] At other times, the court has advanced a "softer" type of separation. Often the court speaks in terms of neutrality when it is discussing this second type of separation. In the 1950s and early 1960s, the court embraced "softer" separation in a number of decisions (e.g., off-campus released time programs, Bible reading in school as long as it is taught as literature, lending textbooks to parochial students, property-tax exemptions).[28]

Eventually, the second approach to separation, couched in terms of neutrality, has prevailed in the court. In the 1971 decision *Lemon v. Kurtzman*,[29] the court held that government involvement with religion might be acceptable provided that programs satisfy three tests. First, a given program must have a secular purpose. Second, it must neither advance nor inhibit religion. Finally, it must not create an excessive entanglement between government and religion.

Since its inception, the *Lemon* test has produced an array of establishment-clause decisions that are akin to watching two top contenders vie for the title at Wimbledon. Members of Congress can hire chaplains, but public school teachers cannot begin their classes with a moment of silence as long as prayer is listed among the options. Professionals can come to parochial schools in order to administer diagnostic tests for eyesight and hearing, but should they discover a problem with some children, they must provide therapy in a building apart from the parochial school grounds. Children attending parochial schools can ride on a government-funded bus to and from school, but the same children cannot use that bus to take a field trip to a local art museum. A school district can lend parochial school children a textbook with a picture of George Washington at Valley Forge, but they cannot lend the school the picture itself (Guliuzza 2000, 72–77).

Generally, the court's post-*Lemon* establishment-clause decisions fall into three larger areas: those that consider (1) government support directly to individuals, (2) government support for religious institutions, and (3) support for religious activities. The court has been fairly willing to allow government to support religion if such support flows directly to individuals (e.g., bus transportation, lending textbooks, interpreters for hearing-impaired students, tuition tax credits, financial support for handicapped students who attend religious colleges).[30] Support that flows directly to institutions is far more difficult to predict. Sometimes the court will allow government to accommodate religious institutions (e.g., hospitals, support for religious colleges and universities).[31] Other times it will not (e.g, support programs for elementary and secondary schools).[32] The court is far less willing to permit government support for (or endorsement of) religious activities (e.g., prayer, posting of religious documents like the Ten Commandments, Bible reading).[33]

Of course, many of the decisions by the national judiciary have an *indirect* effect on religious people by affecting public policy important to them. Judicial decisions related to abortion and obscenity are two prime examples. *Roe v. Wade* (1973) was perceived by many religious conservatives to be judicial activism at its worst, a decision without a strong constitutional foundation, and the decision has triggered widespread political activism among different segments of the religious community. Likewise, when the court started to clarify and constrict its definition of obscenity[34] in the 1950s and 1960s, it not only increased freedom of expression in the United States, but it also provided greater constitutional protection for the burgeoning pornography industry.

Conclusion

Without question, religion has had a substantial impact on America's law and legal system. As this chapter has revealed, religion has affected our judicial system in a variety of ways. It has affected the American legal system by influencing code and common law. Second, it has had an impact on the judicial process itself. It has affected the process from outside the system, as religious activists have sought to shape the process through influencing the nominating process, filing *amicus curiae* briefs, and litigating cases. It is also true that religion has had an impact on the judicial process from within. Many of the justices on the Supreme Court have been openly religious, and studies have suggested that one's religious faith does affect one's voting behavior on the bench. Finally, we examined how the courts can affect religion both directly—for example, in judicial decisions' impact on religious liberty—and indirectly, as the court forges public policies (e.g., issues of abortion and obscenity) that have an indirect impact on people of faith.

However, one should not assume that religion's influence on the judicial system is limited to the topics covered here. While not examined in this chapter, religious thought and texts have also shaped the origin and interpretation of our rights and liberties, and specific components of our criminal and civil law have their genesis in religious texts.

But regardless of religion's past contributions to our judicial system, the courts will continue to be an important factor shaping religious life in America. As judges continue to step into the public policy arena, especially when perceived to be fashioning policy from the bench, the judiciary will remain as important to religious people as the other two branches of government. In fact, over the next several years, as decisions come before the court affecting prayer in schools, reproductive choice, religious expression, gay rights, and education, the judiciary may become to people of faith the most important branch of government.

References

Abadinsky, Howard. 1991. *Law and Justice*. Chicago: Nelson Hall.

Ackerman, Harold. 1980. *Social Justice and the Liberal State*. New Haven: Yale University Press.

Berman, Harold. 1986. "Religion and Law: The First Amendment in Historical Perspective." *Emory Law Journal* 35:777–93.

Brown, Steven. 1998. "The Pornography of the 1990s? Religion, Free Speech, and the New Christian Right in the Courts." Paper presented at the Midwest Political Science Association, Chicago, Ill., 25 April.

Calvi, James, and Susan Coleman. 1989. *American Law and Legal Systems*. Englewood Cliffs, N.J.: Prentice Hall.

Carter, Stephen. 1993. *The Culture of Disbelief*. New York: Basic Books.

Cromartie, Michael, ed. 1993. *No Longer Exiles*. Washington, D.C.: Ethics and Public Policy Center.

Cushman, Clare, ed. 1995. *The Supreme Court Justices*. Washington, D.C.: Congressional Quarterly Press.

den Dulk, Kevin. 1997. "The Legal Mobilization of the New Christian Right: The Supreme Court as a Political Resource." Paper presented at the Wisconsin Political Science Association, Madison, Wis., 31 October.

———. 1999. "Choosing Political Litigation: The Case of Conservative Religion." Paper presented at the annual meeting of the Law and Society Association, Chicago, Ill., 29 May.

Gedicks, Frederick Mark. 1995. *The Rhetoric of Church and State: A Critical Analysis of Religion Clause Jurisprudence*. Durham, N.C.: Duke University Press.

Greenawalt, Kent. 1995. *Private Consciences and Public Reasons*. New York: Oxford University Press.

Guliuzza, Frank. 1999. "Religion and Its Impact upon the American Legal System: Three Examples." Paper presented at the second national conference of Christians in Political Science, Grand Rapids, Mich., 17 June.

———. 2000. *Over the Wall: Protecting Religious Expression in the Public Square*. Albany: State University of New York Press.

Ivers, Gregg. 1998. "Please God, Save This Honorable Court: The Emergence of the Conservative Religious Bar." In *The Interest Group Connection*, edited by Paul Hernson, Ronald Shaiko, and Clyde Wilcox, 289–301. Chatham, N.J.: Chatham House.

Leege, David, and Lyman Kellstedt. 1993. *Rediscovering the Religious Factor in American Politics*. Armonk, N.Y.: M. E. Sharpe.

Levy, Leonard. 1986. *The Establishment Clause*. New York: Macmillan.

Lowi, Theodore, and Benjamin Ginsberg. 1996. *American Government*. New York: W. W. Norton.

McCloskey, Robert. 1960. *The American Supreme Court*. Chicago: University of Chicago Press.

Neuhaus, Richard John. 1984. *The Naked Public Square*. Grand Rapids: Eerdmans.

O'Brien, David. 1996. *Storm Center: The Supreme Court in American Politics*. New York: W. W. Norton.

———. 1997. *Constitutional Law and Politics*. New York: W. W. Norton.

Pasewark, Kyle A., and Garrett E. Paul. 1999. *The Emphatic Christian Center: Reforming American Political Practice*. Nashville: Abingdon Press.

Perry, Michael. 1991. *Love and Power*. New York: Oxford University Press.

Post, C. Gordon. 1963. *An Introduction to the Law*. Englewood Cliffs, N.J.: Prentice Hall.

Rawls, John. 1993. *Political Liberalism*. New York: Columbia University Press.

Ripley, Randall. 1978. *Congress: Process and Policy*. New York: W. W. Norton.

Rossiter, Clinton. 1956. *The American Presidency*. New York: Mentor Books.

Songer, Donald, and Susan Tabrizi. 1999. "The Religious Right in Court: The Decision Making of Christian Evangelicals in State Supreme Courts." *Journal of Politics* 61:507–26.

Tarr, G. Alan. 1994. *Judicial Process and Judicial Policymaking*. St. Paul, Minn.: West.

Thiemann, Ronald. 1996. *Religion in Public Life*. Washington, D.C.: Georgetown University Press.

Van Dervort, Thomas. 1994. *Equal Justice under the Law*. St. Paul, Minn.: West.

Wald, Kenneth. 1997. *Religion and Politics in the United States*. 3d ed. Washington, D.C.: Congressional Quarterly Press.

Walker, Thomas, and Lee Epstein. 1993. *The Supreme Court of the United States*. New York: St. Martin's Press.

Wasby, Stephen. 1988. *The Supreme Court in the American Judicial System*. Chicago: Nelson Hall.

Way, H. Frank. 1981. *Liberty in the Balance*. New York: McGraw-Hill.

Wilcox, Clyde. 1996. *Onward Christian Soldiers*. Boulder, Colo.: Westview Press.

Zane, John. 1998. *The Story of Law*. Indianapolis: Liberty Fund.

Teaching Tools

Discussion Questions

1. What is the distinction between code law and common law? What influence has religion had on each?

2. What evidence do you see in American law to suggest the impact of either code law or common law?
3. How do actors *outside* the process influence the federal judiciary?
4. Describe and critique the "free-speech strategy" for protecting religious freedom.
5. How religious are the justices on the Supreme Court? How might a particular justice's faith be reflected in his or her decisions?
6. What does it mean to suggest that the Supreme Court has engaged in policy making? What are some cases that illustrate this kind of activism from the court?
7. Describe and critique the court's treatment of the establishment clause.

Topics for Student Research

1. Building on the work of Songer and Tabrizi (1999), identify the religious background of the appellate judges in your state. After you have completed this task, look at the some of the decisions rendered by each of the judges to see if there might be a correlation between a judge's religious affiliation and his or her decisions.
2. The chapter describes a certain level of "activism" by the Supreme Court. How would one measure whether or not a particular decision provides evidence of an "activist" court? Develop some measures of judicial activism and its oft-discussed counterpart—judicial restraint. Apply your measures to the leading cases in a given area (those cited in a constitutional law textbook discussing, for example, affirmative action, abortion, symbolic speech, gay rights, or free exercise of religion).
3. The chapter suggests that the Supreme Court unknowingly crafted two theories designed to separate church from state—"strict" separation and "softer" separation (often identified as neutrality). The author also seems to suggest that for the most part, since *Lemon v. Kurtzman* (1971), strict separation has given way to neutrality. Is that true? Review the leading establishment-clause cases to find evidence of the strict separation doctrine articulated in *Everson*. Remember to pay close attention to the concurring and dissenting opinions. Feeling ambitious? You might want to "shepardize" *Everson* (ask your professor how to do this) and to see whether or not there are still pockets of support for the separation doctrine among the lower federal courts and state courts throughout the United States.
4. Consider the following case:

In October 1999, Rod Beatch, a public school teacher in Cheyenne, Wyoming, was ordered by his superiors, on pain of disciplinary action, to remove his personal Bible from his desk where students might see it. He was forbidden to read it silently when his students were involved in other activities. He was also told to remove books on Christianity that he had added to the classroom library, although books on Native American religious traditions, as well as the occult, were allowed to remain. A federal district court imposed an injunction, preventing the disciplinary action taken against Beatch, and held that he did not have to remove any of the religious materials from the classroom since his intent was not to "coerce" the students into embracing a particular religious faith. A federal appeals court struck down the injunction and upheld the decision to remove the Bible and Christian literature, explaining that Beatch could not be allowed to create "a religious atmosphere in the classroom, which it seems might happen if the student knew he [Beatch] was a Christian." Beatch appealed to the U.S. Supreme Court on the grounds that the school district's decision violated the free exercise clause, the free-speech clause, and, ironically, even the establishment clause.

You are an attorney for either the Baptist Life Commission or People for the American Way. You have been asked to write an *amicus curiae* brief to the Supreme Court in *Beatch v. Laramie County School District*. Drawing upon the relevant case law, and sample briefs that you might use as a model, write your brief for the court. Furthermore, prepare to present a ten-minute oral argument before the court (your class). In your brief, please evaluate and discuss each of Beatch's contentions regarding the free exercise, free-speech, and establishment clause claims.

12

Christian Commitment and Political Life

STEPHEN V. MONSMA

Political cynicism and alienation are rife among Americans today. Many are convinced that the political realm is irrelevant at best and a pit of corruption at worse. This attitude seems especially prevalent among those in their twenties, Generation X. One observer reports: "A wide sampling of surveys indicates that Xers are less politically or civically engaged, exhibit less social trust or confidence in government, have a weaker allegiance to their country or to either political party, and are more materialistic than their predecessors" (Halstead 1999). In light of this observation, how should Christian citizens respond? Some might argue that if Americans generally are becoming distrustful of politics, surely Christians ought to be distrustful. After all, Christians—with their high moral standards—ought to be even more outraged than others at the selfishness, naked ambition, and outright corruption that too often mark politics. In addition, all governments exercise coercive power, and are not Christians to exercise love and to "turn the other cheek"? Others, however, argue that part of the Christian's call to be "salt and light" in the world is to enter the political realm to change it for the better, and to assure that public policies pursued by government reflect God's will for human society.

In light of the cynicism toward politics that is common today, and in light of divergent answers to the Christian's role in the political world, this concluding chapter steps back from the analyses and perspectives of the previous chapters and attempts to answer the question of what ought to be the Christian's role in the political realm. The chapter addresses this question in three sections. First, it suggests that Christians indeed ought to be politically active and involved. Next, it considers the basic direction or the goals with which Christians ought to enter the world of politics. The final section outlines three levels of political activism and involvement to which different Christians are called by God.

Why Christians Should Be Involved Politically

The apostle Paul lived under and eventually was executed by the Roman government. At times he made use of his Roman citizenship to protect himself from arbitrary arrest and punishment, and he exercised his right of legal appeal to Caesar's court in Rome.[1] In his letter to the church in the capital city of the Roman Empire he discussed the Christian's duty to obey the civil authorities. Most important for our purposes is the reasoning he used in urging the Roman Christians to obey their government. He argued that obedience was the Christian's duty because the civil authorities "have been established by God"; they are "God's servant[s] to do you good" and are "God's servants, who give their full time to governing" (Rom. 13:1–2, 4, 6). Therefore, Paul argued, Christians ought to obey government, not out of fear of punishment, but out of a good conscience in tune with God's will. Even Jesus Christ himself, when before the civil ruler Pilate, insisted that Pilate's authority came from God: "Jesus answered, 'You would have no power over me if it were not given to you from above'" (John 19:11).

Christians continue to differ on the exact meaning of these and other similar references in Scripture, but most Christians through the centuries have agreed that governments are part of God's ordering of human society and have been established to help shape a just order in society in which all can live in peace and flourish. Although most traditions in Christianity believe government should be viewed as a God-ordained institution that is a part of God's will for human society, they sometimes differ on whether governments were a part of God's original will for human society or whether they entered God's plan only as a result of

256

the fall. The Anabaptist position, in particular, has tended to view government not as a part of God's original intent for humankind, but as a necessary evil that God allows in order to control the effects of sin.[2] But even most Anabaptists believe that in the present, fallen state of the world, civil government is used by God as a means to control or limit evil and to advance a more just order in society.

With this concept of government as a God-established, God-willed institution as a starting point for considering Christian political involvement, I suggest two reasons why it is one's duty as a Christian to be politically involved. But before doing so, I need to clarify what I mean by "political involvement." For many, it may conjure up images of persons spending hours each day reading newspapers, writing members of Congress, attending innumerable meetings, joining a political party, and organizing their neighborhoods in attempts to influence city hall. What I mean by being politically involved encompasses both the simple, undemanding forms of involvement—such as voting once or twice a year—and the much more intensive, time-demanding forms mentioned above. In between these extremes, there are gradations of involvement. Later I discuss in more detail these different levels; here I wish only to be clear that when I write of political involvement, I include the entire range.

Why then is it a Christian's duty to be involved politically? The first reason rests on the Bible's testimony that government is indeed evidence of God's grace—a gift from God intended for the good of humankind. If this is the case, it surely would be, at the very least, appropriate for the Christian to be actively involved with that gift. For God to institute government for the welfare of humankind and then not to want any of God's children to be involved, but to leave government for non-Christians to influence and control, makes no sense. To argue otherwise would be to argue that there is a human institution or structure that God has established and that God intends for human good, but that it is so evil that God does not want his followers to be involved with it.

The second reason rests on the fact that government—intended by God to be a force for justice and the good of humankind—can be either a force for justice and good or a perverted force used for evil ends. Specific governments can be arranged along a continuum, from those that seek a more just order in society—and that do so in an exemplary fashion—to those that not only fail to promote a just order in society, but are themselves destructive of a just order. In a fallen, sinful world, all governments are imperfect and fall short of what they can and should be. Yet there is a difference between the governments of present-day New Zealand and Norway—and, yes, the United States—and the governments of Nazi Germany, South Africa under apartheid, or even present-day Iraq. Given these wide disparities in the nature and character

257

of concrete embodiments of government, one way we can fulfill Christ's command to "love your neighbor as yourself" (Mark 12:31) is by working to assure that the government under which we live is more just, more caring, and less unjust, less callous.

In an earlier book of mine I told an altered version of the parable of the Good Samaritan.[3] It bears retelling here. In this version of the parable, the Samaritan, while going from Jerusalem to Jericho a few days after finding and caring for the beaten and bruised victim of the thieves, found another victim who had been beaten and robbed. The Samaritan again showed love and concern by pouring oil on the victim's wounds, putting him on his donkey, and taking him to an inn. Again he paid the innkeeper to care for the man. A week later he was taking the same trip and came on yet another victim of thieves. Again he cared for him and took him to the inn. By now the good Samaritan was perplexed. He had made the trip from Jerusalem to Jericho many times, and until recently he had never found victims of robbery alongside the road. So he began making inquiries around Jericho. He soon found that the Roman governor had put a new centurion in charge of security along the Jerusalem-to-Jericho road. Many had become convinced that the centurion was receiving kickbacks from the thieves in return for not patrolling the road.

The good Samaritan pondered what to do. Maybe he could make the trip to Jericho more often to look for additional victims, or maybe he could organize some of his friends and fellow church members to patrol the road every day and to provide any victims they came upon with loving, soothing care. But he rejected these possibilities in favor of an idea that attacked the heart of the problem instead of dealing only with its symptoms. He organized a large protest rally and march, whose participants confronted the Roman governor with the problem and demanded the corrupt centurion be replaced with someone who would restore security. The governor, fearing that stories of popular unrest would get back to Rome and reflect badly on his ability to govern, quietly removed the dishonest official and replaced him with one committed to maintaining safety along the Jerusalem-to-Jericho road. The rash of robberies and beatings soon died down.

Evil—as in this retelling of the parable of the Good Samaritan—sometimes takes a structural form. When it does, it is not merely random, accidental, or individual in nature, but is, instead, rooted in certain structures, habits, or patterns of behavior in society. Structural evil creates victims: the already poor and vulnerable who are defrauded by the unscrupulous, who are encouraged by lax laws and a society that says the poor deserve no better; children who are dying of cancer because of improper disposal of industrial chemicals; and children fathered outside of marriage by young men who do not accept parental responsibility for them. All of these cases are evils in the sight of God. Loving others as we love ourselves compels Christians to help and care for the casualties of these sinful actions. But love should also compel Christians to use the legitimate powers of government to stop such evils from happening in the first place. In summary, evil sometimes has a personal face; it sometimes has a structural face.

Individual acts of love and compassion—as important as they are—can sometimes be supplemented by governmental actions designed to deal with underlying causes of evil. This will involve Christians using the coercive powers of government, but they will be doing so, not for their own benefit, but for the welfare of others. To do so is to act no less out of love and compassion than when one seeks directly to "bind up the wounds" of those who are hurting. Theologian Reinhold Niebuhr called on Christians "to relate the religious ideal of love to the political necessity of coercion" (1932, 269). In fact, to sit by and allow structural evils to continue without trying to use the powers of government to stem them is—I am convinced—an offense in God's sight. We are then allowing a means that God has provided to correct evils and to seek a more just society to sit unused. That is not showing love to our neighbors. As Niebuhr has written, "We cannot build our individual ladders to heaven and leave the total human enterprise unredeemed of its excesses and corruptions" (1932, 277).

This second reason for Christian political involvement takes on greater urgency and added compulsion for Christians living in a country such as the United States, in which there are ample opportunities for Christians to influence government policies. One does not need to accept the naive view of the American government as perfectly responsive to the wishes of its citizens to assert that our freedoms are deep and profound and the opportunities to influence government abundant. It is true that money plays too big a role in the political processes, that the media often have an undue influence on the flow of events, and that presidents and members of Congress alike can often be more concerned with their political survival than their pursuit of justice. Nevertheless, the opportunities for ordinary citizens to influence the flow of political decisions, at the local, state, and national levels, are also present and real. As most American government textbooks regularly point out, the American political system is extremely decentralized. This means, at the national level, that work of the two houses of Congress is done in numerous committees and subcommittees, that congressional offices are found in all large cities, and that offices of the executive branch are scattered throughout the nation. But that is only the beginning of the decentralized nature of the American system. State and local governments abound, and they, in turn, incorporate a host of legislative bodies, boards and commissions (elected and appointed), and executive positions. There are school boards, road commissions, township boards, library boards, health department boards, state representatives and senators, city council members, county commissions, and more.

The decentralized nature of the American political system leads to a very complex, often difficult-to-understand system; it also leads to a system with many points of citizen access. There are hosts of positions to which the ordinary citizen can aspire. Many of the numerous governing bodies hold public hearings at which individual citizens or representatives of citizen groups may appear and offer testimony, and that testimony, in turn, is sometimes picked up and reported in the news media. Local officials can be called on the telephone. Yet most citizens never think of taking advantage of these opportunities. The error many persons make, including many Christians, is to think in terms of national political influence—trying to influencing Congress or even the president. When their letters do not have a discernible impact, they give up. What they miss is the host of more modest, yet significant, opportunities to have an impact at the local or state level.

Such opportunities are not something our Lord wants us to throw away with a yawn and a shrug. Christ's command, "Freely you have received, freely give" (Matt. 10:8), surely applies to the gifts of freedom, voting rights, and the right to "petition the Government for a redress of grievances," as the First Amendment movingly expresses it. These are gifts from God that most persons through the centuries—including most Christians—have not had. Not to exercise them would be spurning what God has given and a violation of all Christians' duty to love others as they love themselves.

The Direction of Christian Political Involvement

This leaves two important questions yet to be considered—namely, the basic direction or goal of Christian political involvement, and the forms Christian political involvement can appropriately take.

Before I present what I believe to be the appropriate goal of Christian political involvement, let me first address what I deem to be three inappropriate, yet sometimes pursued, goals. The three inappropriate goals all assume that Christians in the political arena should act similarly to the countless interest groups also operating in the political arena. Most interest groups are there to work for the benefit of their members or to pursue some other specific, defined goal. It may be more benefits for the persons making up the interest group (for example, the American Association of Retired Persons, or AARP, working for more Social Security or Medicare benefits for the elderly) or some other specific goal (the Sierra Club working for a cleaner environment). But Christians have a higher calling in the political arena. More on what that calling is shortly.

The first inappropriate goal of Christian political involvement is enacting Christian moral standards into law, so that Americans—whether Christian or not—would be coerced to conform outwardly to these standards. I do not want to be misunderstood here. There are many Christian moral standards that have a positive societal effect—for example, standards against killing or stealing as well as standards against prostitution and pornography. Christian political involvement can appropriately be aimed at legally enforcing such standards. My key point is that it is not enough to say that our Lord demands a certain standard of behavior of all people, and that we are going to use the coercive power of government to enforce that standard. To do so would be to act as a single-minded interest group seeking to enact into law its desires, irrespective of the rights and needs of others.

Nevertheless, Christians have at times sought to enact laws that require the strict observance of Sunday as a holy day of rest or church attendance, or that make adultery or swearing illegal. Today, some Christians try to impose spoken, teacher-led Christian prayers on all public school students, whether they are Christian or not. School prayer remains a controversial issue, even among Christians.[4] Whatever approach Christians take on prayer in public schools, it ought not to be based on Christians imposing prayer on others by dint of their majority status or political clout. There must be something more. I suggest below that that "something more" ought to be the common good or justice for all in society.

A second inappropriate direction for Christian political involvement is making the protection of the rights of Christians—without regard to the rights of others in society—the primary aim of that involvement. Many Christians today feel under siege, as though their values and practices are under relentless attack by secular forces. In an age when government funds are used to subsidize art that is bitterly anti-Christian or little more than thinly disguised pornography, when naturalistic evolution is often taught in public schools as established fact, and when Christian educational and social welfare agencies are sometime unable to obtain the same governmental funds their secular counterparts receive, such feelings are understandable. It is fully appropriate for Christians, by way of political involvement, to work to correct such wrongs. But that ought not to be the sole or primary aim of their involvement. Christians ought not to act like just another interest group, out to defend their self-interests. Christians ought to be just as concerned for the rights and the welfare of their Jewish, Islamic, or nonbelieving neighbors as they are for their own.

Third, Christian political involvement ought not to be aimed simply at getting more Christians elected to public office. Again, I do not want to be misunderstood. It is good when Christians decide to run for public office; it is good when their fellow Christians come to their assistance with their votes, contributions, and volunteer efforts. But being a committed, biblically based Christian does not necessarily mean that one is qualified to hold public office or is a better candidate than a Jewish, Muslim, or nonbelieving candidate. Again, Christians are not to act like an interest group, trying to get as many of their members into public office as possible, with the expectation that they can then "deliver" for their fellow Christians.

If all these are not proper aims of Christian political involvement, if Christians are not to act like an interest group, what then are the proper goals of their political involvement? I believe Christians are to work for the good of all by seeking greater justice in society. Christians are to work for a just order that is in the public interest, or for the common good. This is the "something more" that ought to set Christian political involvement apart from interest-group politics as usual. But this is not the place for a full-blown discussion of the Christian concept of public justice; others have done that elsewhere.[5] But I wish to make two observations. First, justice has traditionally been defined as assuring that all persons receive their due. This is an excellent start. For Christians, the concept is rooted in their belief that all persons have been created in the image of God and, as such, have the right to fundamental human freedoms, economic and social opportunities, and basic respect as morally responsible beings. Second, for these rights to be realized, there must be a just order in society, in which individuals, economic and social structures, and the laws themselves work to create an order in which the rights of all people are safeguarded. This means that, under a just order, lawbreakers—whether the street-corner dope dealer or the corporate violator of food-safety laws—have to be punished. This, too, is justice.

Christians should be politically involved in order to pursue a more just order in society. That is why I stated earlier that Christians ought to be just as concerned for their Jewish or unbelieving neighbors' rights as they are for their own. Justice should be their aim, not special protections or special consideration for themselves. As God told Moses when the Israelites were about to enter the Promised Land:

Appoint judges and officials for each of your tribes in every town the Lord your God is giving you, and they shall judge the people fairly. Do not pervert justice or show partiality. Do not accept a bribe, for a bribe blinds the eyes of the wise and twists the words of the righteous. Follow justice and justice alone, so that you may live and possess the land the Lord your God is giving you.

Deuteronomy 16:18–20

This pursuit of justice will often mean that Christians will not be fully in the camp of any one political party or of any one interest group. I personally served for twelve years in the political arena in Michigan: eight years in the legislature and four years in policy-making positions with the governor. During that time, I noted how most people and groups who approached me with requests or demands had a very one-sided or narrow point of view. They usually cared about their interests and little else. The environmentalists wanted to protect the natural environment without concern for workers or others who would be displaced; business groups wanted less regulation and lower taxes without regard for the rest of the population; hospitals wanted less regulation and higher payments for care given to the poor; and on and on. All these concerns are good. The environment needs to be protected, businesses should be able to operate without onerous regulations or overly high tax rates, and hospitals deserve adequate compensation for the care they give the poor. But my point is that none of these groups was asking questions of justice, proportion, fairness, and balance. They rarely asked what was the common good, what was in the public interest.

To raise and prayerfully seek answers to such issues, I suggest, should be the awesome, difficult, yet rewarding goal of Christian political involvement. It will involve a weighing and balancing process, in which claims and counterclaims are tested, considered, and evaluated. Doing so is not easy. It requires a wisdom and a sensitivity to others that we must look to and call on God to provide. This is what God expects, whether in the case of a legislator casting what could be a deciding vote on a crucial issue or of an ordinary voter casting one out of millions of votes. Candidates for public office at times try to persuade persons to vote for them by asking, "Are you better off now than you were four years ago?" The implication is that, if they are and if the candidate is an incumbent, they should vote for the incumbent—but if they are not, they should vote for the challenger. For the Christian, this is the wrong question and the wrong decision-making process. One's vote should not be governed by whether or not one is better off economically than he or she was before. The proper question relates to the common good: Is society as a whole more just? Are all segments of the population being treated more or less fairly? These are the sorts of questions Christian voters should be asking.

Christians will often come up with different answers. We ought not expect all Christians to agree on all political issues. The important thing

263

is that Christians start by asking the right questions, that they are seeking what is just. I am convinced that this is what God is calling all Christians to do. And just as Christians sometimes come up with different answers in their personal lives (e.g., some Christians believe that all use of alcoholic beverages is wrong, while others believe the moderate use of alcohol is acceptable in God's sight), Christians will often come up with different political answers as well. Nevertheless, even when Christians are on different sides of a political issue, they can contribute much to the overall discussion (as well as to the positions adopted on both sides of the issue), as they move beyond questions of self-interest and partisan advantage to questions of justice and the common good.

The Meaning of Political Involvement

While I would argue that all Christians are called to be involved politically, I do not contend that all Christians are called to be deeply, actively involved in politics to the point where a significant portion of their time is taken up reading newspapers, attending meetings, and organizing their friends and neighbors. God no doubt calls some to such activism, but God does not call all, or even most, Christians to such a level of involvement. It is important to keep in mind the principle Paul articulated in 1 Corinthians 12, in which he refers to different gifts and callings being allotted to different Christians. He uses the analogy of the body, which is composed of many parts, each with its distinct role, and concludes, "Now you are the body of Christ, and each one of you is a part of it" (1 Cor. 12:27). Thus, God does not expect every Christian to be deeply involved in politics; Christians are called to play different roles.

It is helpful to think of three levels of Christian political involvement, which I have termed the citizen participant, the citizen activist, and the professional activist.[6] The *citizen participant* works to maintain at least a general knowledge of political affairs, votes regularly, and occasionally expresses his or her opinions on political issues by writing public officials, signing petitions, or attending meetings about public policy issues. Such as person will also belong to one or two groups with a political agenda. I would argue that all Christians should at least be citizen participants.

Citizen participants begin by being generally informed on political issues and events. This is not to suggest that they need to spend hours each week learning the details of events in Congress, all aspects of the latest international conflict, the contents of alternative state-tax proposals, or the details of a local zoning dispute. But all Christian citizens should at least know the names of their elected representatives on the local, state, and national levels, and have a basic knowledge of the key policy issues under debate on local, state, and national levels. Spending an hour each week with a national news magazine such as *Time* or *Newsweek*, watching a television news program a couple of times a week, and skimming the local newspaper is likely to be enough to maintain the level of knowledge for which I am calling.

This much is necessary to be a true citizen, to be able to participate in the free, open government that the United States enjoys by God's grace. To be a participating citizen one must have opinions based on knowledge of political events and personalities. Without a basic working knowledge, one's votes and other political actions are as likely to influence events in a wrong, as in a good, direction. If, on the other hand, one is at least minimally informed, one is in a better position to express one's opinions meaningfully, whether through casting one's vote or by other means.

Participating citizens will also avail themselves of other opportunities to influence for good the flow of political events. Examples can be found everywhere: signing a petition circulated at church or at one's place of work, writing a public official, or attending a meeting to educate the public on a particular issue or to call for change in a public policy. My point is not that every Christian citizen, to fulfill his or her obligations, should be constantly writing and attending meetings, but that once or twice a year, when an issue of special concern or importance arises, he or she should be prepared to express those opinions in support of a more just order in society.

The final facet of being a citizen participant is to join one or two organizations that are politically involved. This may sound like an additional, heavy burden on those who already feel that their time and money are stretched to the limit. But I would argue that joining an organization promoting a cause with which one is concerned is a time-saver, not a time drainer. There are an endless number of organizations from which to choose, many of which have a Christian orientation. I am thinking of groups such as Bread for the World, for those who feel a special concern for the problem of hunger; Green Cross, for those with a special concern for environmental problems; various right-to-life committees, for those with a special concern for the continuing tragedy of abortions; and the Center for Public Justice, for those with a broad concern for issues of political justice. I could go on and on listing both secular and Christian organizations worthy of our involvement as Christian citizen participants.

But why is it so important for even the minimally involved citizen participant to join one or two of these organizations? By doing so, one can multiply one's influence with a minimal outlay of time and money.

The American system responds to organized group influence much more than individual attempts. An organized group—even when small and struggling—is generally seen as a legitimate means of citizen influence, and policy makers tend to believe that they should respond to or take into account the wishes of groups more than the wishes of individuals. The time and money needed to join an organized group is usually minimal. Membership fees are normally not more than twenty to thirty-five dollars a year. Many groups have discounted fees for students. The time commitment is also minimal. Members receive periodic newsletters and other mailings, but expectations of attending meetings or doing volunteer work, even for local groups, are usually low or nonexistent. Joining an organization concerned with an issue in which one is genuinely interested can be a time-saver. The organization usually has full-time, paid staff whose job is to keep up with issues and events relevant to the organization's interests. This information is then passed to the members in summarized form in newsletters or other periodic mailings. These groups will sometimes produce voting guides near election time, showing how legislators voted on key issues of concern to the group. Finding in this manner how one's elected representatives have voted on key issues is much easier than checking newspaper articles or doing research at the local library.

The citizen participant, by engaging in the minimal actions outlined here, doubles, triples, and maybe quadruples his or her influence. If all—or even a majority of Christians—would become active at this level, the growth in Christians' influence in the political system would be astounding. And with that growth in influence—if exerted in a loving, justice-promoting manner—American public policies would become much more compassionate, freedom-protecting, and just for all people. The consequences would be huge, and God would be honored.

Not all Christians are called by God to go beyond, and to become *citizen activists*, but some are. Those so called, and who respond, play a crucial role in making possible the political impact of the broader church of Jesus Christ. The citizen activist moves beyond the political involvements of the citizen participant by playing an active role in politically oriented groups, political parties, or candidates' campaign organizations. However, their political involvement stops short of holding full-time or paid positions or of holding a public office themselves. A citizen activist may be deeply involved in an association or organization with a political agenda. This person serves as an officer in the local right-to-life organization or on the board of the state chapter of the Sierra Club, or volunteers to help with a mailing for a welfare-reform group, or organizes his or her precinct for the Christian Coalition. Or a citizen activist may volunteer in a campaign—from a presidential campaign to

266

a campaign for the local school board. Or a citizen activist may be active in the local Democratic or Republican Party organization. Or the citizen activist may make financial contributions to candidates for public office, to his or her political party, or to a politically involved organization. What sets the citizen activist apart in these examples is a willingness to donate significant amounts of time, energy, or money to support political issues or causes that one believes are in keeping with God's sense of justice for the community, state, or nation.

The political system clearly needs more citizen activists. Candidates for public office, campaigns supporting or opposing ballot issues, Christian and secular political associations, and the two political parties are often desperate for money and volunteers. There are countless examples of individuals who, with energy, time, and sometimes money, have made enormous impacts. I know of candidates who have been elected to school boards, city councils, and even state legislatures largely on the basis of the dedicated work of no more than five or six volunteers. In an age of political cynicism and nonstop entertainment, so few people become politically active that those who do are in a position of great influence. This opens up a wonderful opportunity for the Christian activist who desires to move the system toward greater justice.

The highest level of political involvement is that of the *professional activist*—a person who either holds a public office (full- or part-time) or a paid position with a political party or politically oriented group. The public office that a professional activist holds may be an elected or an appointed position on the local, state, or national level. On the local level, such elected positions are often part-time in nature (and sometimes unpaid). I am thinking of local legislative bodies, such as city councils, county governing boards, and local school boards. There are also many appointed positions on local boards and commissions such as zoning boards, highway or road commissions, water- or air-quality boards, and so on. There are also full-time positions on the staffs of state and national elected officials. These are often influential positions, since elected officials rely on their staffs for much of the information and advice on which they base their decisions. One must also mention the large governmental bureaucracies in all three levels of government. These positions are available by way of competitive civil-service examinations and offer their holders opportunities to shape public policies directly.

In regard to these activist positions and their importance, what must be stressed is not the need for a handful of Christian professional activists in a few crucial positions. By depending on a few key persons, the Christian community runs the risk of committing the political-star error. This is the error of believing that a handful of Christian political stars—persons occupying highly visible, strategic positions of political leadership—will be able to effect major policy change. The problem is that any one public officeholder, no matter how highly placed, has only a limited amount of influence. Today Christians can rejoice that outspoken Christian leaders such as Republican Congressman Frank Wolf of Virginia and Democratic Congressman Tony Hall of Ohio are in key positions of leadership. They have done much good. But I am sure they would be the first to admit that, as individuals, their influence is limited.

What is needed is not an isolated Christian here and there in government, fighting lonely battles for greater justice. What is needed is large numbers of Christians committed to justice, occupying many offices on all levels of government. Each one—no matter how high or how modest the office he or she occupies—will have only limited influence in moving society toward greater justice. But cumulatively they can have an influence that will move mountains of injustice.

In the final analysis, that is what this chapter has been all about. It has been about political engagement and the Christian citizen's duty truly to be a citizen, to be engaged instead of on the sidelines. That ought not to be strange or new for those who claim the name of the one who commanded his followers to be a light in a darkening world. When Christians act *as Christians* in the political realm—whether as citizen participants, citizen activists, or professional activists—a more just order may by God's grace be established in society, and the millennium-old prayer of the psalmist may again be answered by our God:

> Endow the king with your justice, O God,
>   the royal son with your righteousness.
> He will judge your people in righteousness,
>   your afflicted ones with justice.

Psalm 72:1–2

References

Brunner, Emil. 1945. *Justice and the Social Order*. New York: Harper.

Halstead, Ted. 1999. "A Politics for Generation X." *Atlantic Monthly* (August): 33.

Marshall, Paul. 1984. *Thine Is the Kingdom*. Grand Rapids: Eerdmans.

Monsma, Stephen V. 1984. *Pursuing Justice in a Sinful World*. Grand Rapids: Eerdmans.

Niebuhr, Reinhold. 1932. *Moral Man and Immoral Society*. New York: Scribner's.

Yoder, John Howard. 1972. *The Politics of Jesus*. Grand Rapids: Eerdmans.

Notes

Chapter 1: Differing Perspectives on Politics among Religious Traditions

1. It is important to add a disclaimer: to talk confidently of a unified Reformed, Anabaptist, Lutheran, Roman Catholic, and Black Protestant perspective on politics is a risky venture. I make generalizations about these perspectives cautiously and with the understanding that they mask a significant degree of diversity and complexity within each.

2. The term *sect* refers to a voluntary religious association that admits persons with specific religious qualifications as members. This is in contrast to the term *church*, in which membership is either compulsory or automatic by birth. In this sense of the term, Roman Catholicism was historically a church, while Anabaptists were a sect. The term also refers, however, to the stance of groups vis-à-vis society at large. There is a high level of tension between the religious values and beliefs of a sect and those of society. This often leads members of the sect to isolate themselves as much as possible from interactions with a culture that they believe will corrupt their religious values (Wilson 1961; Wallis 1982).

Chapter 2: Religion and the Constitution

1. The *National Intelligencer* account garbled other facts as well. The compromise proposal for equal state representation in the Senate came well after Franklin's speech, and the adjournment to which the account referred took place at a different time altogether and was not proposed by Franklin.

2. For other nineteenth-century advocates of this view, see [Frelinghuysen] 1838; McMaster 1832; Baird 1856, 240–61.

3. Also see Marshall and Manuel 1977, 1986.

4. Even in some evangelical pulpits Washington's orthodoxy came under suspicion; in Albany, Episcopal divine Bird Wilson lamented that Washington "was a great and good man, but he was not a professor of religion" (Boller 1963, 15).

5. For a discussion of Wilson's theory of law and its relationship to religion, see West 1996, 41–45; Hall 1997, 35–67. Concerning Wilson's religious beliefs, Bradford claims that Wilson "was more a Deist than a Christian of any sort," but, as Hall points out, there seems to be no evidence for this assertion (Bradford 1982, 83; Hall 1997, 33).

6. Although the amendment on religious tests received a unanimous vote, the final vote on the section of the Constitution in which the ban on such tests appears passed 8–1, with two states divided (when the vote was taken on 30 August, late in the convention, New York was no longer represented).

7. See discussion of the ratification debates below.

8. For an interesting discussion of these clauses and their interpretation by Americans in the nineteenth century, see Dreisbach 1996b, 965–67, 974–86.

9. For attempts to trace the roots of the Constitution back to the Bible, see Beecher 1852, 1:176–90; Barton 1995.

10. For a good introduction to the Christian natural law tradition, see Budziszewski 1997 and Cromartie 1997.

11. Evangelical support for the separation between church and state could be clearly seen in the debate in Virginia over ending tax support of churches (Buckley 1977; Levy 1986, 55–58; Curry 1986, 143–46).

12. For similar arguments, see Mason 1849, 2:59–60; Kendal 1804; Cooke 1825, 13; Bouton 1828, 24–27; Dana 1823, 17–18; Lord 1831; Beecher 1852, 2:79–80, 99–101; Wayland 1963, 320–21.

13. See also "A Pastoral Letter from the Synod of New York and Philadelphia," which was drafted by Witherspoon (Witherspoon 1802, 3:14).

14. The Reverend Martin Luther King Jr. would make a similar argument a century later, calling the Constitution and the Declaration of Independence "those great wells of democracy dug deep by the Founding Fathers" (1991, 302).

Chapter 3: Religion and American Political Culture

1. This argument builds on similar concerns expressed in Skillen 1999.

2. From surveys conducted by the Tarrance Group, Mellman, Lazarus & Lake, and Yankelovich Clancy Shulman as reported in "Faith in America," *The Public Perspective* 5, no. 6 (September–October 1994): 93.

3. As reported by the Roper Organization in ibid.

Chapter 4: Religion and the Bill of Rights

1. City of Hialeah, Florida, Ordinance 87-52.

2. As a state university, a portion of the revenues generated through state taxes are used to support the University of Virginia.

3. Public Law 103-141, 107 Stat. 1488 (codified at 42 *U.S. Code* 2000bb to bb-4 [1994]).

Chapter 5: Religion and American Public Opinion

1. Representatives who adopt the role of delegate believe they should represent their constituents' views regardless of their own views. Those who consider themselves trustees believe their constituents have entrusted them to make decisions that reflect their best judgment and that they should stand accountable to the voters for these decisions in the next election.

2. There are differences in interpretations of classical democratic theory. Some advance a majoritarian model, in which the government is expected to do what a majority of the public wants. Those who advance a more pluralistic model contend that the public, as a whole, rarely holds clear and consistent opinions on the day-to-day issues of government. While this may be true for the public as a whole, pluralists contend that subgroups within the public do express relatively clear and consistent opinions on specific matters, and do so vigorously. For pluralists, therefore, democracy emerges only when opinions by these "minority publics" are expressed and clash openly and fairly over governmental policy.

3. There has been considerable scholarly discussion whether the level of "social capital" has declined within American society over the past several decades. See, for example,
Putnam (1995) and Ladd (1996).

4. Differences in religious beliefs are likely to be captured, in part, by differences in
religious affiliation.

5. The data for tables 5.1 through 5.5 are drawn from the University of Akron Religion
and Politics survey, a national survey of more than four thousand Americans conducted
during the 1996 election.

6. For example, these six traditions do not include those classified as belonging to a
nontraditional conservative tradition (e.g., Jehovah's Witnesses or Mormons) or to a nontraditional liberal group (e.g., Unity or "New Age" affiliations). In addition, these six categories do not include the Eastern Orthodox wing of Christianity (e.g., Greek Orthodox
or Syrian Orthodox) or those who adhere to non-Christian faiths (e.g., Islam or Hinduism).

7. Such physical actions may also include murder, adopted by some extreme elements
in the pro-life movement and morally justified on the grounds that murder of an abortion doctor prevents an even greater number of murders.

8. Caution must be taken in interpreting the percentage of Black Protestants expressing closeness to the Christian Right. It appears that some respondents may be responding to the word "Christian" and not to the groups associated with the Christian Right. In
addition, many of the policy positions adopted by Black Protestants do not coincide with
the positions expressed by groups associated with the Christian Right. Finally, the percentage of Black Protestants who express closeness to Christian Right groups declines as
the level of political knowledge increases (and, by inference, they are likely to be more
familiar with the policy positions of such groups).

9. Because of space limitations, the correlation coefficients are presented for the three
largest religious traditions—the Evangelical Protestant, Mainline Protestant, and Roman
Catholic traditions.

10. An index of political knowledge was constructed from respondents' answers to three
questions. Respondents were asked to identify the following three political figures: Boris
Yeltsin (the leader of Russia), William Rehnquist (Chief Justice of the Supreme Court),
and Newt Gingrich (then Speaker of the House). Those able to correctly identify none or
only one of the figures were classified as "low" in political knowledge; those who correctly
identified two or all three figures were classified as "high" in political knowledge.

11. In addition to the factors of group size and group cohesion, the level of the group's
politicization (e.g., the extent to which the group turns out at the polls) and the relative
salience of the particular issue in forging voting decisions among group members affect
the group's political significance. Even if a group exhibited total unity on one issue, and
even if the group was highly politicized, the group would lose political significance if members made voting decisions on the basis of issues on which the group was far less unified.

12. For a discussion and analysis of social theologies, see Guth et al. 1998.

Chapter 6: Religious Lobbying and American Politics: Religious Faith Meets the Real World of Politics

1. *Lobbying* is the activity that lobbyists do. The term *lobbyist* has its roots from people standing in the entry hall to the British House of Commons, seeking action from members of the House.

2. Baumgartner and Leech (1998, 100–101) review the literature on interest groups
and conclude that the discovery of an interest-group explosion during the 1960s and 1970s
is a recurring theme in the scholarly literature.

3. According to *Washington Post* writer Sally Quinn (quoted in Leo 1992), feminism is dead. Instead of concentrating on political issues, feminists should "concentrate on issues such as intimacy, trust, equality, sharing and child care."

4. See Sapiro 1981.

5. Moreover, congressional leaders such as Newt Gingrich and Bob Dole scored a perfect 100 percent on these targeted roll-call votes.

6. For a more detailed discussion, see Hertzke 1988, chap. 6.

7. I interviewed a range of lobbyists and provide evidence of this perspective in chapter 5 of Hofrenning 1995.

Chapter 7: Religion and American Political Parties

1. This is well described in Conkle 1993.

2. For good general introductions see, for example, Fowler 1985; Fowler and Hertzke 1995; Noll 1988; Reichley 1985; and Wald 1997.

3. This section of the essay relies heavily on Noll 1988 and Dunn 1984.

4. The Scopes trial was the 1925 trial of a public school teacher, John T. Scopes, in Dayton, Tennessee, charged with teaching Darwinian evolution, the teaching of which was against state law. Clarence Darrow was the defense attorney, and William Jennings Bryan aided the prosecution. While Scopes was convicted and the creationists "won" the case, the negative publicity and characterization of Bryan and conservative Christians generally drove fundamentalists away from political action for decades.

5. In urban areas elsewhere in the nation, a more traditional Democratic coalition of African Americans generally mixes with traditionally loyal, mostly Catholic, ethnic communities.

Chapter 8: Religion in American Elections and Campaigns

1. See Wald 1997 for further references to research along a similar vein.

2. For an important discussion of where individual denominations fit into this coding system, see Kellstedt et al. 1997.

3. There is an important difference between whether people *vote* and whether they *say* they vote. For example, the actual turnout rate in the election of 1996 was 51 percent (Stanley and Niemi 2000, 13). In the data we are using, however, the percentage of respondents *reporting* that they voted is 72 percent, more than a twenty-point difference. There are a number of reasons for this phenomenon, including the social pressure to vote (Americans are socialized to believe they should vote, and since many nonvoters do not want to appear as bad citizens to survey interviewers, they lie instead), that being interviewed prior to the election may prompt many to vote on election day, and statistical sampling errors. But the point is that we must be cautious in assuming that all the respondents in this survey are telling the truth when they report having voted.

4. Party identifiers are defined here according to the American National Election Study seven-point partisan identification scale. Democrats and Republicans include respondents who said that they had either "strong" or "weak" identifiers with their respective parties, while independents include those who said they were independents but who leaned toward a particular party, as well as those who said they were "pure" independents. Apoliticals are a separate category and are not included.

5. It lacks a single leader in the earthly sense, that is. Most Christian conservatives would identify Jesus Christ as their real and only leader.

6. However, the harsh rhetoric and personal attacks on Hillary Clinton by religious conservatives at the convention tended to alienate many moderate Republicans, who felt shut out of the party organization. And, while George Bush captured over 60 percent of the white evangelical vote in the 1992 election, he failed to win reelection.

Chapter 9: Religion and the American Presidency

1. One clue to unraveling this question is church denomination. Major religious traditions exhibit distinct attitudes toward government and politics that presidents take with them to office. Many different denominations have been represented in the White House. Almost 30 percent of presidents have been Episcopalian and about 17 percent Presbyterian, with Baptists and Congregationalists each claiming about 10 percent. There have also been changes over time in the denominations that presidents have held. George Washington (1789–97) was an Episcopalian (or Anglican prior to independence); John Adams (1797–1801), Congregational; Thomas Jefferson (1801–9) was "Unitarian by his own statement but Episcopalian by tradition and attendance" (Sharman 1995, 23). John Quincy Adams (1825–29), son of John Adams, is an interesting case, as he attended Unitarian services in the morning and Presbyterian services in the afternoon (Sharman 1995). The twentieth century brought a new dimension in religion to the White House. Herbert Hoover (1929–33) became the first Quaker president, with Richard Nixon being the second Quaker to hold the office. The only Catholic to win office—Kennedy in 1960—came under close scrutiny for his non-Protestant faith. In 1960, some voters were afraid that the young Kennedy, who was forty-three years old when he was inaugurated on January 20, 1961, would take his orders from the Vatican, the independent papal state within Rome. During the campaign against Nixon, Kennedy assured voters that he would not be a tool of the Catholic church. In fact, it appears that Kennedy was never "seized by any religious fervor. From his childhood, Catholicism was right because it was there" (Barber 1992, 350).

2. The Watergate scandal related to the attempt to cover up a break-in by Republican operatives at the Democratic National Committee during the 1972 presidential campaign. The attempt to cover up the event, and subsequent efforts to obstruct justice, was linked to President Nixon and some members of his Republican administration. In the end, President Nixon chose to resign rather than face likely impeachment.

3. In many circles, to be "born again" is to have a religious conversion experience.

4. Casey draws upon Maraniss 1992 and Painton 1993.

Chapter 10: Religion and Congress

1. This historical analysis draws on Grant, Kellstedt, and Rudolph 1995, a massive research effort to assign members of Congress from 1959 through 1995 to broad religious traditions. We have added data from the Eighty-third Congress (1953–54).

2. Although we have kept several categories distinct for purposes of presentation and discussion, our classification accords with both the historical and contemporary realities of religious alignment in the United States.

3. The Black Protestant category includes members of denominations located in the Black Protestant tradition, and does not refer to the race of the congressman per se. Just as black congressmen may theoretically be members of Evangelical (or Mainline) Protestant denominations, or a member of the Roman Catholic church, some white congressmen could theoretically be members of historical Black Protestant denominations. Thus the category refers to the nature of the congressman's religious affiliation, rather than race.

4. Our first resource has been the member's own website. By the end of the 105th Congress, most members had constructed a site, and many listed a religious affiliation. Less frequently, members described their religious involvement, such as holding leadership positions in their church, serving on special committees and task forces, or teaching Sunday school. Others simply noted that they were "regular attenders," or in some other way indicated high commitment. We took such claims at face value. Similarly, we found a good bit of additional self-reported religious involvement in the online publications of *Project Vote Smart*, which in recent years has asked members and candidates to fill out a long standardized questionnaire before elections, which includes queries on their most important organizational memberships and commitments. Not all candidates answered this query, but many provided detailed lists of outside affiliations and activities, including religious ones. In addition, we undertook an extensive search of the media. Although the more prestigious national press tends to ignore religious activities of legislators, specialized religious publications and local newspapers show much more interest. By thorough searches in the *Dow Jones News Retrieval Service*, *Newsbank*, and the *Public Affairs Information Service*, we found a treasure trove of information about members' religious life, their interaction with churches and religious organizations other than their own, and information about their personal religious "constituency." These sources ranged from articles discussing the religious life of individual members, to accounts of private devotionalism, such as small-group prayer sessions on Capitol Hill (National Prayer Breakfasts do not count), to income-tax returns showing substantial religious contributions. We also interviewed a few past members of Congress, contacted some congressional offices, and talked to knowledgeable observers—primarily to clarify problematic cases.

Chapter 11: Religion and the Judiciary

1. For a thorough discussion of the historical development of civil and common law—in Babylon, Egypt, Rome, Jewish law, and Great Britain—see Zane 1998.

2. The development of equity reveals a separate source of influence for religion. As suggested above, in the absence of an extensive code, common law judges made decisions in particular cases. One problem with the British common law was that it was cumbersome and reactive (Post 1963, 40–41). For instance, in the English countryside, Mr. Johnson looks over the fence to see his neighbor, Mr. Smythe, walking away with his prize breeding bull. Smythe is planning a family barbecue and Johnson's bull will be a nice addition to the feast. As hard as he tries, Johnson cannot persuade Smythe to relinquish the bull. So Johnson takes his case to court. Unfortunately, Johnson learns that the judge can do nothing at this time. The judge tells Johnson that after Smythe butchers the bull, Johnson can return to court and sue for damages. But Johnson does not want damages. He wants the bull. Such was the weakness of the common law. Plaintiffs could not stop the defendant from undertaking an objectionable action. As a result, some people would bypass the courts and seek justice directly from the king. The king would generally assign the case to a cleric. Over time, people would go directly to the clerics. Hence, a separate system developed alongside the common law. The clerics, known as chancellors, were empowered to hear the pleas of citizens and to provide specific relief, such as an injunction or the requirement that a defendant perform a contract (Van Dervort 1994, 17–18).

3. U.S. Constitution, art. 3, sec. 2.

4. 5 U.S. 137 (1803).

5. I will discuss the establishment clause and the free exercise clause in greater detail in the next section.

6. 454 U.S. 263 (1981).

7. 496 U.S. (1990).

8. See *Lamb's Chapel v. Center Moriches Union Free School District*, 508 U.S. 384 (1993).

9. *Rosenberger v. The Rector and Visitors of the University of Virginia*, 515 U.S. 819 (1995).

10. Although efforts were made to ensure Catholic and, later, Jewish representation on the court, the practice is no longer followed. Walker and Epstein (1993, 39) note that "for both of these religious groups, the idea of a designated 'seat' has lost most of its political power. In part this has coincided with a breakdown in the political cohesiveness of these populations."

11. I would very much like to thank Margaret Pilcher for her hard work in "coding" Cushman's book for religious references among the various biographies.

12. This historical distinction is made clear in McClosky 1960.

13. 330 U.S. 1 (1947).

14. Again, these biographical data come largely from Cushman 1995.

15. 410 U.S. 113 (1973).

16. 384 U.S. 436 (1966).

17. Ibid.

18. Ibid.

19. 408 U.S. 238 (1972).

20. *Reynolds v. United States*, 98 U.S. 145 (1878).

21. *West Virginia v. Barnette*, 319 U.S. 624 (1943).

22. See, for example, *U.S. v. Seeger*, 380 U.S. 163 (1965).

23. 374 U.S. 398 (1963).

24. 406 U.S. 205 (1972).

25. 494 U.S. 872 (1990).

26. 117 S. Ct 2157 (1997).

27. *McCollum v. Board of Education*, 333 U.S. 203 (1948); *Engel v. Vitale*, 370 U.S. 421 (1962); *Grand Rapids v. Ball*, 474 U.S. 373 (1985). In *McCollum v. Board of Education* (1948), the U.S. Supreme Court held that students could not be released to receive religious instruction on school premises, even if attendance was voluntary, classroom space available, and instructors were not paid with tax dollars.

28. *Zorach v. Clauson*, 343 U.S. 306 (1952); *Abington Township v. Schempp*, 374 U.S. 203 (1963); *Walz v. U.S. Tax Commission*, 397 U.S. 664 (1970). In *Zorach v. Clauson* (1952), the U.S. Supreme Court ruled that students could be released *during school hours* to receive religious instruction off-campus.

29. 403 U.S. 602 (1971).

30. *Everson v. Board*, 330 U.S. 1 (1947); *Board of Education v. Allen*, 392 U.S. 236 (1968); *Zobrest v. Catalina Foothills School District* (1993); *Mueller v. Allen*, 463 U.S. 388 (1983); *Witter v. Washington*, 474 U.S. 481 (1986).

31. *Bradfield v. Roberts*, 175 U.S. 291 (1899); *Tilton v. Richardson*, 403 U.S. 672 (1971).

32. *Lemon v. Kurtzman*, 403 U.S. 602 (1971); *Meek v. Pittenger*, 421 U.S. 349 (1975); *Aguilar v. Felton*, 473 U.S. 402 (1985).

33. *Engel v. Vitale*, 370 U.S. 421 (1962); *Stone v. Graham*, 449 U.S. 39 (1980); *Abington Township v. Schempp*, 374 U.S. 203 (1963).

34. See, for example, *Roth v. United States*, 354 U.S. 476 (1957).

Chapter 12: Christian Commitment and Political Life

1. See, for example, Acts 16:37–39; 22:24–29; and 25:10–12.

2. For a good explication of an Anabaptist perspective on government, see Yoder 1972. For a contrast from the Reformed perspective, see Marshall 1984.

3. This altered version of the parable is one I first heard Lewis Smedes of Fuller Seminary tell many years ago in a lecture. See Monsma 1984, 9–10.

4. Let me mention that I favor a moment of silence at the beginning and, perhaps, at the end of public school days for the purpose of silent, personal prayer or meditation, which would respect the various religious and nonreligious beliefs among students. Another approach would be student-led prayers, with strict provisions for excusing students who do not wish to take part in the prayers.

5. See, for example, Brunner 1945 and Marshall 1984, especially chapter 3.

6. I first used these terms in an earlier book. Portions of the following section have been adapted from that work. See Monsma 1984, 83–95.

Index